15 Q

lark

lark

COOKING WILD IN THE NORTHWEST

John Sundstrom

Photography by Zack Bent

SASQUATCH BOOKS
SEATTLE

Printed in China

Published by Sasquatch Books
20 19 18 17 16   9 8 7 6 5 4 3 2 1

Editor: Susan Roxborough
Production editor: Emma Reh
Design: Joyce Hwang
Copyeditor: Rachelle Longé McGhee

Library of Congress Cataloging-in-Publication Data is available.

ISBN: 978-1-63217-070-5

Sasquatch Books
1904 Third Avenue, Suite 710
Seattle, WA 98101
(206) 467-4300
www.sasquatchbooks.com
custserv@sasquatchbooks.com

*To all the moms and chefs who
showed me the way, thank you*

contents

mist

evergreen

bounty

lark larder

mist

NOVEMBER TO MARCH

evergreen

APRIL TO JULY

bounty

AUGUST TO OCTOBER

lark larder

a book in three seasons

JOHN SUNDSTROM

WHEN I BEGAN WORK ON THIS COOKBOOK, I knew it needed to be firmly located in the Pacific Northwest, my chosen home. It feels to me that we have three distinct seasons of food: Mist, Evergreen, and Bounty. Within each, there are waves of seasonal foods; there are fewer in the long gray months of Mist and we treasure them dearly. Evergreen comes on slowly, the forests and farms waking up from a long wet winter to unfurl their leaves and hope for some sun. Then for a brief window in the late summer and early fall, we struggle to keep up with the season of Bounty—the choices are overwhelming, and in the kitchen we try to stay out of the way and let each ingredient sing.

I love the Japanese idea of micro-seasons: appreciate the cherry blossoms for a week in the spring or eat eels at their best during six midsummer days. I bring that idea to the restaurant by changing our menu every week. It means I can work with suppliers even at very small scale. If a farmer has twenty pounds of the most perfect fingerling potatoes, or one beautiful lamb, then I can make it work. And for the weeks in June that our local strawberries are incomparable, I don't mind using them two or three ways.

It takes a lot of people to run a restaurant, and a lot of guests to make it last. When we opened Lark in 2003, it was thrilling when guests flocked in for dinner, and deeply gratifying when so many returned. We had been confident that we could make ends meet; being a success was a dream come true. Before long, people started saying, "You ought to write a cookbook," and I knew I wanted to. I started organizing my recipes, figuring out how to make them work in home kitchens.

The kitchen was pretty top-heavy then, with three cooks that had the talent to be chefs themselves. Our restaurant was packed most nights, my wife and I had our son a month after we opened, and there was so little free time. It was exhilarating to run a new, successful restaurant. Lark got great reviews, and I won the James Beard Award for Best Chef: Northwest, which brought in guests from around the country. Being congratulated and celebrated by our guests gave me a big personal boost too.

To go with the grain is to do the expected, and I can certainly do that, but in many ways with Lark we went against the grain. I chose Twelfth Avenue for Lark because the potential of the space and the neighborhood inspired me, and now we have many great shops and restaurants as neighbors. After more than ten years in our original location, it's been a thrill settling in to our new building just a few blocks away. Lark has been shined and brightened up just a bit, and sharing the space is Bitter/Raw, our crudo, shellfish, and amaro cocktail lounge, and Slab Sandwiches and Pie, for coffee, slab pies, sandwiches, and JM's salted chocolate chip cookies.

Serving small plates was a little bit risky when we opened, yet the gamble has paid off—our guests love building a meal from our broad menu, just as I had hoped.

And that cookbook that people kept asking about? A person needs a home life, travel, and time in the hammock, right? But I kept planning, reading cookbooks, food magazines, and industry publications. I talked about it with a couple of great writers and editors whose work I love and thought I'd eventually work with one of them. Then the stock market went south and the publishing world began to change. Luckily, our strong core of regular customers at Lark helped us weather the worst of it, but the cookbook was put aside for a few years. Finally I got together with a great cook and former chef Jared Stoneberg to talk about the idea, and it began to take shape. He builds websites now, and suggested we produce a Lark cookbook app at the same time as the book. We decided to Kickstart it, and once again I felt such a grand upswell of support and interest from the community, especially from so many of our regulars. The original self-published hardcover edition was such a pleasure to work on. I learned so much, and throughout its creation, my connection to the Lark community just grew and grew. Despite having a great team to handle development and production, it was still a ton of work! I'm thrilled to have partnered with Sasquatch Books on this new and improved edition, and so grateful to have some pros behind me every step of the way.

This book is more than a collection of recipes we cook at Lark; it is a picture of life in the Pacific Northwest and the rhythm of the seasons. Some of the recipes I've included here aren't simple, and the ingredients can be hard to find or downright intimidating. But making a meal that sings with of-the-moment ingredients and then sharing it around a table is such fun. I am proud to present this book and hope it will give you a taste of the good life, from our kitchen to yours.

from the front of the house

KELLY RONAN

O NE OF THE FIRST TIMES I MET JOHN, he joined JM (now his wife and our business partner) and me on a hike in the Cascades. They worked together at Dahlia Lounge, but I didn't know him very well. It was February, cold but not very snowy, and he talked a lot about food and traveling. What might be growing out there in the forest, best foraging practices, how the Northwest is a lot like parts of Europe, though he'd never been there. (He wasn't like the cooks I knew: he didn't drink as much, and he collected cookbooks. Twenty years ago, that wasn't normal.) We returned home famished, to a typically empty refrigerator. John stepped in and made the most delicious sandwiches from uninspiring ingredients. He was in the right business. Later, when he was wooing waitress JM, she would rave about the staff meals he cooked. You can always tell when a cook likes a server.

In the following years, we three traveled together in Japan, then in Italy and France, and John thrived. He brought back flavor memories like tattoos, faded a little but permanently seared in his memory. He thought about food all the time. The accolades started coming for him. John and JM invited me to open a restaurant with them, and we looked at spaces on and off for a few years, never finding a place that inspired all three of us. But we'd sketch out a plan, imagine the décor, and John would write a new menu, always from scratch. I thought he'd run out of new ideas, but he didn't, and doesn't. He would always write the right meal, finding new inspiration. And then we signed a lease, taking a big risk on an old building in a marginal neighborhood.

Many chefs are screamers. John is not—he's a Zen chef. Once, when a celebrity host promised a boat to carry the food for fifty people and equipment for eight courses to a remote location, and then that boat didn't show up? He didn't make a fuss—he made it work. The grill and charcoal were the worst part; I'm not sure how many times I passed it along the footpath on the twenty-minute walk between the vehicles and the table, John moving it a little farther along every trip. Hours later, he happily walked a plate of wriggling spot prawns around the tables, reveling in their freshness before cooking them.

One of the greatest things about restaurant work is that we meet the most incredible people, spend dinnertime with them, and often we get to celebrate their big events. We have helped welcome babies; brought an extra dozen oysters when the kids scarfed the first; fed the family sending their child off to college, and later for their graduation as well. And we've suffered a few losses with them, and hopefully helped a small bit. It is an honor. Sometimes a regular shows up with a treat for John and me—produce they grew, something they made that tastes great—and then we know that we've been doing things right.

One question we still are asked is how we chose the name Lark. It's hazy, but I think it was the only one that we all agreed on one evening when the pressure was on. A lark isn't precious or beautiful, but it has a gorgeous song. When we three still liked it in the sober light of day, we knew it was perfect. Taking a chance felt like a lark—equal parts adventurous and harmonious. More people began to help us: JM's dad determined the perfect angle for comfortable booths; Bob found the right tool for each job I tried to tackle.

Lark is handmade. Family and friends built it, and John and I worked full-time at our jobs during the build-out. Friends showed up and offered to run to the lumberyard or paint for a few hours. Many of them fed us.

One Monday morning a few years back, I came to Lark and found our friend Hannah cooking for her catering company, former server Rachel juicing fifty pounds of lemons for her excellent Rachel's Ginger Beer, and a big group of current employees and their friends sitting around a table with five bottles of wine doing a blind tasting. Oh, and John was sitting at the bar flipping through the *Noma* cookbook while calling suppliers. That's restaurant life: the front door is open six hours a night, but the kitchen door is seldom closed. About a year later, in the middle of this cookbook's creation, I came in a few hours before a Tuesday shift. Zack was shooting photos, lights and reflectors around the room, tables akimbo. I walked the rest of the way in and there was a pig carcass on a prep table in the middle of the dining room. That's restaurant life too. Sometimes the kitchen is a bit too small.

the road to lark

I GREW UP IN SALT LAKE CITY, UTAH, where scallions on a baked potato was considered exotic and the pizzas were square. Mormon families are not particularly known for reaching great heights when it comes to food and presentation. Our dinners were pretty plain, mostly white (or brownish-white) and fairly sweet. My favorite meals before the age of seventeen were Swiss steak with mashed potatoes, pan-fried pork chops, and the very rare treat of shrimp cocktail when we dined out. I loved doughnuts, especially apple fritters, and my childhood photos tell the tale. Some things never change.

The first time I made éclairs with my grandmother from *Amy Vanderbilt's Complete Cookbook* I was ten or eleven years old. I didn't recognize that I was taking a first step toward becoming a chef, but I liked the feeling of sharing the plate with the family. Grandma Estrid was a great baker, and she held epic canning parties where my mom and her sisters would gather to put up peaches, apricots, pears, pickles, and zucchini relish.

My first restaurant job was at the 47 Samurai, a Benihana-like Japanese restaurant in Salt Lake City. I was there covering a friend's dishwashing shift, but I pushed the chef to let me do more. I was a rube, but he let me peel fifty-pound sacks of onions, pull the skin off of chickens by the case, and race the cooks to see who could slice five pounds of button mushrooms the fastest. Eventually I earned the trust and respect of chef Yasu, and I was one of the few gaijin cooking tableside for customers. I had some pretty good moves with the knives and pepper mills, and never caused anyone serious injury.

At the time, I was thinking about pursuing a college degree in a more practical field, but I kept returning to what I enjoyed the most. I started buying

Gourmet magazine, and purchased the copy of Jacques Pépin's *La Technique* that I still have on my shelf at home today. When I began to consider cooking school, I tried my luck for a winter season cooking breakfast at Deer Valley's Snow Park Lodge. Those first shifts at Snow Park were scary as hell for me, as I knew nothing about cooking French continental hotel food. I was assigned to help out an old-timer whose arm was in a plastic-wrapped cast. My first week there I reached into a giant toaster and burned my hand pretty badly. He berated me, then barked, "Go clarify the butter on the flat-top!" He screamed when he returned to find all that butter melting away on the surface—in hindsight, I really should have thought to put it in a pan.

Somehow, I liked cooking, and after flying to Vermont for a tour of the New England Culinary Institute, I signed up. I had a great time those two years at NECI, a classic college experience: mischief in the dorms, new friends, lots of beer, and swimming holes. I paid my own way (well mostly, right Mom?) and was committed to getting my money's worth from the experience: I arrived early to classes and stayed late, and I thrived. One of my internships was a stint at the Ritz-Carlton in Laguna Niguel. That was quite an experience, especially in lifestyle voyeurism: I marveled at the copper pots and pans, the fabulous china, and the glamorous customers . . . what a world.

After graduation I moved to Seattle because my girlfriend's sister lived there, and so I had a place to stay. The grunge years in Seattle were in full swing, and what self-respecting cook doesn't seek out music? I took a job as breakfast cook at the much-loved and mostly forgotten raison d'être. Owners Stacy and Shelly were mad genius types, redecorating the restaurant several times per year and always surrounded by drama, but also sweet and protective of twenty-three-year-old me. I met several waiters whom I still see around town; I moodily slurped lattes at Kurt Timmermeister's Cafe Septieme in Belltown; I worked with some pre–Pearl Jammers; and I never saw Nirvana.

I wanted to work for Tom Douglas, who was already The Man in Seattle, but it wasn't until after he left Café Sport that I got a job there as a line cook. It was steadily declining, and one Sunday I went in for a drink only to find the GM giving the staff the "we're closing the doors after this shift" talk. The silver lining was that Tom and his wife, Jackie Cross, came by for a farewell cocktail, and I got a quick introduction. Fortune smiled, and I started working at Dahlia Lounge.

I spent six years at Dahlia as a line cook, sous chef, then chef de cuisine (though we didn't call it that—Tom wasn't one for formalities). I grew in many ways there as a cook and as a leader. It was a giddy time, with so much remarkable talent in that kitchen: Holly Smith, Matt Costello, Eric Tanaka, and Shelley Lance. I met my wife, JM Enos, at Dahlia, and our friend and partner Kelly Ronan through JM.

The menu was built around authentic international flavors. It was inspiring to research the world's great cuisines through cookbooks and to glean ideas from my own travels and those of my fellow cooks. If someone had just returned from Mexico or Thailand full of new ideas, we'd replicate those dishes. My first trip to Europe and a three-week visit to Japan kept me inspired for an entire year.

I began to want to do things differently. It happens to every cook, right? Most leave restaurant work for a more settled life: Microsoft, Amazon, and every game company on the Eastside is staffed with former cooks and waiters. Many great cooks stay, and some of those get a little too cranky. I left, staged around Manhattan and San Francisco for inspiration, then came back to chef at a vegetarian restaurant.

Imagine that. My friends thought I was crazy for limiting myself. "It was great, but something was missing," they'd rib me after a dinner at Carmelita. But that was nothing compared to the surprise they got when I took my next job later the same year: I'd been recruited to take over as executive chef of Earth & Ocean, at the W Hotel Seattle.

It had been a very difficult opening year for that restaurant. The hotel had opened to much fanfare and has been a hit ever since. Earth & Ocean had a much rougher go. It struggled with a very ambitious opening menu, terrible reviews, and then chefs and cooks leaving in droves. Myriad Restaurant Group ran the show and threw their considerable resources behind me and the restaurant. It was the first chance I got to distill and focus all of my ideas and ideals and put them out for the public to see. I introduced an all foraged and wild prix fixe menu, along with a vegetarian market menu.

We worked hard, and staff morale improved immediately, cover counts started going up, the hotel staff started encouraging guests to check out what we were doing rather than sending them elsewhere, and we started seeing some positive press and new reviews. It never could have happened without the dedicated and talented coworkers who remained from the opening days to help me rebuild: Maria Hines, Sue McCown, Angie Roberts, Rob Larcom, and Gregg Nelson, and of course Drew Nieporent and Michael Bonadies from the Myriad team. We had a lot of fun taking trips to New York and Aspen (this was my *Food & Wine* Best New Chef year), Boca Raton and Toronto, all the while improving our service and quality at Earth & Ocean. I spent three years there and learned a ton (and went to a ton of meetings), but I knew that the life of a corporate hotel chef wasn't what I wanted. The quest for Lark was about to begin.

In early 2003, JM and I decided we had to make the move and figure out how to open our own place, and Kelly said she was in. We got to work on our business plan, then started looking at restaurants for sale and buildings for lease. We didn't see much that we could afford or that we liked, but finally one day our attorney called and said he'd noticed a restaurant that was closed up, apparently evicted from the property. And then it was ours.

This book is about our neighborhood restaurant and living the good life in the Pacific Northwest. Behind each recipe there are the stories of many players in this frolic we decided to call Lark, and it's a thrill for me to play a central role in all of it. We opened Lark in December 2003, and our lives changed forever. Our son Owen was born in January 2004, and then things got really interesting. This book tells the tale of the journey we've been on ever since.

how to cook from this book

I'VE NEVER BEEN ONE FOR HARD-AND-FAST RULES in the kitchen. I'm an intuitive cook. A touch of this, some more of that. If there's a formula for crème fraîche I don't know it, though we've been making it weekly for years. When it came time to write this cookbook, committing the recipes in my head to the page was a daunting task—thank goodness for the patience and expertise of Lauren, former Lark cook and sous chef and integral member of the cookbook team.

At Lark we take notes when we're working on a new dish, otherwise my cooks would lose their minds trying to replicate them correctly. It can be difficult when things aren't consistent at the restaurant. My cooks have a solid foundation in technique, so they are able to be very flexible and adaptable when cooking. A ribeye in Seattle is going to taste different from a ribeye in Buenos Aires. Sometimes garlic is incredibly spicy. But not always. Cooks know that source and season play a big role in flavor.

Learning to work with these variations is liberating for a cook. My hope is that this book will give you the tools to become an even better and more confident cook, striking a balance between precision and accuracy on one hand, and adaptability and more free-flowing cooking on the other. We've laid out accurate recipes, but we encourage you to play with them. It's all about tasting; taste often and adjust whenever necessary.

When I cook dinner at home, I usually first ask JM what we have on hand. There might be a chunk of halibut from my last fishing trip thawing, so I'll start with that and build the meal around it. Maybe I start thinking "peas, pea vines, and mint." If it's a farmers' market day, we'll go shopping and see what's available. If English peas or pea vines aren't available but there are sugar snap peas and new-crop spinach, it's an easy substitution as those "families" of ingredients can be approached in the same way.

A well-stocked larder can save the day when you're puzzling over what to make for dinner. If you have some good olive oil, a can of anchovies, a head of garlic, a chunk of Parmigiano-Reggiano, potatoes, and eggs on hand, I guarantee that a delicious meal is possible. Even better if you have some fresh herbs in your backyard.

Try the recipes as written, then play around to make them your own. If you love the steak tartare at Lark just the way we serve it, then stick closely to the recipe. Hazelnut cake always sounds good, but you might choose to serve it with softly whipped cream in place of salted caramel ice cream. It'll be quick and delicious. In many of our recipes, types of ingredients can be swapped for others. Some examples:

CHARDS, KALES, MUSTARDS, SPINACH: They all have some differences in flavor but can be interchangeable in the way they are prepared and cooked.

ROOT VEGETABLES: If a recipe calls for turnips and you prefer parsnips or have carrots, it's an easy substitute. Or you might consider using pumpkin or butternut squash to add a fruitier flavor.

MUSHROOMS: There are huge differences in flavor, but they will contribute to a dish in similar ways. Use what's seasonally available.

Always read a recipe all the way through before beginning to cook, including any component recipes. The Chef's Notes will give you clues as to things you can do to make cooking a dish easier and more efficient.

AT LARK (AND THROUGHOUT THIS BOOK):

BUTTER is unsalted and high butterfat (82 percent)

SALT is kosher, unless otherwise specified (I use Alaska Pure fleur de sel, a flaky sea salt, for finishing, and some other finishing salts for specific dishes)

PEPPER is freshly ground black Tellicherry

WINE is dry

FLOUR is unbleached all-purpose

SUGAR is granulated and made from sugar beets

EGGS are large, organic, and very fresh

MILK is whole and organic

CREAM is 36 to 40 percent fat and organic

MIX & MATCH RECIPES

Depending on what you have on hand or what is in season, feel free to experiment with different combinations of the recipes in this book. For example:

Pommes de Terre Robuchon,
page 53

Creamed Nettles *from*
Neah Bay Halibut with Creamed
Nettles and Morels, page 97

+

+

Hanger Steak *from*
Hanger Steak with Porcini Butter
and Mizuna Salad, page 125

Salmon *from Wild Salmon*
with Fingerling Potatoes and
Two Sorrels, page 100

+

+

Wild Mushrooms with Garlic,
Olive Oil, and Sea Salt, page 199

Wild Rice Polenta *from*
Duck Leg Confit with Wild
Rice Polenta, page 45

mist

NOVEMBER TO MARCH

Cold, hazy, damp, gray. The outsider's view of Seattle is somewhat accurate. The veterans of Northwest winters seem to jet off every year, to Hawaii or Palm Springs, or to a ski paradise such as Sun Valley. The lack of blue can be relentless.

It is the trickiest time in the kitchen. You can't just drizzle a chestnut with olive oil and have its glory shine. Frisée wants to be wilted and sauced instead of lightly dressed. Even the potatoes need extra attention after they've aged four months in the cellar. It takes coaxing, prodding, some tough love, and lots of time to bring out the best qualities of the season of Mist. You need to be a rutabaga-whisperer. You need butter too.

But there are riches in this mist, and they are often cooked slowly in our favorite weathered Staub iron pots. We can play with fat ducks and geese, elk and wild boar. Some portions are roasted in the hottest oven, and the Lark kitchen feels like the warm heart of the restaurant, glowing. The waitstaff congregates near the rotisserie, soaking up the heat, the scents, and the inspiration to share with our guests.

Dried, pickled, or preserved months before, the bounty of autumn returns transformed. Mushrooms bring the earthiness that connects us with the land, and we've stashed foraged huckleberries in the freezer to brighten the rich meats of the season.

As the holidays approach, I bring in a bigger variety of game meats and experiment with recipes for our Wild Beast supper. There is grouse dressed with truffles, celeriac, winter squash, quince, hazelnuts, and spices. The planning leaves me fired up and thirsty for Syrah.

We can't have it all in one night, though. So the wide-ranging lists of foods I want for Wild Beast become the inspiration for many of the winter items at Lark, and for entertaining at home. Our friend Andy Stout showed up for Thanksgiving one year with a massive amount of king and Dungeness crab, and ever since we love to start every winter occasion with shellfish.

Northwest oysters are at their prime during these chilly months; they are so crisply sweet and briny that we plan a dozen or more per person at our celebrations. I always eat the first few simply shucked: no sauce, no distractions. I grew up in a landlocked state, so I was taught to disguise the suspects. Here in the Puget Sound, we get these fresh jewels and they need no polish. But the lightest sauce complements the second half dozen: a squeeze of low-acid Meyer lemon or a drop of mignonette. In Mist we get our crab on too.

More, now, please.

This was one of our opening dishes at Lark and we have served it every year since. A nod to the timeless Normandy combination of apple cider, smoky bacon, mussels, and cream, this is our version. Since the menu is constantly changing and evolving at Lark, we usually run this dish between November and February when my favorite blue-shelled mussels from the Jefford brothers at Penn Cove Shellfish are fat and firm. I see many similarities between our climate in the Pacific Northwest and the western coast of Europe, and sometimes when I'm researching a new dish, I'll look through one of my favorite French country cookbooks by Patricia Wells or Anne Willan to find inspiration.

mussels

WITH BACON, APPLE, AND SHALLOT

1   Over medium heat in a wide saucepan, cook the bacon until it is rendered and crisp.

2   Drain off all but 1 tablespoon of the fat. Add the apple and shallot and cook until slightly caramelized. Increase the heat to medium-high. Add the mussels and stir to coat them with the bacon, shallot, and apple.

3   Deglaze the pan with the wine, apple cider, and vinegar. Reduce the liquid slightly. Add the cream, thyme, salt, and pepper. Be careful how much salt you add as the bacon and mussels are naturally on the salty side.

4   Cover and cook for 2 to 4 minutes, or until all of the mussels are open and the sauce is reduced and slightly thickened. Discard any mussels that do not open.

5   Serve with toasted country bread directly from the pan or transfer to a large bowl.

MAKES 2 SERVINGS

4 ounces smoked bacon, cut into ¼-inch lardons

¼ cup peeled and diced Granny Smith apple

2 tablespoons thinly sliced shallot

1 pound mussels, washed and debearded

2 tablespoons dry white wine

2 tablespoons apple cider

1 tablespoon apple cider vinegar

¼ cup heavy cream

Leaves from 1 sprig thyme

Kosher salt and freshly ground black pepper

4 thick slices toasted Lark Country Bread (page 253)

CHEF'S NOTE: Before cooking, wash and swish your mussels around in a bowl of cold water and scrub off any barnacles. Discard any mussels that do not close or are cracked or damaged. Gently remove the "beard" by pulling it up along the seam of the shell. Store the mussels in a pan or bowl covered with a wet towel but not submerged in water.

I first cooked this dish while at Earth & Ocean. Looking back I was really going through an "obsessed with Alsace" phase, especially the classic choucroute garnie, which is basically a giant pile of sauerkraut with all kinds of smoked pork, potatoes, and mustard. I was playing around with the "earth meets ocean" idea and this was the result.

Fresh diver scallops are best for this dish; most often they'll be from the New England coast, but when Alaskan Weathervane scallops are available, I always choose them. Sometimes I add a drizzle of pumpkin seed oil, or maybe a foie gras vinaigrette—made with the melted fat from our foie gras terrine balanced with some champagne vinegar—but I never go wrong with this tangy, leeky, luscious butter sauce.

scallops choucroute

WITH HAM HOCK AND PICKLED MUSTARD SEEDS

MAKES 4 SERVINGS

FOR THE BUTTERY
LEEK SAUCE

1 quart water

1 cup diced celery

1 cup diced fennel

1 cup washed and diced
  leek whites

1 cup diced onion

½ bottle dry white wine

½ cup (1 stick) unsalted
  butter, cut into
  tablespoons

1   To make the buttery leek sauce, in a stockpot, combine the water with ½ cup of the celery, ½ cup of the fennel, ½ cup of the leek whites, ½ cup of the onion, and 5½ ounces of the wine and bring to a boil. Simmer and reduce by 25 percent. Strain the mixture, saving the liquid; discard the vegetables.

2   Combine the strained liquid with the remaining celery, fennel, leek whites, onion, and wine, and repeat the simmering process, again reducing by 25 percent before straining.

3   Let the strained liquid cool and refrigerate it until ready to use, or move right on to the next step. This sauce can be made up to 2 days ahead of time.

4   When you are ready to make the sauce, boil the strained liquid for about 1 minute to reduce 1 quart of the liquid down to 1 cup. While it's hot, whisk in the butter, salt, and white pepper to taste. Immediately before serving, blend the sauce with an immersion blender to achieve a frothy consistency.

5   To make the pickled mustard seeds, place the mustard seeds into a glass or metal bowl. In a small saucepan, bring the water, champagne vinegar, sugar, salt, and bay leaf to a boil. Pour the mixture over the mustard seeds. Let them cool to room temperature.

6   Once they have cooled, they are ready to use. To store, keep the seeds submerged in the brine and place them in an airtight container in the refrigerator, where they can be saved for several weeks.

7   To make the braised cabbage, in a dry medium sauté pan, toast the fennel and caraway seeds and set aside.

8   In a large saucepan, melt the butter. Add the onion and cabbage and sauté them until lightly wilted but not browned, 10 to 15 minutes.

9   Add the apple, apple cider vinegar, wine, and fennel and caraway seeds. Add a little salt and pepper. Simmer uncovered, stirring frequently, for 30 to 40 minutes, or until the cabbage is tender.

10   Add the ham hocks just prior to serving. Adjust seasoning to taste.

11   To prepare the scallops, pat the scallops dry with paper towels and season them with salt and pepper.

12   Heat a medium sauté pan over medium-high heat. Add the oil and butter to the pan, and once they are very hot, sear the scallops on one side until crispy, 2 to 3 minutes. Turn them over and baste for 2 to 3 minutes, or until the scallops are medium-rare. Remove them from the pan and let them rest for 2 minutes before serving.

13   To serve, mound the braised cabbage in the center of a serving bowl. Place the seared scallops on top of the cabbage. Spoon some of the blended buttery leek sauce around the cabbage and top the scallops with some drained pickled mustard seeds. Sprinkle with chives.

½ teaspoon kosher salt

Freshly ground white pepper

FOR THE PICKLED MUSTARD SEEDS

¼ cup yellow mustard seeds

½ cup water

½ cup champagne vinegar or white wine vinegar

2 tablespoons granulated sugar

1 teaspoon kosher salt

1 bay leaf

FOR THE BRAISED CABBAGE

½ teaspoon fennel seed

½ teaspoon caraway seed

1 tablespoon unsalted butter

1 cup very thinly sliced onion

4 cups loosely packed savoy cabbage, cut into ¼-inch-thick slices

1 cup peeled and grated green apple

½ cup apple cider vinegar

1 cup dry white wine

Kosher salt and freshly ground black pepper

½ cup smoked ham hocks, cooked until tender and shredded (bacon or smoked pork sausage will also work)

FOR THE SCALLOPS

16 extra-large U16 sea scallops (about 1 pound total)

Kosher salt and freshly ground black pepper

1 teaspoon extra-virgin olive oil

1 tablespoon unsalted butter

1 tablespoon very thinly sliced chives, for finishing

*Yellowtail (*hamachi *in Japanese) is one of my favorite fish to eat raw. I love its fatty rich-ness and clean, very light taste. The first time I had it was while working at my first kitchen job as a prep cook at 47 Samurai, the Benihana-like restaurant. It had a pretty decent sushi bar considering the time (mid-'80s) and the place (Salt Lake City). Chef Yasu flew fish in a couple of times per week and I'd watch, entranced, as he turned these beautiful, exotic sea-foods into exquisite bites. Years later when opening Lark, I knew it had to be on the menu.*

Crudo is a term meaning "raw" in Italian and is used to describe raw fish or seafood with a Western rather than a Japanese preparation. This combination of picholine olives, pre-served lemon, and wild fennel pollen with the hamachi is spectacular.

hamachi crudo

WITH PRESERVED LEMON, GREEN OLIVES, AND WILD FENNEL SALT

1 First, prep the fennel salad ingredients. Slice the fennel very thinly by hand or using a mandoline. Slice the sides of the olives away from the pits. Quarter the lemon and remove the flesh from the rind. Discard the flesh and cut the rind into small dice.

2 In a bowl, mix the fennel, olives, lemon, and 1 tablespoon of the chives. Add the olive oil and lemon juice and toss to coat. Season to taste with salt and pepper.

3 Thinly slice the yellowtail across the grain and divide it equally among four plates.

4 In a small bowl, mix together the wild fennel pollen and fleur de sel and sprinkle a small amount over the yellowtail. Reserve the leftover for another use.

5 Sprinkle the remaining 1 tablespoon chives over the yel-lowtail. Dress each plate with a drizzle of the lemon-infused extra-virgin olive oil. Mound a quarter of the fennel salad in the center of the yellowtail on each plate and serve.

MAKES 4 SERVINGS

½ fennel bulb

8 picholine olives

1 Preserved Lemon (page 273) or store-bought

2 tablespoons very thinly sliced chives, divided

1 tablespoon extra-virgin olive oil

1 teaspoon freshly squeezed lemon juice

Kosher salt and freshly ground black pepper

8 ounces sashimi-grade yellowtail (hamachi) loin, trimmed

1 tablespoon wild fennel pollen

1 tablespoon fleur de sel

1 tablespoon lemon-infused extra-virgin olive oil

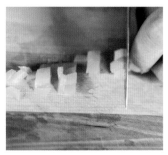

This is a dish I like to serve in late autumn, a time when shellfish is gorgeous and both razor clams (usually from the Quinault Reservation on the Olympic Peninsula) and Manila clams are plentiful and plump. Shave fresh Oregon or Washington truffles over the top to give the dish a luxurious scent without spending a fortune. Local truffles can be bought for about one-tenth the price of their European counterparts.

razor clam chowder

WITH TURNIP, TRUFFLE, AND THYME

MAKES 4 SERVINGS

¼ cup peeled and diced turnip

¼ cup peeled and diced celery root

¼ cup peeled and diced Yukon Gold potatoes

1 tablespoon unsalted butter

2 cups Clam Stock (recipe follows)

1 cup heavy cream

Leaves from 6 sprigs thyme

Kosher salt and freshly ground black pepper

¼ pound razor clams, chopped

¼ pound Manila clams, reserved from Clam Stock, chopped (optional)

1 teaspoon truffle oil, for finishing

1 Oregon black truffle, shaved, for finishing

1   In a large saucepan over medium heat, sweat the turnip, celery root, and potato in the butter without browning, 5 to 6 minutes. Add the stock, cream, and thyme. Season to taste with salt and pepper. Simmer until the vegetables are tender. Add the razor and Manila clams and cook for 30 seconds. Adjust seasoning to taste.

2   To serve, spoon into four bowls, drizzle each serving with ¼ teaspoon truffle oil, and top with truffle shavings.

clam stock

1 In a stockpot over medium heat, melt the butter and add the onion, leek, and fennel. Sweat them gently until soft but not browning, 5 to 6 minutes.

2 Add the clams and wine and bring to a boil. Simmer until the wine is reduced by half. If you are reserving the clams for another use, remove them once they have opened. Add 2 cups water, the garlic, peppercorns, and bay leaf and simmer gently for 15 minutes. Strain through a fine mesh strainer. The stock can be made up to 2 days ahead of time.

CHEF'S NOTE: In the Clam Stock recipe, the intention is to extract as much flavor from the Manila clams as possible, so they will be overcooked when the stock is made. If you want to reserve those clams for another use or add them to the chowder, just be sure to remove them from the stock once they have opened so that they don't overcook. Shell the clams before adding them to the chowder.

MAKES 2½ CUPS
OF STOCK

1 teaspoon unsalted butter
½ cup diced yellow onion
½ cup washed and sliced
    leek whites
½ cup sliced fennel
2 pounds Manila clams
1 cup dry white wine
2 cups water
1 head garlic, halved
10 whole black peppercorns
1 bay leaf

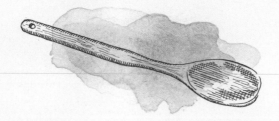

ALWAYS BE MAKING STOCK

Always be making stock. It's an essential part of cooking, at home or in a restaurant. With a little planning and a few minutes of prep time you'll improve your cooking and the tastiness of your dishes exponentially by making your own stock. Whether it's your grandmother's tried-and-true chicken broth recipe or a modernist chef's pine needle tisane, flavored broth, stock, jus, and infusions all provide a foundation or focal point in any great dish.

At Lark, we buy forty pounds of chicken bones and feet every week; we roast them, drain off the fat, deglaze the roasting pans, and simmer the bones for hours with a full mirepoix of carrots, celery, and onions and a sachet of thyme, parsley stems, bay leaf, and peppercorns.

Here is how we make our chicken stock at lark:

1   Roast the chicken backs and necks at 400 degrees F until golden brown.

2   Cool slightly and drain excess fat from the roasting pan.

3   Place the roasted bones in a stockpot.

4   Deglaze the roasting pans with water or white wine; pour over the bones and then top up to 1 inch above the bones with cold water.

5   Bring just to a boil, then immediately reduce the heat to simmer for 30 minutes, skimming any foam or fat from the surface.

6   Add the mirepoix and aromatics (don't forget the parsley stems!) and simmer for 3 to 4 hours.

Often the leavings of one preparation can become the start of another. At home, my wife keeps a freezer bag with trimmings for stock, always collecting them. She adds the bones of last night's roast chicken and trimmings from vegetables like onions, carrots, and celery. When the bag is full, she starts the stockpot to simmering.

Chicken and beef are the workhorses, but I like making a light and intensely flavored spot prawn stock when live spot prawns are available. It might end up as a lovage-infused broth served with those same prawns, or I might reduce it to a rich concentrate that will flavor our shellfish mayonnaise that accompanies a grilled squid salad.

Fresh beet juice reduced to a syrup and seasoned with just a pinch of salt is an incomparable companion to a soft, tart goat cheese and some candied pistachios.

Good stock-making has been covered countless times by many talented chefs and cooks. Don't like measurements so much? See the first few pages of Fergus Henderson's *The Whole Beast* for some great stock guidelines. If you prefer exact measurements, check out Daniel Humm's *Eleven Madison Park* cookbook, which has a great formula. And best of all, the pressure cooker is back in style, so you can make your broth in a quarter of the time.

CLOCKWISE FROM TOP LEFT:

LEEK SAUCE from Scallops Choucroute, page 24

CORN BROTH from Wild Sockeye Salmon, page 172

PARMIGIANO-REGGIANO BRODO from Ricotta Gnudi, page 128

CLAM STOCK from Razor Clam Chowder, page 29

MUSHROOM STOCK from Wild Mushroom Risotto, page 194

One of my hopes when opening Lark was to serve classic dishes better than anywhere else. So while we clearly are not the only restaurant serving steak tartare, we often hear that ours is the best in Seattle. Try this with our Onion–Poppy Seed Crackers (page 75) or some toasted Lark Country Bread (page 253) and all's well!

wagyu sirloin tartare

WITH QUAIL EGGS AND ONION–POPPY SEED CRACKERS

1 Finely dice the sirloin. Place in a mixing bowl and season with salt and pepper. Stir in the aioli and a few drops of lemon juice.

2 Add the mustard, ½ teaspoon each of the shallot and chives, the capers, and the pickle. Mix until well combined. Adjust seasoning to taste. Mound the steak tartare on four plates.

3 In another mixing bowl, combine the lemon juice and oil and mix well. Add the parsley, frisée, and the remaining 1 teaspoon each shallot and chives. Season with a little salt and pepper. Gently toss the salad and adjust seasoning to taste.

4 Separate the quail eggs by trimming off the top of the shell with a paring knife. Pour an egg into your hand, keeping the yolk intact. Using a melon baller, separate the yolk from the white. Discard the white.

5 Top each mound of steak tartare with a raw quail egg yolk, and season the yolk with salt and pepper.

6 Place a quarter of the salad on each plate beside the tartare. Serve with the crackers.

> CHEF'S NOTE: Dicing the sirloin is much easier if it is extremely cold or even partially frozen. You can dice the sirloin a few hours in advance but do not progress with the recipe until you are ready to serve it. Be careful when separating the quail egg yolks as they are small and sometimes very delicate; using a spoon or melon baller can be easier than using your hands.

MAKES 4 SERVINGS

½ pound Wagyu top sirloin, trimmed of any silverskin

Kosher salt and freshly ground black pepper

2 tablespoons aioli (from Albacore Ventresca, page 175)

½ teaspoon freshly squeezed lemon juice, plus more for the tartare

1 tablespoon Dijon mustard

1½ teaspoons minced shallot, divided

1½ teaspoons minced chives, divided

1 teaspoon minced capers

1 teaspoon minced cornichon pickle

1 tablespoon extra-virgin olive oil

1 bunch Italian parsley, washed, spun dry, and trimmed into small sprigs

1 bunch frisée, yellow parts only, washed and spun dry

4 quail eggs

Onion-Poppy Seed Crackers (page 75)

Spot prawns are the Maine lobster of the Northwest, though if you ask me they are even better: so sweet and tender, they melt in your mouth. They are recreationally caught start-ing in May most years, with short commercial seasons then and in late autumn. I buy spot prawns, octopus, and blue king crab from John and Sylvia of Sylver Fishing Company out of Wrangell, Alaska. Everything they catch is top-notch. Spot prawns are really delicate, so cook them with great care, and serve on the rare side. The smoked butter is something we started doing after reading the Noma *cookbook; it's such a simple idea, I can't believe we didn't think of it ourselves since we've put a lot of crazy things in the smoker over the years.*

spot prawns

WITH BRUSSELS SPROUT LEAVES, SMOKED BUTTER, AND RYE CRUMBLE

MAKES 4 SERVINGS

3 tablespoons cold unsalted
   butter, divided

½ cup dark rye bread, torn
   into very small pieces

Kosher salt

1 tablespoon caraway seeds

1 tablespoon fleur de sel

½ pound brussels sprouts

Smoked Butter
   (recipe follows)

1   In a small sauté pan over medium heat, melt 2 tablespoons of the butter. Sauté the rye bread until it is crispy all the way through. Drain the toast on paper towels and season it with a pinch of salt right away. Once the rye toast has cooled, pulse it in a food processor until it resembles bread crumbs. Set aside until ready to use.

2   In a small dry sauté pan over medium-high heat, toast the caraway seeds for about 2 minutes. Toss them frequently so that they toast evenly. Grind the toasted seeds in a spice grinder. Mix with the fleur de sel and store the caraway salt in an airtight container.

3   Bring a medium saucepan of water to a boil and season with a generous amount of kosher salt. Prepare an ice bath.

4   Remove the outermost leaves of the brussels sprouts and discard them. Cut a piece of the core out of the sprouts and pull the leaves off, keeping them intact. Continue to cut off a small piece of the core and pull off the leaves until each brussels sprout has been pulled apart into separate leaves.

5   Blanch the leaves in the boiling water until just tender, about 1 minute. Shock the blanched leaves in the ice bath to stop cooking. Set aside.

6   Cut the chilled Smoked Butter into cubes. Heat the wine in a small sauté pan over medium-high heat and let it reduce slightly. Turn the heat down to low and slowly whisk in the Smoked Butter, a third at a time, until it is emulsified. Taste the smoked butter sauce and adjust seasoning with salt, pepper, and lemon juice. Keep the sauce warm for poaching the prawns. Be careful not to let the sauce get too hot, which will cause the butter to separate.

7   Peel the spot prawns, and season to taste with salt and pepper. Gently poach the prawns in the warm smoked butter sauce until they are just cooked, 2 to 3 minutes.

8   In a medium sauté pan over medium heat, combine the remaining 1 tablespoon butter with the water. Add the blanched brussels sprout leaves and gently reheat. Adjust seasoning to taste.

9   To serve, place the poached prawns on a serving plate and arrange the brussels sprout leaves around the prawns. Scatter the bread crumbs over the top. Drizzle some smoked butter sauce over the leaves and around the plate. Sprinkle with 2 teaspoons of the caraway salt and the dill.

smoked butter

1   Place the butter on a small plate and freeze it for about 1 hour.

2   Find a pot or a container with a tight-fitting lid that can hold both the smoker and the plate of butter.

(CONTINUED)

2 tablespoons dry white wine

Freshly ground black pepper

Juice from ½ lemon

1 pound spot prawns

1 teaspoon water

1 tablespoon minced dill sprigs, for finishing

MAKES 1 CUP BUTTER

1 cup (2 sticks) unsalted butter

1 handful dry wood chips

3 Place the wood chips in a mini smoker box and place on the stove over medium-high heat to get the wood chips smoking. Once the wood chips have started to give off an abundance of smoke, place the smoker box in the pot. Place the plate of chilled butter on top of the smoker. Very quickly place the lid on the pot and let it sit for at least 20 minutes, or until the smoke has subsided.

4 Smell the butter to verify that it has taken on a smoky aroma. You can even taste a little to make sure that it has taken on a smoky flavor to your liking. If you don't feel it is smoky enough, place the butter back in the freezer for another hour and repeat the smoking steps.

5 Place the butter in the refrigerator until chilled all the way through.

Trotters? Exactly what do you mean by that? It's a common question tableside at Lark.
We've been serving pork feet successfully for many years now and usually once people try
them they're hooked. We live in a wealthy country, where most of us enjoy the "premium"
cuts of meat, but in many cultures the "off" cuts, such as the feet, head, and organs, are highly
prized for their deep flavor, nutritional value, and interesting texture. Pork trotters take all
of a cook's skill to bear, but the time and energy spent bring delicious rewards!

crispy pork trotters
WITH TRUFFLE AIOLI AND MIZUNA SALAD

1   Place the trotters in a bucket or tub large enough to fit
them. Pour enough cold brine over the trotters to completely
cover them. Make sure the trotters are fully submerged; use a
plate to help weigh them down. Refrigerate in the brine for
2 to 4 days.

2   Transfer the trotters to a large stockpot or saucepan and
discard the brine. Cover them with water or stock. (If you have
chicken stock, this makes an amazingly jellied stock to use
for sauces.) Add the onion, carrot, celery, thyme, and bay leaf.
Bring to a boil, then immediately turn down to a simmer. Cook
until the meat is very tender and pulls apart easily, 3 to 4 hours.
Be sure to keep an eye on the liquid level in the pot, and if it
goes below the trotters, add more to keep them covered.

3   When fully cooked, remove the trotters from the liquid
and allow them to cool enough to handle, about 30 minutes.
Strain the liquid through a fine mesh strainer and reserve
it for another use. (See page 30 for more about making and
using stock.)

4   Gently pull the meat, fat, and skin off the bones and place
in a mixing bowl. Tear into bite-size pieces and season to taste
with salt and pepper.

5   Line a baking tray or cake pan with parchment paper. Press
the pork into a uniform layer about 1 inch thick in the pan.
Cover with a piece of parchment paper, and place another
baking tray or cake pan that is small enough to fit on top. Press
down to flatten and smooth the pork. Refrigerate and chill for
at least 4 hours or overnight.

6   Remove the parchment paper and flip the meat onto a cutting board. Remove the other piece of parchment and cut the
meat into 2-inch squares.

(CONTINUED)

MAKES 8 SERVINGS

4 pork trotters

½ gallon Basic Brine (see
   recipe on page 120)

1 onion, cut into 1-inch dice

1 carrot, peeled and cut into
   1-inch dice

1 celery rib, trimmed and
   cut into large dice

½ bunch thyme

1 bay leaf

Kosher salt and freshly
   ground black pepper

2 tablespoons canola oil

½ cup all-purpose flour

1 teaspoon minced shallot

1 teaspoon extra-virgin
   olive oil

½ teaspoon freshly squeezed
   lemon juice

1 bunch mizuna (or water-
   cress, arugula, or another
   peppery green), washed
   and dried, stems trimmed

FOR THE TRUFFLE AIOLI

2 egg yolks

½ teaspoon freshly squeezed
   lemon juice

3 tablespoons canola oil

½ teaspoon black or white
   truffle oil

½ teaspoon minced
   black truffle

Kosher salt and freshly
   ground black pepper

Fleur de sel, for finishing

7   Heat the canola oil in a medium sauté pan over medium-high heat. Dust the pork cakes lightly with flour and season to taste with salt and pepper. Sauté the cakes until crispy and golden brown on both sides, 2 to 3 minutes per side. Be careful when turning the cakes over in the pan; they are delicate and can easily break apart.

8   In a medium bowl, combine the shallot, olive oil, and lemon juice. Season to taste with salt and pepper. Add the mizuna and toss gently to coat.

9   To make the truffle aioli, in a medium bowl, combine the egg yolks and lemon juice. Whisk until pale yellow and thickened, about 1 minute. Continue to whisk while slowly drizzling in the canola oil until fully incorporated and fluffy. Add the truffle oil and minced truffle and whisk well. Season to taste with salt and pepper.

10   To serve, smear 1 tablespoon of the truffle aioli across each of eight plates. Place the pork cakes on top of the truffle aioli. Divide the salad among the plates. Sprinkle with fleur de sel.

CHEF'S NOTE: The trotters will need to remain in the brine for 2 to 4 days before cooking, and the cooked pork needs to press overnight, so be sure to plan ahead when making this recipe. The brine itself can be made up to 3 days in advance; just store in the refrigerator.

A rare and rich treat, foie gras is celebration food when the occasion calls for something special. It's controversial, certainly, but accurately portrayed? That's up for debate. The heart of the argument tends to be more about eating meat and less about eating fattened duck livers. I buy the foie gras for Lark from Pleasant View Farm in Puyallup, Washington, and I trust that Rose and her family raise their ducks responsibly and with great care.

seared foie gras

WITH SHAW ISLAND QUINCE AND DUCK CRACKLINGS

MAKES 4 SERVINGS

2 cups granulated sugar

2 cups water

2 quince

2 teaspoons freshly
  squeezed lemon juice

1 cup duck fat trimmings
  and skin pieces

Kosher salt

8 ounces duck foie gras

Freshly ground
  black pepper

1 teaspoon sherry vinegar

2 teaspoons white wine

1   To make the poached quince, first prepare a simple syrup by combining the sugar and water in a small saucepan. Place over high heat and bring to a simmer, making sure the sugar fully dissolves. Let the mixture simmer for about 1 minute, then remove from the heat. Cool the syrup to room temperature and refrigerate until ready to use. If kept in a tightly sealed container, it will keep for a week.

2   Peel and core the quince. Quarter each quince and place in enough water to cover them, then add the lemon juice. Keep them in the water until you are ready to poach them.

3   When ready to cook, strain the quince quarters and transfer to a saucepan. Cover with the simple syrup and gently simmer until the quince is tender when pierced with a paring knife,

25 to 30 minutes. Remove the saucepan from the heat and reserve the quince in the poaching liquid. Once cooled, slice the quince quarters in half lengthwise.

4   To make the duck cracklings, place the duck fat trimmings in a pot with ½ cup water and simmer over very low heat, stirring occasionally, until the duck fat has rendered and the water has evaporated. Continue to cook over low heat until the duck skin is golden brown and crispy.

5   Remove the duck cracklings from the pan and drain on paper towels. Season them immediately with salt. Strain and reserve the rendered duck fat for another use. Once the cracklings have cooled to room temperature, store them in an airtight container until ready to serve.

6   To prepare the foie gras, first slice it into 2-ounce portions. Score one of the flat sides of each piece in a cross-hatch pattern by cutting into it about ⅛ inch. Season each piece generously with salt and pepper. Keep the foie gras slices cold until you are ready to cook them.

7   Place a dry medium sauté pan (no oil or butter is needed because of the foie gras fat content) over high heat. Place the seasoned foie gras, scored side down, in the pan.

8   Cook until the scored sides are seared, golden brown, and crispy, 60 to 90 seconds. Using a fish spatula, gently turn them over and cook the other side for 30 to 60 seconds. They are ready when they are just tender to the touch but the very centers are still slightly firm. Transfer the foie gras from the pan to a plate to rest while you make the sauce.

9   Reduce the heat to medium and pour off all but 1 teaspoon of the fat. Deglaze the pan with the sherry vinegar.

10   Add the wine, 1 teaspoon of the reserved poaching liquid, quince slices, and stock and simmer for 2 to 3 minutes, or until slightly reduced. Add the butter and stir it into the sauce.

11   To serve, place 1 teaspoon of the quince preserves on each plate and run a spoon through it to spread it on the plate. Add a piece of foie gras and a few quince slices. Drizzle with a little of the sauce and top with three or four duck cracklings. Drizzle with a little of the foie gras juices that were released while resting and garnish with some watercress leaves.

- 2 teaspoons rich chicken or duck stock
- 1 teaspoon cold unsalted butter
- 4 teaspoons quince preserves, for finishing
- ½ cup watercress leaves, picked, washed, and dried, for finishing

I've been intrigued by wild boar for years now, dreaming of joining some Italian noble on their annual hunt through the foothills of Tuscany in search of the mysterious, elusive, and ultimately delicious cinghiale. Boar meat tends to be lean, but rich and deep in flavor. Often I'll look to the cuisines of France, Italy, and Eastern Europe when deciding how to prepare boar for Lark. This recipe is rich with the flavors of autumn and is worthy of bringing a special bottle of wine up from the cellar, a deep amarone or a favorite Châteauneuf-du-Pape.

wild boar shoulder

WITH CHESTNUTS, SUGAR PUMPKIN, AND PORCINI MUSHROOMS

MAKES 4 SERVINGS

1 pound wild boar shoulder, cut into large cubes

Kosher salt and freshly ground black pepper

2 tablespoons extra-virgin olive oil

1 cup sliced onion

10 cloves garlic, crushed

1 bunch rosemary

1 bunch thyme

2 cups red wine

2 quarts chicken stock

1 tablespoon heavy cream

FOR THE PUMPKIN-CHESTNUT MIXTURE

4 ounces fresh porcini mushrooms, well cleaned

2 tablespoons unsalted butter, divided

½ sweet onion, cut into ½-inch dice

1 cup peeled and diced sugar pumpkin

Kosher salt and freshly ground black pepper

12 chestnuts, roasted, peeled, and halved

2 tablespoons thinly sliced (chiffonade) Italian parsley

1   Season the boar with salt and pepper. Heat the oil in a large pan over medium-high heat. Add the boar and brown on all sides. Add the onion and garlic and cook until softened, 2 to 3 minutes. Add the rosemary, thyme, and wine. Simmer until reduced by half.

2   Add enough stock to cover the boar completely. (You may not need all of the stock.) Bring to a simmer. Cover and cook at a bare simmer until the boar is very tender, 2 to 3 hours.

3   Remove the herb branches from the liquid and discard. Remove the boar meat from the liquid, bring to a boil, and reduce by two-thirds. Return the boar to the pan, add the cream, and heat just until warm. Be very careful not to let the sauce boil. Adjust seasoning to taste.

4   To make the pumpkin-chestnut mixture, trim and slice the mushrooms.

5   Heat a medium sauté pan over medium heat and melt 1 tablespoon of the butter. Add the onion and cook until soft, 4 to 5 minutes. Add the pumpkin and season to taste with salt and pepper. Sauté until golden and cooked through, 5 to 7 minutes.

6   Add the remaining 1 tablespoon butter to the pan. Add the mushrooms and cook for 2 to 3 minutes. Add the chestnuts and cook for another 2 to 3 minutes. Stir in the parsley and adjust seasoning to taste.

7   To serve, divide the braised boar among four plates and spoon the pumpkin-chestnut mixture over the top. Spoon sauce around the boar.

CHEF'S NOTE: The boar can be prepared a day ahead of time. Store it in its braising liquid (with the herbs) in the refrigerator, and when you're ready to finish the dish, gently reheat the meat before resuming the recipe.

The crispy duck leg confit has been on the menu at Lark since we opened. All it takes is a little planning, some quick prep, slow cooking in the oven, and then cold storage to deepen in flavor. I serve it eight to ten ways throughout the year: with red wine cherries in July, with maple-glazed delicata squash in November, and with this wild rice polenta, which is great anytime there's a chill in the air.

 # duck leg confit

WITH WILD RICE POLENTA

1 To make the duck leg confit, trim and shape the duck legs, removing any extra fat, and pat them dry. Arrange the duck legs in a 3-inch-deep roasting pan in a single layer. Sprinkle half of the salt evenly over the duck. Turn the duck over and cover with the remaining salt. Add the garlic, thyme, peppercorns, and bay leaves. Turn the duck legs so that the aromatics are mixed throughout the meat; be sure to position the legs skin side up. Cover and refrigerate for 24 hours.

2 Remove the pan from the refrigerator and leave at room temperature for 1 hour. Meanwhile, preheat the oven to 275 degrees F.

3 Cover the duck legs with the lukewarm (not hot!) duck fat. Press parchment paper directly on the surface of the legs and then cover the pan with a lid or foil. Place in the oven and cook for 3 to 4 hours, or until the duck is tender when pierced with a fork near the bone. Uncover the pan and cool for 1 hour.

4 Remove the duck from the fat, and if not serving right away, place in a similarly sized heatproof pan for storage. Strain the fat through a fine mesh strainer and cover the duck legs. Cover and chill until ready to serve. The duck will keep for 1 week in the refrigerator.

5 To make the wild rice polenta, grind the wild rice in a spice or coffee grinder for several minutes until very finely pulverized.

6 Bring the chicken stock to a boil in a medium saucepan. Stir in the ground wild rice, whisking constantly, until well incorporated. Add the salt. Turn the heat down to low and very slowly raise the temperature to about medium-high, whisking frequently, until the polenta begins to thicken.

(CONTINUED)

MAKES 8 SERVINGS

FOR THE DUCK LEG CONFIT

8 duck legs, including thighs

¼ cup kosher salt

10 unpeeled cloves garlic, cracked

½ bunch thyme

1 tablespoon whole black peppercorns

4 bay leaves

2 quarts lukewarm duck fat

FOR THE WILD RICE POLENTA

½ cup wild rice

2 cups chicken stock or water, plus more as needed

½ teaspoon kosher salt

1 tablespoon unsalted butter

2 tablespoons grated Parmigiano-Reggiano, for finishing

7 Cook until the liquid has been absorbed, 20 to 25 minutes, and the polenta is tender. If all the liquid has been absorbed but the polenta is not quite tender, add some more chicken stock and continue to cook. Fold in the butter and adjust the seasoning.

8 Preheat the oven to 400 degrees F. Meanwhile, remove the pan with the confit from the refrigerator and warm gently, either in the oven or on the stovetop, until the fat is mostly melted. Remove the duck legs from the fat. Strain and reserve the duck fat for another use.

9 Place the duck in a heavy-bottomed, ovenproof pan skin side down over medium heat for several minutes and then into the oven for about 8 minutes, or until the skin is crispy and golden brown.

10 To serve, place a dollop of polenta on each plate and top with a crispy duck leg. Finish with Parmigiano-Reggiano. If desired, drizzle some reduced chicken or duck stock on the plate.

CHEF'S NOTE: Begin this recipe at least a day ahead of when you plan to serve it. Although the duck does not require much active time, it does need to cure overnight. You can choose to serve it the same day as you confit it, but I suggest that you leave it at least a day in the fat as the flavor improves with time. You could use lard instead of duck fat, but the flavor will be a little different. Remember if you buy a whole duck, rendering the fat from any trim will yield a fair amount of duck fat, which will keep refrigerated for at least a month. The polenta can also be made up to a day in advance, although you will need to add a little more chicken stock or water when reheating it.

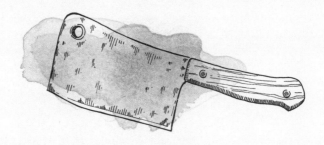

USING THE WHOLE BEAST

Cooking with whole animals is part of what we do at Lark. Whether it's a whole hog, lamb, rabbit, game bird, or fish, we love to break it down and challenge ourselves to find delicious uses for everything, even the odd little bits. It's especially important in this compartmentalized world we live in for our customers and even for my cooks. Though many of them have attended cooking schools or have solid experience prior to joining the team at Lark, many have never seen a whole lamb or a twenty-five-pound Chinook salmon.

Our strategy when we get a whole pig is to break it down according to how it will be cooked or cured and when it will be used. Most of the kitchen staff want to help; the more experienced cooks learn how to handle the whole beast, the novices skin the bellies and grind the sausage.

There are many approaches to this. Here's my typical list:

1 Break the pig down into primal sections (large muscle groups), making it easier to handle and maneuver. These in turn get broken down into smaller pieces: trotters/hocks and hind legs (hams); bellies, loin, and ribs; shoulders and head; tenderloin and skirt.

2 Skin everything except the hams, which get cured for prosciutto, and trotters. Save the skin for chicharrones or cotechino sausage.

3 Brine the trotters, hocks, and head for a few days, then braise for headcheese, trotter cakes, and smoked hocks.

4 Brine the bellies for menu pork belly, or cure for pancetta or pancetta tesa.

5 Remove coppa from shoulder/neck and slice into thick steaks for tonight's special, or cure and hang to dry.

6 Portion and marinate tenderloins and skirt steak for the menu. Sear the hanger steak for a quick snack.

(CONTINUED)

7   Cut the loin into bone-in pork chops, or brine the whole thing to roast, or cure and dry for lomo.

8   Either cure and confit the shoulder for rillettes, or use for fresh or dried sausage.

9   Cure the fatback as lardo or incorporate it into sausages.

While it's unlikely that most home cooks will take home a two-hundred-pound hog, you'll use the same approach when working with a smaller animal. For example, one duck can be turned into several meals for my family of three.

Here's how:

1   Bone whole duck into breasts, legs, and thighs. Trim fat from the edges of each piece and reserve.

2   Trim all excess fat from the carcass and place in a saucepan with some water to render. Simmer slowly until all the water has evaporated and you are left with clear fat and crispy cracklings. Strain the fat into a glass jar and refrigerate to use for confiting the legs or roasting potatoes or vegetables. Toss the hot cracklings into a salad and top with a poached egg.

3   Score one breast and eat it for dinner that night. Sear with the skin side down until crispy, draining extra fat off a couple of times. Turn over and cook for just 1 minute, then let it rest for a few minutes and slice thinly to serve.

4   Cure the other breast for duck prosciutto (see recipe on page 61).

5   Cure and confit the legs. Once cooked, these will last quite a while in the refrigerator.

6   Roast the duck bones until golden brown and make duck stock for sauces or a soup with leftover duck breast sliced into it (see page 30 for more on stock).

One twenty-dollar duck just turned into three or four meals. If I had purchased each of these pieces separately I could easily spend forty dollars or more.

We do two annual dinners at Lark. The Whole Beast is a feast that usually falls somewhere during the season of Mist, usually February or March, and is a celebration of all things piggy, with some lamb or goat to round it out. It's a family-style feast, with wave after wave of dishes, ranging through fried snouts, pickled tongue, milk-braised pork loin, and crispy trotter cakes, just to name a few. The Wild Beast takes place in November, and the focus is on wild game and rich autumn flavors.

WHOLE BEAST SUPPER

FIRST WAVE

Lark coppa, mortadella, goose prosciutto, and rabbit rillettes
Chicharrones *with malt vinegar salt*
Bacon-wrapped dates *with Fourme d'Ambert*
Pig snouts Milanese *with pickle aioli*
Marcona almonds and marinated olives

SECOND WAVE

Split pea soup *with pea shoots and crispy pig ear*
Rabbit and foie gras terrine *with rhubarb, hazelnuts,
and pickled mustard seeds*
Pork belly *with butter lettuce, green papaya, and nuoc cham*

THIRD WAVE

Crispy pig tails as a salad *with watercress,
sunchokes, and mustard vinaigrette*
Cold lamb neck bagna càuda *with artichokes and fennel*
Lamb sweetbreads *with smoked potato and pork fat–shallot crumble*
Meyer lemon granite

FOURTH WAVE

Offal pie *with pork, lamb tongue, rabbit kidneys, truffle, and beef fat crust*
Pork schnitzel *with fried egg, braised cabbage, and caraway*
Lamb loin *with vadouvan curry, apple, and red dandelion*
Goat crepinettes *with taggiasca olives, dandelion greens, and black garlic*

DESSERT

Fernet Brancamenta ice cream *with chocolate cookie crumble*

I've been fortunate to work with the Lucy family over the past few years. Brooke and Sam own and operate Bluebird Grain Farms in Winthrop, Washington. I had been featuring farro (or emmer) on the menu at Lark since our first year, sourcing from Ritrovo, a high-quality Italian importer. It had always been a delicious and popular dish. The Lucys and I met at the Farmer-Fisher-Chef Connection one winter, and I immediately started ordering their farro, as well as their rye and wheat flours. The farro that the Lucys grow is the best that I've tried, and locally sourcing one of my favorite ingredients is very important to me. And my family can't get through winter without their Old World Cereal Blend.

farro

LARK
CLASSIC WITH RED WINE–BRAISED SALSIFY AND WILD MUSHROOMS

1   In a large saucepan over medium heat, heat the olive oil. Add the onion and a pinch of salt and cook until the onion is translucent. Add the farro and stir until all the grains are coated with oil. Add the white wine. Season to taste with salt and pepper. Add the water. Bring to a boil, then lower the heat to a simmer.

2   Cook until the water and white wine have been absorbed and the farro is tender but still chewy, 30 to 40 minutes. If the farro is not tender enough before the water has been absorbed, add more water a little at a time and continue cooking. You don't want any extra water remaining in the farro. Stir in the mascarpone until it melts and is incorporated. Taste and adjust seasoning if necessary.

(CONTINUED)

MAKES 6 SERVINGS

2 tablespoons extra-virgin olive oil

½ onion, cut into small dice

Kosher salt

2 cups farro

1 cup dry white wine

Freshly ground black pepper

4 cups water, plus more as needed

1 cup mascarpone

1 pound salsify

2 cups red wine

1 tablespoon unsalted butter

1 teaspoon minced garlic

2 cups wild mushrooms, such as morels, black trumpets, or porcini (cultivated cremini or oyster mushrooms will also work), cleaned

1 tablespoon thinly sliced chives, for finishing

3   Meanwhile, braise the salsify. Peel the salsify and slice it on the bias about ¼ inch thick by 2 inches long. Place the salsify in a medium saucepan and cover it with the red wine. Season very lightly with salt and pepper. Bring the wine to a boil and then turn the heat down and simmer until the wine is reduced and syrupy and the salsify is tender, 15 to 20 minutes. Check the salsify for tenderness periodically; if it becomes tender before the wine has reduced to a syrup, remove it, keep simmering the wine, and return the salsify to the pan at the end to reheat. Adjust seasoning to taste.

4   In another medium saucepan over medium heat, melt the butter, and then add the garlic. Add the mushrooms and cook until the garlic is just golden, about 5 minutes. Season to taste with salt and pepper.

5   To serve, divide the farro among six small casserole dishes (or one large one). Spoon the mushrooms and salsify around. Drizzle some of the red wine syrup over the top and sprinkle with chives.

CHEF'S NOTE: Salsify is a root vegetable that is usually very dirty. Be sure to give it a good wash before you even start to peel it. All the components of the recipe can be made on the same day, although the salsify and farro (up until adding the mascarpone) can be made 1 to 2 days ahead of time and reheated. If making the salsify in advance, store the red wine syrup and salsify separated, then reheat them gently together.

This potato dish is of course a nod to the great French chef Joël Robuchon. Several years ago I decided to try this dish here in Seattle, even going so far as to have my friend Andy at Full Circle Farm grow the La Ratte fingerling potatoes from seed potatoes I'd acquired so it would be entirely authentic. At Lark we cut the proportion of the butter back to about one-quarter versus the one-third ratio that Chef Robuchon uses, and they are still very rich. We fill a small cast-iron pot and gently feather the top into a spiral design to finish.

pommes de terre robuchon

1   In a large saucepan, cover the potatoes with cold water. Add 3 tablespoons of the kosher salt. Bring the water to a boil and simmer the potatoes until tender.

2   Drain the potatoes and pass them through a fine mesh food mill or ricer into a large bowl. Once nearly all of the potatoes have been passed through the mill, add the butter with the remaining potatoes to be passed through with them.

3   Heat the cream in a large heavy-bottomed saucepan over medium heat. Add the mashed potatoes and heat through, stirring frequently. When the cream is fully incorporated, adjust the seasoning with the remaining 1 tablespoon salt. The potatoes should have a thoroughly pureed consistency.

4   Transfer the potatoes to a bowl and smooth, and using the curved edge of a small rubber scraper or spatula, feather the top. Sprinkle with the chives and serve.

MAKES 4 SERVINGS

2 pounds La Ratte fingerling potatoes (or other small waxy variety), scrubbed

4 tablespoons kosher salt, divided

1 cup (2 sticks) unsalted butter, at room temperature

1 cup heavy cream

1 tablespoon minced chives, for finishing

Rosti are a staple in Switzerland and there are some variations in style. We use mini frying pans made by Staub at the restaurant, but a small cast-iron pan works great too. I used to make one large rosti, and after it cooled down a bit, I'd cut it into wedges to serve alongside a ribeye steak. At Lark we serve rosti with clabber cream or crème fraîche and minced chives as a side dish, or with sustainably raised Yellowstone River paddlefish caviar on top as a starter. If you're feeling extra decadent, try it with American white sturgeon caviar, a great alternative to the delicious (yet overharvested) caviars of Russia and Iran.

 # rosti potatoes

LARK CLASSIC — WITH CLABBER CREAM AND PADDLEFISH CAVIAR

1 Preheat the oven to 450 degrees F. Place either four mini frying pans or one small cast-iron skillet in the oven to preheat.

2 Shred the potatoes into about ¹⁄₁₆-inch pieces on a mandoline with a julienne attachment. Use your hands to squeeze out as much water as you can from the julienned potatoes. (This will help them brown and crisp when cooking.) Season the potatoes generously with salt and pepper. Let the potatoes sit at room temperature for about 10 minutes, then again squeeze out as much water as you can with your hands.

3 In a small saucepan, melt the duck fat. Drizzle about ¼ cup of the melted fat over the potatoes. Mix well to incorporate. Place about 1 tablespoon of the remaining duck fat in each mini frying pan, or the full remaining ¼ cup if using a cast-iron skillet. Divide the potatoes evenly among the mini pans, or spread them all evenly in the cast-iron skillet, and place the skillet(s) back in the oven.

4 Cook for 12 to 15 minutes, or until the rostis are golden and crispy on the bottom. Flip them over and cook for another 6 to 8 minutes, or until golden and crispy on the other side.

5 Serve the rostis with a generous amount of clabber cream, caviar, and a sprinkling of chives.

CHEF'S NOTE: I think this recipe is best made with duck fat, but it certainly could be made with clarified butter or vegetable oil.

MAKES 4 SERVINGS

6 medium Yukon Gold potatoes, peeled

Kosher salt and freshly ground black pepper

½ cup duck fat

¼ cup clabber cream

2 ounces paddlefish caviar

1 tablespoon finely sliced chives

I usually have this salad on the menu starting in July or August when baby Chioggia beets come into season, but it's great in colder weather too. The full-size beets in winter have a deep earthy flavor, and once roasted, a subtle caramelized sugar note makes them irresistible!

chioggia beet salad
WITH TOASTED HAZELNUTS AND ROGUE SMOKEY BLUE CHEESE

MAKES 4 SERVINGS

6 baby Chioggia beets (1 to 1½ inch diameter), well scrubbed

½ tablespoon canola oil

Kosher salt and freshly ground black pepper

2 tablespoons sherry vinegar

1 tablespoon minced shallot

1 clove garlic, minced

½ teaspoon Dijon mustard

½ teaspoon chopped thyme leaves

¼ cup grapeseed or canola oil

¼ cup extra-virgin olive oil

2 bunches frisée, trimmed of the greenest leaves

1 bunch watercress, torn into bite-size pieces

1 small head radicchio, thinly sliced

1 cup hazelnuts, toasted and roughly chopped

½ red onion, thinly sliced

2½ tablespoons very thinly sliced chives, divided

6 ounces Rogue Creamery Smokey Blue cheese, cut into ⅓-inch dice, for finishing

1 tablespoon tangerine or blood orange oil, for finishing

Fleur de sel, for finishing

1 Preheat the oven to 350 degrees F. Place the beets in a roasting pan and coat them with the canola oil, salt, and pepper. Add ½ cup water. Cover the pan with foil and place in the oven.

2 Roast the beets until tender, 45 minutes to 1 hour. (Bigger beets may take longer.) When you can easily insert a paring knife into the centers, they are done.

3 Let the beets cool until just warm enough to handle and use a towel to gently rub off their skins. (This is easiest when they are still warm.) Cut them into bite-size pieces: quarters or eighths depending on their size.

4 Meanwhile, make the vinaigrette. Place the sherry vinegar in a small mixing bowl. Add the shallot, garlic, mustard, and thyme and whisk well. Whisk in the grapeseed oil. Slowly whisk in the olive oil. Season to taste with salt and pepper.

5 Combine the frisée, watercress, and radicchio in a bowl of cool water. Wash and spin dry.

6 In a large bowl, toss together the frisée, watercress, radicchio, hazelnuts, red onion, and 2 tablespoons of the chives. Season to taste with salt and pepper, and toss with the vinaigrette. Mound the salad on a serving platter or divide among four plates. Dot the salad with the blue cheese.

7 Toss the baby beets with the tangerine oil. Sprinkle the remaining ½ tablespoon chives and a pinch or two of fleur de sel on the beets. Adjust seasoning to taste. Position the beets across the salad and serve.

CHEF'S NOTE: The vinaigrette can be made a couple of days ahead of time. Just bring it to room temperature and mix it well before using. The beets take a while to roast, cool, and peel, so be sure to give yourself plenty of time. Like many recipes in this book, this recipe contains steps you can do ahead of time that make the final preparation a snap (e.g., roasting and cleaning the beets or making the dressing). Just check seasoning before using or serving, as subtle changes can occur in acidity or saltiness that may need to be adjusted.

In the middle of the cold and misty Seattle winter, delightful salad ingredients are sparse. This quick, easy, and satisfying recipe is there to fill the void. These are all greens and vegetables that overwinter nicely—and together they sing.

white salad

WITH FENNEL, CELERY, FIORE SARDO, AND WHITE TRUFFLE VINAIGRETTE

1   Trim off the greenest part of the frisée until you are left with just pale green and yellow leaves. Tear them into small pieces. Wash the frisée and parsley and spin dry.

2   Peel the celery ribs and slice them thinly into ⅛-inch pieces. Peel the outer layer of the fennel. Using a mandoline, thinly shave the fennel bulb. Remove any core pieces.

3   Combine the frisée, parsley, celery, fennel, 1 tablespoon of the shallot, and the chives in a large bowl. Using a peeler, shave the cheese very thinly into the bowl.

4   To make the vinaigrette, in a small mixing bowl, combine the remaining 1 tablespoon shallot, 1 teaspoon water, the vinegar, and thyme. Whisking constantly, slowly pour in the grapeseed oil. Continuing to whisk, slowly add the truffle oil. Season to taste with salt and pepper.

5   To serve, drizzle 3 tablespoons of the vinaigrette over the salad and toss gently to mix. Adjust seasoning to taste. Place the salad on a platter or divide among four plates. Shave extra Fiore Sardo over the top.

> CHEF'S NOTE: The vinaigrette can be made in advance and refrigerated for up to 2 days. Just bring it to room temperature and whisk well before using. I add water because champagne vinegar is usually very high in acidity, and I find the vinegar on its own overwhelms the truffle flavor; cutting the vinegar with water results in a more balanced vinaigrette. I also use grapeseed oil in this recipe because it is a neutral-flavored oil and will not overwhelm the delicate truffle flavor. If you don't have grapeseed oil, another neutral-flavored oil like canola will work.

MAKES 4 SERVINGS

2 bunches frisée

Leaves from 1 bunch Italian parsley

4 celery ribs

1 fennel bulb

2 tablespoons minced shallot, divided

½ teaspoon very thinly sliced chives

6 ounces Fiore Sardo or Pecorino Romano, plus more for finishing

1 teaspoon champagne vinegar

Leaves from 1 sprig thyme, chopped

⅓ cup grapeseed oil

1 teaspoon white truffle oil

Kosher salt and freshly ground black pepper

The compote that accompanies this dish uses only ingredients that were available during the Middle Ages in Europe, with black pepper and cinnamon being chief among them. I started making this chutney specifically to serve it alongside cured meats like salami and prosciutto. In the middle of winter I often find inspiration in the Old World Kitchen *cookbook when odd (or old) ingredients are abundant: pork fat, turnips, or in this case, storage apples and pears.*

goose prosciutto
WITH TWELFTH-CENTURY CHUTNEY

1   Rinse, dry, and trim the goose breast. Pack the goose in the salt, making sure it is covered with at least ¼ inch of salt on all sides. Refrigerate for 48 hours.

2   Remove the goose from the salt. Brush and rinse the goose and pat dry. You will notice that it has changed color to a darker hue and the breast has shrunk a little.

3   Cut a generous piece of cheesecloth and open it completely. Place the dry goose on the cheesecloth, roll it up, and twist the ends to secure it. Hang the bundle in the back of the refrigerator. After about 4 weeks (3 weeks if using a duck breast), squeeze the meat to test for firmness. If it feels firm and dry, remove it from the refrigerator and unwrap. The flesh should resemble a more moist beef jerky. If it does not, rewrap it and hang it for another 1 to 2 weeks. Larger breasts might take longer. The finished prosciutto should have a rosy hue and the fat should be firm and white.

4   To make the chutney, in a medium saucepan, combine the pear, apple, shallot, and cider vinegar. Stir in the sugar until somewhat dissolved.

5   Using a peeler, remove the outer rind of the orange, being careful not to take any of the bitter white pith. You should have eight to ten pieces of orange peel. Juice the orange to get about ⅓ cup. Add the peels and juice to the saucepan.

(CONTINUED)

MAKES 6 SERVINGS

- 1 goose breast (Muscovy duck breast will also work)
- 2 cups kosher salt, plus more for seasoning
- 1 Anjou or Bartlett pear, peeled and finely diced
- 1 Granny Smith apple, peeled and finely diced
- 1 tablespoon minced shallot
- ¼ cup apple cider vinegar
- ½ cup granulated sugar
- 1 medium navel orange
- 1 teaspoon poudre douce

6   Add a pinch of salt and the poudre douce to the pan and place over medium-high heat. Bring to a simmer, and then turn the heat down so the liquid it is barely bubbling. Cook, stirring occasionally, until the apples and pears are tender all the way through but still hold their shape.

7   Remove from the heat and cool to room temperature. The chutney will keep in the refrigerator for up to 5 days in an airtight container.

8   To serve, slice the prosciutto paper-thin. Fan the slices on a platter and garnish with a scoop of chutney and a strip of orange peel.

CHEF'S NOTE: This is a great curing project to try at home. The best way to determine if the goose breast is cured all the way is to feel it. It should be firm but not as dry as jerky, and the flesh should feel a little tacky. Keep an eye on it while curing, and if it feels like the cheesecloth is getting very moist, replace it. Too much moisture around the duck breast can slow the curing process and cause mold. If you see any mold, I recommend you discard the meat and try again.

Poudre douce means "strong and sweet" and is a ground blend of cinnamon, ginger, nutmeg, and cloves. With the addition of Tellicherry black and cubeb peppers it becomes poudre fort.

This chicken liver pâté is a classic French dish that I think we've really perfected over the years. My dear friend and former sous chef Joseph Margate, now a very fine chef in his own right, spent many hours tinkering with this recipe until it was just so. The Armagnac prunes are my favorite, but we serve many other preserves with this throughout the year: red wine–poached cherries, pickled wild huckleberries, cipolline agrodolce, and black figs with Madeira, to name a few. We usually seal our parfaits with a spoonful of rich chicken or duck consommé, but this melted butter version works really well too.

chicken liver parfait

LARK CLASSIC WITH ARMAGNAC PRUNES AND WALNUT BREAD CROSTINI

1   Remove any dark spots from the chicken livers, but there is no need to remove membranes or veins. Place the chicken livers in a medium mixing bowl and sprinkle with 1 tablespoon of the salt. Add the milk, making sure the livers are covered. Chill for 24 hours. (This helps to draw out any excess blood from the livers.)

2   Using a fine mesh strainer, drain the livers for a few minutes until no liquid remains.

3   Preheat the oven to 400 degree F. In order to taste-test the parfait, you will need to bake a little bit.

MAKES ABOUT TWO 4-OUNCE JARS; 1 JAR SERVES 2 PEOPLE

- ½ pound chicken livers, rinsed
- 1 tablespoon plus 1 teaspoon kosher salt, divided
- 2 cups whole milk
- 1 cup brandy or Armagnac, plus more as needed
- 6 tablespoons cold unsalted butter

(CONTINUED)

Freshly ground white
pepper

¼ cup heavy cream

¼ cup unsalted butter,
melted, or wine jelly,
melted but cool

8 slices walnut bread,
for finishing

1 tablespoon extra-virgin
olive oil, for finishing

12 Armagnac Prunes (see
recipe on page 208), for
finishing

4   In a small saucepan over medium heat, simmer the brandy
until it is reduced to about ⅓ cup. If it flares up, cover it with
another pan to smother the flames and then turn down the
heat. Cool the brandy reduction to room temperature.

5   Place the livers, brandy reduction, and cold butter in a
blender. Season with the remaining 1 teaspoon salt and a pinch
of white pepper. Blend on medium speed, then gradually
increase to high so that the mixture is very finely pureed. Turn
the blender back down to medium speed and add the cream in
a thin stream.

6   Pass the liver mixture through a fine mesh strainer. At
this point you should have a smooth, pale-pink, some-
what-thick puree without any lumps or white bits of butter.

7   Test the seasoning by spooning a teaspoon or two of the
liver mixture into a small ramekin. Place in the oven for a couple of minutes, or until it looks set and has darkened in color.
Taste and adjust the seasoning with salt, white pepper, and a
splash of uncooked brandy, if needed. Repeat this step to check
the seasoning again, if necessary.

8   Fill two 4-ounce tempered glass jars or heatproof glasses
to ¼ inch from the top. Gently tap the jars on the counter to
remove any air bubbles.

9   Fill a heavy-bottomed roasting pan or a saucepan (large enough to hold both jars) with hot water, just enough so that the it comes about halfway up the sides of the jars. Do not place the jars in the water yet.

10   Place the pan with the water on a burner, and over medium heat bring the water up to 175 degrees F. Turn the heat down to maintain the 175-degree temperature. Be sure the temperature holds before adding the jars.

11   Carefully place the jars into the 175-degree water bath and leave uncovered for 20 to 25 minutes, or until the liver mixture barely jiggles when shaken slightly. Depending on how high the sides of the pan are, it might take a little less time or a little longer, so be sure to check the consistency frequently.

12   Remove the jars from the water bath, let cool to room temperature, and then chill for at least 2 hours or overnight.

13   Cover the parfait with the melted butter about ⅛ inch thick to seal it. Chill until ready to serve. After being covered with the butter, it will keep in the refrigerator for up to 5 days.

14   When ready to serve, preheat the oven to 350 degrees F. Brush the walnut bread with the oil and sprinkle with salt. Toast in the oven until crispy, about 10 minutes.

15   To serve, place a jar of liver parfait in the middle of a large plate. Surround it with the prunes and walnut crostini.

CHEF'S NOTE: This is a dish that takes some planning as the livers marinate overnight and then the next day there is a lot of cooking and chilling time before it can be eaten. I recommend starting this dish 2 days before you plan to serve it. I love to serve this with Armagnac prunes that we make in-house (page 208). We serve it with walnut bread crostini, but crusty bread or crackers also work well.

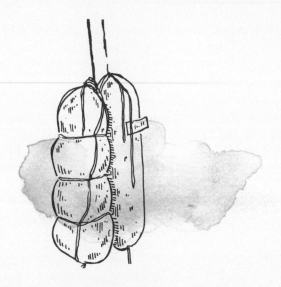

CHARCUTERIE

If you follow tradition, charcuterie starts with the slaughter of a pig in the winter months to take advantage of the cold and often less humid winter conditions for processing and curing, and because the fully grown animal is expensive to feed over the winter. There were often holiday celebrations where pork dishes would play an important annual role. Of course that was during an age when people lived on farms and led more self-sufficient lives.

These days it's easy for me to get a whole hog almost anytime of the year, and I tend to buy two or three during the season of Mist. I source beautiful Tamworth/Hampshire cross hogs from Nick and Sara of Jones Family Farms on Lopez Island—a nice mix of flavorful, lean, and well-larded meat. When I get in a whole hog, it quickly gets divided up into categories according to how I want to use it (see Using the Whole Beast on page 47). There are always parts reserved for our house-made charcuterie.

At Lark, we use the term *charcuterie* to cover the whole family of prepared meats. Bacon, hams (wet and dry), fresh and cured sausage, pâté, terrines, and confit, smoked or not, are all porky versions; there is also a wide variety using beef, lamb, wild game, and poultry. Even cured and smoked fish are forms that we include in the charcuterie family. The idea has always been to preserve and extend the shelf life of these meats. Most are cured with salt and spices and, for longer curing items, nitrates or nitrites. Salamis and chorizos fall into the fermented and cured/dried category and are really best left in expert hands, as they require very careful handling and management of moisture, pH level, and specific environmental conditions to avoid harmful bacteria.

Here are some items we make at Lark:

BACON: Pork belly for a week in salt, brown sugar, and maple, then smoked with apple or pear

TESA: Spice-cured pork belly, unsmoked (an unrolled version of pancetta)

GUANCIALE: Cured hog jowl, smoked and unsmoked, bacon-like, but more refined and delicate

LARDO: Cured thick fatback, seasoned with herbs, black pepper, or cinnamon

DUCK BREAST PROSCIUTTO: Salted, spiced, and dried for a few weeks

GOOSE PROSCIUTTO: Salted, spiced, and dried for a month or more (see recipe on page 61)

FOIE GRAS TERRINE: Soaked in salted milk, deveined, salted and spiced, poached, pressed, and capped with fat

FOIE GRAS TORCHON: Salt-cured, rolled in cheesecloth, dried for a week

CHICKEN LIVER PARFAIT: Soaked, seasoned with butter, cream, and brandy, and gently poached in jars (see recipe on page 63)

RILLETTES: Pork, pheasant, rabbit, wild boar cured in salt, garlic, and herbs; poached in duck or pork fat; shredded and potted (see pork recipe on page 136)

VENISON PÂTÉ: Seasoned with salt, juniper, pork fat, and red wine, then cooked in a terrine

WILD BOAR PÂTÉ: Seasoned with salt, spices, toasted hazelnuts, and cream, then cooked in a terrine

We also buy a wide variety of high-quality hams throughout the year: Italian prosciutto and speck, jamón Ibérico, jamón Serrano, American La Quercia prosciutto, and domestic and European salami and chorizo.

(CONTINUED)

A Few Favorite Combinations:

Salumi coppa *with marinated olives*

Warm lardo on toast *with Sylvetta arugula and fig jam*

Speck *with pickled apples and candied walnuts*

La Quercia prosciutto *with truffled green nectarines and Parmigiano-Reggiano* (see recipe on page 213)

Boccalone nduja on olive oil–fried bread

Salumi mole salami *with cherry tomatoes*

Fra' Mani Salame Nostrano *with mostarda d'uva*

Olli Salumeria salame piccante *with Marcona almonds and quince preserves*

Chorizo *with anchovy-stuffed cherry peppers* (see recipe on page 218)

Wild boar and hazelnut terrine *with persimmon*

Smoked venison heart *with volkorn bread, Lark butter, and green alder cone*

This cake recipe is an adaptation of a favorite financier recipe we used at Licorous. Classic financiers are made with ground almonds, almond flour, sugar, and butter. I use hazelnuts instead for a Northwest twist and brown the butter to make it even toastier and deeper in flavor. The salted caramel toffee ice cream is pure decadence—a treat anytime of year.

hazelnut brown butter cake

WITH SALTED CARAMEL TOFFEE ICE CREAM

1   To make the salted caramel toffee ice cream, grease a baking tray with butter or line with a nonstick baking mat.

2   In a small saucepan over medium-high heat, spread ½ cup of the sugar in an even layer. Cook until it becomes a golden-brown caramel. As the sugar starts to brown in one area, spread it around by gently and lightly swirling the pan. Watch it closely and be careful as sugar burns quickly.

3   Add the salt and then spread the toffee onto the baking tray. Set aside and cool to room temperature. Chop into small pieces.

4   In a large saucepan over medium-high heat, spread the remaining 1 cup sugar in an even layer. Cook until it becomes a golden-brown caramel. Again, watch it closely and swirl gently

(CONTINUED)

MAKES 6 SERVINGS

FOR THE SALTED CARAMEL TOFFEE ICE CREAM

¼ cup unsalted butter, plus more for greasing

1½ cups granulated sugar, divided

¾ teaspoon kosher salt

2 cups milk

1 cup heavy cream

5 egg yolks (use the whites to make the cake)

FOR THE HAZELNUT BRITTLE

1¼ tablespoons unsalted butter, plus more for greasing

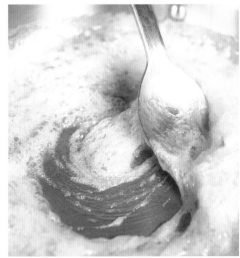

¼ cup water

⅔ cup granulated sugar

⅓ cup light corn syrup

¼ teaspoon baking soda

½ teaspoon kosher salt

¾ cup hazelnuts, roasted, peeled, and roughly chopped

FOR THE HAZELNUT CAKE

½ cup (1 stick) unsalted butter, plus more for greasing

4 egg whites (save the yolks to make the ice cream)

1⅓ cups confectioners' sugar

½ cup hazelnut meal or finely ground hazelnuts

⅓ cup all-purpose flour

3 tablespoons hazelnuts, toasted, skinned, and cracked or roughly chopped

½ cup pitted and sliced dates, for finishing

for even color. Whisk in the butter—the caramel will spatter, so be very careful. Gradually whisk in the milk and cream and bring the mixture just to a simmer. Remove from the heat.

5   Prepare an ice bath.

6   In a large bowl, whisk the egg yolks thoroughly. While whisking, add ½ cup of the hot milk mixture to the bowl to gently temper the eggs. Whisking constantly, add in another ½ cup of the hot milk mixture. (Continuous whisking prevents the eggs from scrambling.)

7   Now begin whisking the milk mixture in the saucepan and slowly pour in the tempered egg yolks. Place the saucepan over medium heat and stir constantly with a wooden spoon or heat-proof spatula. Continue stirring until the mixture has reached a temperature of 180 degrees F and is thick enough to coat the back of a spoon. Strain the custard through a fine mesh strainer into a metal bowl or container. Immediately place the metal bowl into the ice bath. Stir occasionally until the custard cools to room temperature, then refrigerate the custard until thoroughly chilled, at least 4 hours.

8   Process the custard in an ice cream maker according to manufacturer's instructions. In the last few minutes of processing, add ⅓ cup of the chopped toffee and churn until it is evenly incorporated. Transfer the ice cream to a lidded container and freeze for at least 8 hours before serving.

9   To make the hazelnut brittle, grease a baking tray with butter or line with a nonstick baking mat.

10   In a small saucepan over medium heat, combine the water, sugar, corn syrup, and butter. Cook until it is a light caramel

color, about 10 minutes. Remove the pan from the heat and stir in the baking soda and salt. Fold in the hazelnuts.

11   Working quickly, spread the brittle mixture evenly on the baking tray. Cool to room temperature. Chop the brittle into pieces and store in an airtight container at room temperature for 1 to 2 weeks.

12   To make the hazelnut cake, preheat the oven to 350 degrees F. Grease six 3-inch ring molds or an 8-inch cake pan with butter. If using ring molds, place them on a parchment-lined baking tray.

13   In a small saucepan over medium heat, cook the butter until it is golden brown. Cool to room temperature.

14   Using an electric mixer on medium-high speed, whip the egg whites in a large bowl until they reach stiff peaks. In a separate bowl, combine the confectioners' sugar, hazelnut meal, and flour. Gently fold the dry ingredients into the egg whites. Fold in the brown butter and hazelnuts.

15   Pour the batter into the molds. Bake for 20 to 25 minutes, less if using a cake pan. The cake is done when a toothpick inserted in the center comes out clean.

16   To serve, unmold or slice the cake and serve with a scoop of salted caramel toffee ice cream and some hazelnut brittle. Garnish with the dates.

CHEF'S NOTE: Caramel ice creams need as much time in the freezer as possible because the sugar content alters their ability to freeze quickly. Read through Ice Cream and Sorbet on page 78 for some other general rules of thumb. Ice cream custards can be made a day or two in advance or can be made then frozen for a couple of weeks (if they last that long!).

Sorry, I'm not including a recipe for actually making a terrine here. It's a complicated three-day process that doesn't easily lend itself to description; it's more suited to a private lesson or years of looking over the chef's shoulder. My favorite way to eat foie gras is served cold; I love spreading it over a crusty baguette or toasty brioche, with just a pinch of fleur de sel. The kumquat preserve is a very adaptable condiment, delicious here but also with cheeses or as part of dessert.

foie gras terrine

WITH VANILLA KUMQUAT PRESERVE AND TOASTED BRIOCHE

1   Heat a large sauté pan over medium heat. Add 1 tablespoon of the butter to the pan and let it melt and foam. Add one or two pieces of the brioche, depending on how many will fit in the pan. When it is toasted on the first side, flip the brioche over and toast the second side. Repeat with another tablespoon of the butter and continue until all the brioche slices are toasted. Trim the crusts and cut the brioche slices into triangles.

2   Cut the foie gras terrine into two portions and place one piece in the center of each plate. Top with a little sprinkle of fleur de sel. Garnish with a spoonful of kumquat preserve and four triangles of the toasted brioche.

MAKES 4 SERVINGS

4 tablespoons (½ stick) unsalted butter, divided

½ loaf brioche, cut into 8 slices about ⅓ inch thick

2 slices (about 4 ounces each) foie gras terrine

Fleur de sel, for finishing

Vanilla Kumquat Preserve (recipe follows)

vanilla kumquat preserve

1   Thinly slice and seed the kumquats. Combine the kumquats with ½ cup water and the sugar in a medium sauté pan. Halve the vanilla bean, scrape out the seeds, and add them and the pod to the pan. Cook over medium-high heat until the kumquats are tender and the liquid has thickened to a syrup, 8 to 10 minutes. The kumquat preserve will keep covered in the refrigerator for up to 1 week.

MAKES 1 CUP PRESERVE

1 cup kumquats

½ cup granulated sugar

1 vanilla bean

CHEF'S NOTE: If you don't want to buy foie gras terrine already sliced, purchase about 8 ounces of an intact terrine or torchon and slice it just before serving. Be sure to keep any foie gras terrine tightly wrapped until you are ready to serve it. See Sources on page 277 for Seattle Caviar Company, D'Artagnan, Corfini Gourmet, and Nicky USA to purchase prepared foie gras.

We started making our own crackers in our second year of business, and depending on where you work in the restaurant you either love them or hate them. For newer cooks, it's the most challenging thing to make consistently and correctly and is a hard-earned badge of honor when you can do them as well as Saul Perez, a long-time prep and pasta cook. We go through hundreds every week: they're great with cheese and pâté, and our Onion–Poppy Seed version (see variation on page 75) is always served alongside our steak tartare.

Dinah's cheese is a delicious, creamy, rich soft-ripened cheese named after the lead Jersey cow at our friend Kurt Timmermeister's Kurtwood Farms on Vashon Island. Kurt and I have collaborated for years, from dinners on the farm (sometimes as a cook, mostly as a guest) to long mornings as a customer over numerous cafe au laits at Cafe Septieme, Kurt's former restaurant.

dinah's cheese

WITH HONEYCOMB AND LARK CRACKERS

MAKES 4 SERVINGS

1¼ cups all-purpose flour

½ cup pastry flour

1½ tablespoons malt powder

1 tablespoon baking powder

1 teaspoon kosher salt

¼ cup (½ stick) unsalted butter, at room temperature

½ cup ice-cold water

1 wheel Dinah's Cheese

3 tablespoons (2 ounces) raw honeycomb

1 In a food processor, combine the flours, malt and baking powders, and salt. Pulse to mix. Add the butter in small pieces and pulse again. The mixture should be crumbly and hold together slightly. While pulsing, slowly add the cold water and continue to pulse until the dough forms a ball. Transfer the dough to a lightly floured counter or board and knead it for about 1 minute. Wrap the dough in plastic and let it rest for 30 minutes at room temperature.

2 Preheat the oven to 400 degrees F.

3 Cut off one-quarter of the dough, keeping the rest tightly wrapped in plastic. Knead it for about 1 minute. This helps to prevent large bubbles in the crackers. Using a pasta roller, roll

the dough until it is about $\frac{1}{16}$ inch thick. Dock each strip of dough generously with a fork.

4   Using a pasta cutter or a knife, cut the strips into 2-by-3-inch rectangles and lay them out on a baking tray. Repeat with the remaining dough, kneading, rolling, and cutting one-quarter at a time.

5   Bake the crackers until the edges are golden brown, about 4 minutes. Rotate the pan and bake for another 3 to 4 minutes. Transfer the crackers to a rack to cool. The crackers will keep for up to 2 days in an airtight container at room temperature.

6   To serve, arrange the cheese, honeycomb, and crackers on a board with a spreader.

ONION-POPPY SEED VARIATION

Follow the instructions, but after docking the dough, sprinkle each strip with 1 tablespoon minced red onion and 1 teaspoon poppy seeds. Cut the dough strips into triangles instead of rectangles and bake as directed.

CHEF'S NOTE: We roll our crackers out with a pasta roller because we have found that it is the quickest and most consistent way to achieve the right thickness. You can certainly use a rolling pin instead.

An easy and wonderful appetizer, this is especially delicious with a Manhattan when dinner is an hour away (a couple favorite cocktail recipes are included below). Guanciale is pork jowl cured with salt and spices and then hung to dry for a few weeks. We make our own at Lark, sometimes smoked and sometimes not, but either way it's magical: it tends to be more delicate in texture than pancetta but more porky in flavor. Ask your butcher to slice the guanciale as thinly as they possibly can.

guanciale-wrapped dates
WITH FOURME D'AMBERT

MAKES 4 SERVINGS

12 Medjool dates

3 ounces Fourme d'Ambert

12 paper-thin slices guanciale (about 4 ounces
total); thin-sliced bacon
or pancetta will also work

1 Preheat the oven to 400 degrees F.

2 Carefully slice the sides of the dates just enough to open them and remove the pit. Fill each date with ¼ ounce of the Fourme d'Ambert and close the dates back up. Wrap one slice of the guanciale around each date. Place the wrapped dates in a small roasting pan.

3 Bake until the guanciale is rendered and crispy, 6 to 8 minutes.

4 When serving, warn guests that the dates will be very hot and are filled with molten cheese.

MANHATTAN ROCKS

2 ounces bourbon or rye whiskey
1 ounce sweet vermouth
1 dash Angostura bitters
1 cherry

Fill a tumbler with ice. Add the bourbon, vermouth, and bitters. Stir briefly, then add the cherry. The first gulp will be boozy and bracing, the next few easy and cold. As the ice melts, you'll finish with more scent than flavor—a sweet memory.

THE LARK

1 ounce Campari
½ ounce freshly squeezed orange juice
3 ounces sparkling wine
1 orange twist

Pour the Campari and orange juice into a champagne flute. Add the sparkling wine and garnish with the orange twist.

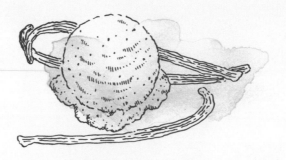

ICE CREAM AND SORBET

Making your own ice creams and sorbets is extremely satisfying, and it's not as complicated as you might think. The best part is once you know the basics you can create any flavor you want. Both ice creams and sorbets need time to chill before churning, and then they need at least eight hours to freeze completely.

ice cream

When I'm training a new cook, I run through these tips to help make the process successful. I hope they help you too.

Once you start making the ice cream custard, it's important not to walk away, at the risk of making scrambled eggs. This can happen at several stages.

1   **When tempering the eggs.** Slowly add the hot milk to the yolk mixture, whisking constantly. If you add the hot liquid too quickly, the yolks can scramble, so adding just ½ cup at a time will raise the temperature of the yolks gently.

2   **While the custard is cooking.** If the heat is too high, the egg yolks can be overwhelmed with heat and can scramble. It is also important to keep stirring so that the heat is evenly distributed.

3   **After the custard has thickened.** After the custard has been strained, if the mixture is left to sit without being cooled quickly in an ice bath, the residual heat can scramble the eggs.

It's also important to make sure you have cooked the custard long enough that it reaches the right consistency, which is called nappé. Many cooks and pastry chefs dip a wooden spoon into the custard and run their finger along the back to create a path through the custard. If the custard is thick enough, it will easily coat the back of the spoon and will not fall into the path. The best way to know the custard has cooked long enough is to make sure it has reached 180 degrees F. While stirring the custard, measure the temperature with a thermometer, and as it approaches 180 degrees F you'll know it's almost ready. If the custard does not reach the right temperature and consistency, the custard will form ice crystals when it freezes instead of maintaining the lovely creaminess of a well-made ice cream.

Have all of your equipment in place before you get started:

1 A whisk to mix the egg yolks when tempering

2 A heatproof cup or ladle to gently pour the hot milk into the yolks

3 A wooden spoon or heatproof spatula

4 A thermometer

5 A fine mesh strainer

6 A metal container or bowl to hold the finished custard for cooling

7 An ice bath large enough for the metal container to fit into easily without tipping over

8 Any flavorings to be added to the custard once it has been strained

sorbet

Sorbet is similar to ice cream in that it is churned in an ice cream maker, and getting the texture right is sometimes tricky. Sorbets are flavored liquid that is mixed with a simple syrup (sugar-water that is boiled and then chilled). The flavor can be pureed fruit, pureed vegetable, melted chocolate, or even a liqueur, to name a few. The most important thing about a sorbet, besides the flavor, is the sugar content. Too much sugar, and your sorbet will not freeze when churned. Too little, and you'll create a block of ice.

Because not all of those flavored liquids have the same sugar content, it is hard to know exactly how much sugar is in the mixture. Many professional pastry chefs use a tool called a refractometer to check for sugar content, but we use a little trick known as the "egg test." Once the flavored liquid and the simple syrup are combined, gently place an uncooked egg (washed and in its shell) into the mixture. If the egg floats, you don't need to add any more simple syrup. If the egg doesn't float, remove it, add a little more simple syrup to the mixture, and place the egg back into the mixture. Repeat until the egg floats. The sugar content is just right when the egg begins to float. You are now ready to chill and churn the mixture.

recipes in this book

(CONTINUED)

vanilla bean ice cream

MAKES 1 QUART

2 cups whole milk	½ cup granulated sugar
¾ cup heavy cream	½ teaspoon kosher salt
1 vanilla bean	1 teaspoon pure vanilla extract
8 egg yolks	

1   In a medium heavy-bottomed saucepan over medium-high heat, combine the milk and cream. Halve the vanilla bean, scrape out the seeds, and add them and the pod to the pan. Bring the mixture just to a simmer. Remove from the heat.

2   Meanwhile, prepare an ice bath.

3   Thoroughly beat together the egg yolks and sugar in a large bowl. While whisking the egg mixture, add ½ cup of the hot milk mixture to the bowl to gently temper the eggs. Whisking constantly, add in another ½ cup of the hot milk mixture. (Continuous whisking prevents the eggs from scrambling.)

4   Now begin whisking the milk mixture in the saucepan and slowly pour in the tempered egg mixture. Place the saucepan over medium heat and stir constantly with a wooden spoon or heatproof spatula. Continue stirring until the mixture has reached a temperature of 180 degrees F and is thick enough to coat the back of a spoon.

5   Strain the custard through a fine mesh strainer into a metal bowl or container. Stir in the salt. Immediately place the metal bowl into the ice bath. Stir occasionally until the custard cools to room temperature.

6 Add the vanilla extract, then refrigerate the custard until thoroughly chilled, at least 4 hours.

7 Process the custard in an ice cream maker according to manufacturer's instructions.

8 Transfer the ice cream to a lidded container and freeze for at least 8 hours before serving.

Ah, the chocolate madeleines . . . one of our most beloved desserts. No visit to Lark is complete without an order to share with the table. While staging at Café Boulud years ago, I saw mini madeleines being prepared to order as an accompaniment to the coffee service. I swore then that I'd serve these wonderful little cakes once I had my own restaurant. It took a few years, but here's my version.

chocolate madeleines

WITH THEO DARK CHOCOLATE SAUCE

MAKES 6 SERVINGS

- 1 cup (2 sticks) unsalted butter
- 6 large eggs
- ¾ cup granulated sugar
- 2 tablespoons light brown sugar
- 1¼ cups all-purpose flour
- ½ cup pastry flour (Bob's Red Mill makes a great one)
- ¼ cup Valrhona cocoa powder
- 2½ teaspoons baking powder
- ½ teaspoon kosher salt
- Powdered sugar, for dusting

1 In a medium saucepan over medium heat, brown the butter slowly, stirring occasionally. It will foam up and then start darkening—you want it to be medium brown and smell nutty. Remove from the heat and cool to room temperature.

2 Preheat the oven to 350 degrees F.

3 Using an electric mixer on medium-high speed, whip the eggs and sugars until the mixture doubles in volume. It should be pale yellow and fluffy. Be patient; this takes a little while.

4 In a medium bowl, sift together the flours, cocoa powder, baking powder, and salt. In three additions, gently fold the dry ingredients into the egg mixture. Stir by hand between additions just until incorporated. Drizzle in the butter and gently fold it into the batter.

5   Fill a pastry bag with the batter; twist and tie the end. Pipe the batter into a mini madeleine mold pan, filling each about three-quarters full.

6   Bake for 4 to 8 minutes, depending on the size of the mold. Our molds hold about 1 tablespoon of batter and we bake them for 4 to 5 minutes. If you are using larger molds, let them bake for a few minutes longer. They will puff up and should be cooked all the way through, not wet in the center.

7   Very carefully flip the pan over onto a board or plate to release the madeleines. Dust them with powdered sugar.

8   Meanwhile, make the chocolate sauce. In a small saucepan, heat the cream and hot water to just under boiling. Place the chocolate in a heatproof bowl. Pour the hot mixture over the chocolate and whisk to melt it and incorporate. Hold the sauce in a warm spot, or chill and warm gently before using.

9   Serve the madeleines right away, nestled in a cloth napkin or towel and dusted with a little more powdered sugar. Place the warm chocolate sauce on the side for dipping.

FOR THE CHOCOLATE SAUCE

¼ cup heavy cream

¼ cup hot water

4 ounces Theo Pure 70 percent dark chocolate, chopped into small pieces

CHEF'S NOTE: You can make the batter up to a day ahead and keep it in the piping bag in the refrigerator. Just pull it out about an hour before you are ready to bake. The madeleines are best served right after they come out of the oven and they don't take long to bake, so I suggest popping them in the oven while you are making after-dinner coffee or tea.

Lemons, while available year-round, tend to be best from December to March. The fragrant and mild Meyer lemon works great for this recipe, though I use half regular and half Meyer lemon juice to keep the tartness. At Lark, we use this lemon curd recipe for a number of desserts, from this satisfying tart to a blood orange parfait layered with lemon curd and a Lillet-soaked sponge cake. And make sure to try this during the summer with loads of fresh berries.

lemon curd tarts

WITH GREEK YOGURT AND CANDIED GRAPEFRUIT PEEL

1 To make the lemon curd, fill a medium saucepan about one-third with water and bring just to a simmer.

2 In a large metal bowl, combine the whole eggs, egg yolks, and sugar. Stir in the lemon juice and zest.

3 Place the bowl over the simmering water, making sure the bottom of the bowl is not touching the water. Whisk the egg mixture vigorously until it is thick and smooth, being careful to avoid scrambling the eggs. Mix in the butter and salt. Strain and chill. You can keep the curd covered in the refrigerator for up to 5 days.

4 To make the candied grapefruit peel, prepare a simple syrup by combining 1 cup of the sugar and 1 cup water in a small saucepan and bringing it to a boil for about 1 minute. Remove from the heat and cool to room temperature.

5 Remove the peel and pith from the grapefruit. Keep the grapefruit flesh rounded. Carefully separate the grapefruit sections from the membranes and set aside for serving.

6 Put the grapefruit peel in the simple syrup and simmer gently for 40 minutes. The grapefruit peel will become candied and translucent and the syrup will thicken. Remove the pan from the heat and let the mixture cool to room temperature. Roll the grapefruit peel in the remaining 1 cup sugar. It can be stored in the refrigerator for up to 1 week. Slice the grapefruit peel thinly before using.

7 To make the tarts, in a large bowl, combine the flour, butter, shortening, and salt. Using clean hands, mix until it resembles coarse meal. Add the cold water and blend the mixture until the water is incorporated. Stir until a smooth dough is formed,

(CONTINUED)

MAKES 4 SERVINGS

FOR THE LEMON CURD

3 whole eggs

3 egg yolks

½ cup granulated sugar

Zest from 1 lemon

½ cup freshly squeezed lemon juice

¼ cup (½ stick) unsalted butter, at room temperature, cut into cubes

⅛ teaspoon kosher salt

FOR THE CANDIED GRAPEFRUIT PEEL

2 cups granulated sugar, divided

1 grapefruit

FOR THE TARTS

2½ cups all-purpose flour, plus more for dusting

¾ cup (1½ stick) cold unsalted butter, cut into small cubes

¼ cup vegetable shortening

½ teaspoon kosher salt

¼ cup ice-cold water

½ cup plain Greek yogurt

1 tablespoon honey

being careful not to overwork it. Form the dough into a disk, wrap it in plastic wrap, and chill it for 1 hour.

8   Preheat the oven to 350 degree F. Set four individual tart molds on a baking tray.

9   Cut a piece of the dough large enough to roll out a tart shell. Lightly dust the counter or a board with flour. Using a rolling pin, roll the dough into a circle that is $\frac{3}{16}$ inch thick and slightly larger than the tart mold. Gently place the rolled dough into the mold and form it into the shell, being careful not to tear the dough. Trim any excess dough from the shell. Using a fork, dock the dough. Place the tart mold in the refrigerator for about 20 minutes to chill. Repeat with the remaining dough.

10   Place a piece of parchment paper large enough to cover the dough in each shell, and place pie weights (or dry beans) on top of the parchment to weigh the dough down while it bakes.

11   Bake for 15 to 18 minutes. Remove the parchment paper and weights, then return the shells to the oven and continue to bake for another 3 to 5 minutes, or until golden brown. Let the shells cool to room temperature.

12   Fill the shells with the lemon curd. Bake for 2 to 3 minutes to set the curd. Let the tarts cool to room temperature, then remove from the molds.

13   To serve, in a small bowl, whisk together the yogurt and honey. Place each tart on its own dessert plates. Garnish the tarts with the yogurt mixture, thinly sliced grapefruit peel, and grapefruit segments.

CHEF'S NOTE: The tarts can be prepared in 45 minutes or less, but they require additional unattended time. We use small tart shells to make smaller tarts. You can use this same recipe to make a larger tart; just note that the cooking times might be a little longer.

The lemon curd can take up to 20 minutes to thicken; be patient and switch hands if your arm starts to get tired. If the bowl seems like it is getting too hot, remove it from the water bath for 30 seconds and then return it, whisking continuously.

We have an outstanding array of great apples once harvest season rolls around. One of my favorite heirloom varieties is the King apple, originally from New Jersey but grown around the Northwest since the early 1900s. My friends Caryn and Andy Buck discovered that they had this apple growing on their family farm on Shaw Island. Now, I'm lucky enough to get most of the crop each year. Yellow-and-red striped, sweet, crisp, juicy, and great for eating and baking. This easy apple cake stays moist with the addition of some homemade applesauce. And the green apple sorbet? Yes!

spiced apple cake

WITH CARAMELIZED APPLE, CANDIED WALNUTS, AND GREEN APPLE SORBET

1   To make the candied walnuts, preheat the oven to 350 degrees F. Butter a baking tray or line with a nonstick baking mat.

2   Arrange the walnuts on a baking tray and bake for 5 to 6 minutes, or until golden brown and fragrant. Set aside to cool.

3   In a wide, heavy-bottomed saucepan over medium heat, spread the sugar in an even layer. Cook until it becomes a golden-brown caramel. As the sugar starts to brown in one area, spread it around by gently and lightly swirling the pan. Watch it closely and be careful as sugar burns quickly.

4   Stir in the walnuts and quatre épices until the nuts are evenly coated. Pour the mixture onto the baking tray. Using a fork, quickly separate the walnuts so they are not touching each other or sitting in excess caramel. Sprinkle them with a little fleur de sel.

(CONTINUED)

MAKES 8 SERVINGS

FOR THE CANDIED WALNUTS

Unsalted butter, for greasing

½ cup walnut halves

½ cup granulated sugar

¼ teaspoon quatre épices

Fleur de sel

FOR THE GREEN APPLE SORBET

4 skin-on Granny Smith apples, quartered and cored

Juice from 1 lemon

1 cup granulated sugar

½ cup water

FOR THE CARAMELIZED
APPLES

¼ cup granulated sugar

1 Granny Smith apple,
   peeled, cored, and
   finely diced

FOR THE APPLE CAKE

2 cups peeled and diced
   apples

½ cup water

2 tablespoons calvados
   or brandy

2 cups all-purpose flour

¼ cup cocoa powder

1 tablespoon ground ginger

1 teaspoon kosher salt

½ teaspoon baking powder

½ teaspoon freshly ground
   black pepper

1 cup (2 sticks) unsalted butter, at room temperature

1 cup brown sugar

4 large eggs

1 cup molasses

2 teaspoons confectioners'
   sugar

5   Set aside at room temperature to cool completely. They will keep for up to 1 week stored in an airtight container at room temperature.

6   To make the green apple sorbet, toss the apple quarters with the lemon juice. (This prevents them from browning.) Arrange the apples in a single layer in a large dish and place in the freezer for 1 hour.

7   Meanwhile, make a simple syrup by combining the sugar and water in a small saucepan over high heat. Bring to a boil, and then turn off the heat and let the syrup cool completely.

8   Remove the apples from the freezer, place them in a food processor, and pulse. Add 1 cup of the simple syrup to the food processor. Puree until very smooth and pale green. Strain the puree through a fine mesh strainer; using a ladle, push as much through the strainer as possible (you are trying to separate out the skin). To make sure that there is the right amount of sugar in the puree for freezing, complete the "egg test" described on page 79.

9   Immediately process the puree in an ice cream maker according to manufacturer's instructions. The quicker you do the whole process from pureeing the apples to churning the sorbet, the more the sorbet will maintain its nice green color. Transfer the sorbet to a lidded container and freeze for at least 8 hours before serving.

10   To make the caramelized apples, in a wide, heavy-bottomed saucepan over medium-high heat, spread the sugar in an even layer. Cook until it becomes a golden-brown caramel. Again, watch it closely and swirl gently for even color. Stir in

the apple. (Note that the caramel will steam and possibly seize and turn very sticky or brittle, but it will soften again as the apples cook.) Cook for 2 to 3 minutes, or until the apples take on a golden-brown caramel color and are just tender.

11 Spread the apples on a plate in a single layer and cool to room temperature until ready to use.

12 To make the apple cake, first, cook the applesauce. In a small saucepan over medium-high heat, combine the apples and water and bring to a simmer. Turn the heat down to low and cook until tender. Puree the mixture with a hand blender or in a food processor. Stir in the calvados and set aside to cool.

13 Preheat the oven to 350 degrees F. Arrange eight 4-ounce silicone muffin molds on a baking tray, or butter and flour an 8-inch cake pan.

14 In a medium bowl, sift together the flour, cocoa powder, ginger, salt, baking powder, and pepper and set aside.

15 Using an electric mixer on medium speed, cream together the butter and brown sugar. Beat in the eggs one at a time, scraping down the sides of the bowl in between each addition. The mixture will look broken by the time all the eggs are added. Fold in the molasses, 1 cup of the applesauce, and the dry ingredients.

16 Pour the batter into the muffin molds or cake pan and bake for 20 to 25 minutes for muffin molds or 30 to 35 minutes for a cake pan, or until a skewer inserted into the center of the cake comes out clean. Cool the cakes on a rack.

17 To serve, sprinkle the warm cakes with a little confectioners' sugar. Place a cake on a plate and spread some of the candied walnuts around it. Also place a small pile of walnuts on one side of the plate. Arrange some of the caramelized apples and caramel around the plate. Place a quenelle (an egg- or football-shaped spoonful) of the apple sorbet on top of the pile of walnuts.

CHEF'S NOTE: Quatre épices is also known as four-spice. It comes in a number of blends and it usually contains ground pepper, nutmeg, cinnamon, and ginger. We get ours from World Spice Merchants (see Sources on page 277).

You can make some of these components, such as the applesauce and candied walnuts, ahead of time; they keep well and can be used in a number of other ways. The sorbet can also be made in advance.

This recipe has become a must-have every winter at Lark. Sweet, fragrant Meyer lemons, egg yolks, and cream—whipped and frozen—bring sunny brightness to our dark nights. Meyer lemons are best when you get them by the sackful from your father-in-law!

meyer lemon parfaits

WITH VANILLA KUMQUAT PRESERVE AND MEYER LEMON JUS

MAKES 6 SERVINGS

1½ cups granulated sugar

9 egg yolks

½ cup freshly squeezed Meyer lemon juice, strained

2 teaspoons finely grated Meyer lemon zest

2 cups heavy cream, whipped to stiff peaks and chilled

FOR THE MEYER LEMON JUS

¾ cup granulated sugar

½ cup freshly squeezed Meyer lemon juice, strained, plus more as needed

1   Arrange six ring molds (about 3 inches in diameter) on a parchment-lined baking tray that will fit in the freezer.

2   In a small saucepan, combine the sugar and ½ cup water. Place over medium-high heat and cook until it reaches the hard-ball stage, about 255 degrees F.

3   Meanwhile, using an electric mixer with a whip attachment at medium-high speed, beat the egg yolks until pale in color.

4   Turn the mixer down to low speed and very slowly pour the hot sugar mixture into the mixing bowl, aiming to drizzle it down the side of the bowl and avoid the whip. There will be some sugar that hardens and collects on the whip and side of the bowl before it incorporates into the yolks. Once all the hot sugar is incorporated, turn the mixer up to high speed and whip until the mixing bowl is no longer hot to the touch, just slightly warmer than room temperature.

5   Add the lemon juice and zest and whip slowly until the juice is fully incorporated. Gently fold in the cream in three batches.

6   Pour the mixture into the molds and transfer to the freezer, making sure the tray lays flat. Freeze the parfaits completely before serving, about 8 hours.

7   To make the Meyer lemon jus, in a small saucepan, combine the sugar and 1 cup water and bring to a boil for about 1 minute. Remove from the heat. Stir in the lemon juice and zest and let the jus cool to room temperature. Taste and adjust with more juice if it is too sweet.

8   Transfer the jus to an airtight container and store in the refrigerator until ready to serve. The jus will keep in the refrigerator for up to 1 week.

9   To serve, unmold one of the parfaits and place it in the center of a bowl. Pour some of the jus around the parfait and add a few lemon segments. Top the parfait with a spoonful of kumquat preserve. At Lark we also serve the parfaits with sweetened whipped cream and a lace cookie.

2 teaspoons finely grated
   Meyer lemon zest

Meyer lemon segments
   (optional)
Vanilla Kumquat Preserve
   (page 73), for finishing

CHEF'S NOTE: The parfait needs time to freeze before it is served, so it's best to make it a day or two in advance. We make them in ring molds about 3 inches in diameter and fill them about 1½ to 2 inches deep. However, this parfait can be frozen in containers or molds of various sizes. You can freeze it in individual glasses or even one larger dish and just scoop to serve. The Vanilla Kumquat Preserve and Meyer lemon jus can also be made a day or two ahead.

evergreen

APRIL TO JULY

Oh the longing for something bright green and crisp after months of celeriac and potatoes. Suddenly, there are hundreds of shades of green outside. The Douglas firs, alders, and hemlock that seem timeless have new buds at the tips of their branches. Apple, cherry, and peach trees leaf out in greens blushed with red. Young wheat in the Palouse looks like a new lawn, and everything else is about to explode in shades of green we scarcely remember. Great eating is on the way, yet the menu changes slowly in spring.

The first greens on our menu this time of year are stinging nettles, wood sorrel, miner's lettuce, and wild watercress, all foraged from the Cascade or Olympic ranges. Then comes the asparagus from the Yakima Valley and Walla Walla. The first Western Washington farms start delivering sometime late May or early June with radishes, mizuna, and Tom Thumb and Little Gem lettuces. And the snap peas . . . sweet, fresh sugar bombs. I taste them as they arrive in the kitchen and it seems a shame to add dressing or cook them. But I get over it.

As the green garlic and spring onions arrive, we still rely on the pantry, and my farmer friends are sick of me calling to see what's popping up next. When sea urchin, razor clams, and spring porcini and morels make their way onto the menu, the change of season feels real. Rhubarb and strawberries paired with fresh goat cheese and thick cream make desserts a breeze. And suddenly we have fresh halibut, black cod, and then salmon to cure again.

I've been lucky enough to spend a few days fishing for salmon and halibut each year. My friend Riley, the former owner of the Willows Inn on Lummi Island, is one of the last remaining reef net fishers in the world. It's an amazing process where two crews on rafts collaborate to catch sockeye and pink salmon as they migrate from the ocean to the Fraser River, resulting in unmatched quality. I've also learned to troll for salmon farther north at Sund's Lodge in the Queen Charlotte Strait of British Columbia. Great fun, hard work, and very little sleep. Perfect.

For a few weeks in April, we have a lovely convergence of spring delights: fresh halibut, young and tender stinging nettles, and the first true morels of the season. I bring them together in this bright, earthy, and creamy dish. After months of root vegetables and cabbage we Northwesterners are craving something green, and usually the first stinging nettles fill the void. At Lark I have a network of hard-working foragers who bring them right to me, but nettles grow wild all over. Whidbey Island's bucolic setting is known for having nettles galore, and many a part-time forager takes revenge on this weed. They do sting, so use tongs to move them from the storage container to the pan for cooking. Cooking removes the stinging properties. Nettles are highly nutritious, full of vitamins and minerals, and delicious. And if this is all just too much, spinach is a great substitute.

neah bay halibut

WITH CREAMED NETTLES AND MORELS

1   Season the halibut on both sides with salt and pepper.

2   Heat the oil and 1 tablespoon of the butter in a large sauté pan over medium-high heat. Add the halibut fillets and cook on one side until golden brown, 3 to 4 minutes. Turn them over gently and use a spoon to baste the fillets. Continue cooking until they are just cooked through and translucent in the center, 2 to 3 more minutes. Transfer the halibut to a warm plate until ready to serve.

3   In a medium sauté pan over medium-high heat, melt the remaining 1 tablespoon butter. Add the morels with a pinch of salt and pepper and cook them until just soft and tender, 2 to 3 minutes. Add the garlic and sauté for 1 to 2 minutes until softened but not browned. Using tongs, add the nettles to the pan and stir them into the morels and garlic. Add the wine to deglaze the pan and let it reduce slightly. Stir in the cream and adjust seasoning to taste. Simmer until the cream has reduced to a slightly thickened sauce. Adjust seasoning to taste.

4   To serve, spoon the creamed nettles and morels onto a serving platter. Place the halibut on top and garnish with the chives.

MAKES 4 SERVINGS

1½ pounds halibut fillets (or cheeks), cut into 6-ounce portions

Kosher salt and freshly ground black pepper

1 tablespoon extra-virgin olive oil

2 tablespoons unsalted butter, divided

¼ pound morels, trimmed, washed, dried, and sliced

1 teaspoon minced garlic

½ pound stinging nettles, picked and washed

2 tablespoons dry white wine

¾ cup heavy cream

1 tablespoon minced chives, for finishing

CHEF'S NOTE: When cleaning morels, it is best to use a brush or towel to gently remove the dirt. Sometimes they can be especially dirty and hard to clean completely with a brush and need to be washed in water. It is important not to soak them; dunk them in the water, toss them around briefly and then dry immediately in a salad spinner before laying them out on paper towels.

Be very careful when handling the stinging nettles. At Lark we double up on latex gloves when cleaning them.

This Spanish-inspired dish would be wonderful made with some home-canned tomatoes on a cool night. It will get you dreaming of the Costa Brava. Baby octopus are quite small, fitting in the palm of your hand, with a head about the size of a walnut. If you use a larger octopus, cut it into bite-size pieces and simmer longer to get them tender. In the warmer months, use vine-ripened Big Beef tomatoes.

baby octopus

WITH SMOKED PAPRIKA AND OLIVE OIL—SMASHED POTATOES

1   Heat the oil in a large saucepan over medium heat. Add the onion and sauté until light golden brown, about 10 minutes. Add the garlic and cook until softened but not browned. Add the tomatoes and white wine. Cook until the wine has reduced slightly (this will happen quickly). Add the octopus, water, pimenton, and summer savory and season to taste with salt and pepper. Bring to a boil, and then immediately turn the heat down to maintain a simmer. Cook uncovered until the octopus is tender, 1 to 1½ hours.

2   Remove from the heat and serve, or chill for later. To reheat, bring the octopus and sauce to a gentle simmer over medium heat.

3   Meanwhile, prepare the smashed potatoes. Place the potatoes, garlic, salt, and 2 quarts cold water in a large saucepan over medium heat. Bring to a simmer and cook until the potatoes are tender when pierced with a fork, about 20 minutes. Drain off the water. Peel the garlic cloves and return to the pan. Crush the potatoes with their skins and roughly smash the garlic with a fork. Drizzle with the oil and sprinkle with fleur de sel.

4   To serve, spoon the hot octopus and sauce over the smashed potatoes. Sprinkle with a little pimenton.

CHEF'S NOTE: The octopus can be made up to 1 day ahead of time. That's what I did when I served it for JM's and my wedding party. If your octopus are not pre-cleaned, make sure to remove the eyes, beak, and innards.

MAKES 4 APPETIZER SERVINGS

2 tablespoons extra-virgin olive oil

1 small yellow onion, diced

3 cloves garlic, slivered

1 cup ripe tomatoes, cored and diced, or canned diced tomatoes

¼ cup dry white wine or dry rosé

1 pound baby octopus

2 cups water or chicken stock

2 teaspoons pimenton (sweet smoked paprika), plus more for finishing

½ teaspoon fresh summer savory or rosemary, chopped

Kosher salt and freshly ground black pepper

FOR THE SMASHED POTATOES

6 small skin-on Yukon Gold potatoes

3 unpeeled cloves garlic, cracked

2 teaspoons kosher salt

2 tablespoons extra-virgin olive oil

Fleur de sel

May means the beginning of salmon season to me. It begins with the big Chinook (or king) salmon and moves through the other four species: coho (or silver), sockeye, pink (or hump-back), and chum. One of my favorites is marbled salmon, a genetic cousin to red Chinook with half orange and half white flesh, and it's just as fatty and succulent. Northwest runs begin in mid-May and last through September, with each species making their appearance as summer progresses.

wild salmon
WITH FINGERLING POTATOES AND TWO SORRELS

MAKES 4 SERVINGS

½ pound fingerling potatoes

2 tablespoons kosher salt, plus more for seasoning

1½ pounds skin-on wild king salmon, scaled, trimmed, deboned, and cut into 4 (6-ounce) portions

Freshly ground black pepper

1 tablespoon plus 2 tea-spoons extra-virgin olive oil, divided

1 tablespoon unsalted butter

1   Place the potatoes in a medium saucepan that will fit them easily. Cover with cold water, add the salt, and bring the water to a simmer over medium heat. Simmer gently until the potatoes are tender throughout but not falling apart. Drain the potatoes and let them cool enough to be handled.

2   While the potatoes are still warm, peel off the skins. (They are much easier to peel while warm.) Cut the potatoes into ¼-inch-thick coins. Set aside.

3   Season the salmon fillets on both sides with salt and pepper.

4   Heat a medium ovenproof sauté pan over high heat and add 2 teaspoons of the oil. Place the salmon, skin side down, in

the pan and cook until the skin is crispy, 2 to 3 minutes. Turn it over and add the butter. As the butter melts, use a spoon to baste the salmon. Continue cooking the salmon until it is medium-rare to medium, 1 to 2 more minutes. Transfer the salmon to a plate and let it rest for 2 minutes before serving.

5   Drain off half of the fat in the pan and add the potato coins to heat them through.

6   To make the sorrel sauce, in a large saucepan, bring 4 quarts salted water to a boil. Prepare an ice bath. Blanch and shock the spinach. Squeeze out any extra water. In a blender, puree the spinach and French sorrel together.

7   Meanwhile, in a small saucepan, bring the wine, shallot, bay leaf, and peppercorns to a simmer and reduce the mixture by two-thirds. Whisk in the butter a few cubes at a time. The sauce will thicken up a little. Strain the sauce through a fine mesh strainer and season to taste with salt. Mix the spinach puree into the sauce. Set aside in a warm (not hot) place until you are ready to serve.

8   In a small mixing bowl, combine the lemon juice and the remaining 1 tablespoon oil. Add a pinch of salt and pepper. Gently toss the sheep sorrel and frisée with half of the vinaigrette. Taste and add more vinaigrette if necessary.

9   Gently reheat the potato coins. Add the chives and toss. Spoon the potatoes onto four plates. Top with a salmon fillet, crispy skin side up, and a bundle of sorrel salad. Spoon the sorrel sauce around the salmon.

CHEF'S NOTE: The sorrel sauce is temperature sensitive and cannot be made too far in advance. Make the spinach and sorrel puree close to the time you are ready to complete the sauce or it will turn brown. The best place to keep the finished sauce is in a warm area of the kitchen.

Cooking salmon is a gentle process and it is best done medium-rare or medium. If your salmon pieces are more than 1 inch thick in the center, as king salmon can sometimes be, place them in the oven at 350 degrees F after you have basted them so that they can continue to cook.

FOR THE SORREL SAUCE

8 ounces baby spinach

4 ounces French sorrel, cleaned

1 cup dry white wine

1 shallot, sliced

1 bay leaf

8 black peppercorns

¾ cup (1½ sticks) cold unsalted butter, cut into cubes

Kosher salt

½ teaspoon freshly squeezed lemon juice

¼ cup wild sheep sorrel, or a mixture of chopped tender herbs such as parsley, chives, tarragon, or basil

¼ cup frisée, yellow and pale-green leaves only, washed and spun dry

1 tablespoon minced chives, for finishing

I love this combination of bright, lively green garlic, salty bottarga, and creamy, briny sea urchin. Bottarga is the salted and dried roe of tuna or mullet, often dipped in beeswax to preserve its moisture and texture. Sea urchin roe (or more properly, gonads) is called uni in Japanese and was probably first seen or tasted by most of us in a sushi bar. In the Mediterranean, it's often served with just a squeeze of lemon. When green garlic is at its prime, you should be able to use nearly the entire stalk: the white and the light-green parts right on up to the darker green. If the bulb looks almost like a regular head of garlic (individual cloves forming), or if the woody center stalk is forming, it's no longer green garlic.

spaghettini

WITH GREEN GARLIC, BOTTARGA, AND SEA URCHIN ROE

1   Fill a large saucepan with salted water and bring it to a boil over high heat. Once boiling, cook the spaghettini until just al dente according to the package directions, about 6 minutes.

2   Drain the spaghettini and toss it with 1 tablespoon of the oil. Lay the noodles on a baking tray to cool. If you are going to serve it soon, leave the spaghettini at room temperature. Otherwise store in the refrigerator and bring it back to room temperature before continuing with the recipe.

3   Heat the remaining 1 tablespoon olive oil in a medium sauté pan over medium heat. Add the garlic, season with a little salt, and sauté until softened but not browned, about 2 minutes. Add the white wine and reduce it by half. Add the lemon juice and butter and swirl the pan to incorporate. Add the cooked spaghettini to the pan and toss to coat it with the sauce. Season to taste with salt and pepper.

4   Turn off the heat. Add the uni and gently mix to incorporate and warm them. Try not to break up the pieces.

5   To serve, transfer the pasta to a warm serving platter or divide it among four warmed plates. Sprinkle the parsley over the top. Carefully arrange the sliced bottarga on top of the spaghettini.

MAKES 4 SERVINGS

12 ounces spaghettini

2 tablespoons extra-virgin olive oil, divided

2 tablespoons sliced green garlic

Kosher salt

2 tablespoons dry white wine

1 teaspoon freshly squeezed lemon juice

2 tablespoons unsalted butter

Freshly ground black pepper

8 uni (sea urchin roe), torn into bite-size pieces

1 tablespoon thinly sliced (chiffonade) Italian parsley leaves, for finishing

16 very thin bottarga (tuna or mullet) slices, wax coating or casing removed

AROMATICS

In my kitchen the word *aromatics* refers to a whole group of flavorings that include fresh herbs, garlic, shallots, and sometimes chiles. I divide herbs into two camps according to how they're used in cooking: *tender* and *resinous*. I think of dry spices as a separate category. By no means is this a complete list; there are many more varieties used throughout the world for specific cuisines, but these are the most common and widely available.

Growing your own herbs is a great idea and much more economical than purchasing them; even in a small space it's possible to grow a few favorites. One plant each of thyme, sage, and rosemary will provide more than enough for most home cooks, while parsley, chives, and basil might require two of each if you cook with them often. Snip and wash just before throwing them in.

At Lark we use a pound or two of parsley, chives, and thyme every week, and our own backyard garden could never keep up with what we need. Instead I choose to focus on offbeat, harder-to-find herbs like lovage (it has a savory, celery-like flavor that is great with tomatoes), lemon verbena (with its bright, sweet, citrusy fragrance), and borage (we use the new leaves and flowers, which are mild and cucumbery).

TENDER HERBS should be snipped or torn just before using, and they will lose color and change in character the longer they are cooked. Used in cold dishes, they hold up very well. Tender herbs can be used as whole leaves, torn, sliced chiffonade, minced, or roughly chopped. Often the stems are edible and delicious in some recipes, especially cilantro and parsley stems.

Basil	Dill	Parsley
Borage	Lemon verbena	Rose geranium
Chervil	Lovage	Shiso
Chives	Mint	Sorrel
Cilantro	Nasturtium	Tarragon

RESINOUS HERBS are heartier, tougher, and generally can be cooked longer without losing their potency. They can be picked as whole leaves, sliced chiffonade, or roughly chopped. They are generally used in smaller quantities compared to the tender herbs, as the resinous oils they contain tend to be more potent and can easily overpower a dish if not used judiciously.

Bay	Oregano	Summer savory
Lavender	Rosemary	Thyme
Marjoram	Sage	Winter savory

garlic

Garlic is one of the backbones of nearly every great cuisine. There are many varieties, all with different levels of intensity and fragrance; try them all, play around, experiment, and always buy whole heads and peel as you need them. The pre-peeled or semi-preserved garlic is never going to be as fresh and bright.

At Lark we use garlic in many different forms. Crushed and smashed garlic releases the essential oils and will make a formidable aioli with an assertive garlic pungency. Thinly sliced and stewed with octopus and tomatoes for a couple of hours, the garlic will be present but not overwhelm the other flavors. The following are a few ways we use garlic at Lark.

WHOLE HEADS: Split in half and added to stocks. Top removed and gently baked with olive oil for roasted garlic to flavor soups, sauces, or vinaigrettes.

SKIN-ON WHOLE CLOVES: Cracked with the flat side of a knife to smash slightly. Cooked alongside large cuts of meat, such as a leg of lamb or pork roast, or added to a sauté pan with a sprig of thyme and a knob of butter for basting a hanger steak or thick slab of halibut.

THIN SLICES: Quick stews or braises, where you want garlic flavor and presence but not overwhelming sharpness. Great in shellfish dishes like clams with chorizo.

SLIVERS: Sliced and then julienned for a stronger garlic flavor but still not overpowering. Perfect for many uses, such as when sautéing mushrooms, hearty greens, or green beans, or in pastas.

MINCED: Similar intensity as slivers, but used when the goal is to have the garlic to disappear and blend in to the finished dish. Great as a foundation for a pan sauce or dressing.

(CONTINUED)

CRUSHED AND FINELY CHOPPED: When you smash a clove with the side of a knife and chop it very finely, you'll notice the cutting board becomes wet as the oils are released. This will result in garlic flavor that is spicy, hot, and pungent and is perfect for aioli, pasta puttanesca, or anywhere you want the garlic flavor front and center. Be sure to warn your dinner guests.

BLACK GARLIC: Black garlic is a relatively new product originally from Korea, but it's now being made in the United States. Black garlic is the result of whole heads being very slowly fermented and dried over a couple of days. The process gives the cloves a sweet, smoky, slightly caramelized flavor. The texture is pliable and soft, almost like roasted garlic, but the cloves are sliceable. We use them whole, sliced, slivered, or pureed into a paste to flavor dressing and sauces. It's pretty expensive but fun to try, and a little goes a long way.

shallots

Shallots—the smaller, milder, and sweeter cousin to onions—play a huge role at Lark. We use ten to fifteen pounds of them every week as the foundation for many of our dishes. It's our mid-level sauté cooks' job to cut all of the herbs, shallots, and garlic for the rest of the kitchen every day—a task that takes at least 30 minutes. It's one of the proving grounds in the Lark kitchen, day after day mincing, slicing, and chopping—and believe me no one's going to let a less-than-perfect sliced chive or bruised, watery minced shallot slip past. If it's not up to our standard, it gets turned back for use in our stocks or thrown out. Cooks learn fast to get it right. We always prep them by hand, never with a food processor.

WHOLE: Roasted slowly in their skins, shallots are great alongside a pan-roasted steak, as a puree to flavor vinaigrette, or as a spread under some crispy-skinned Spanish mackerel.

SLICES: Sliced into thin rings for use in dishes where you want the shallots to have presence but a milder flavor. We use these in our mussel and clam dishes, pastas, and sautéed greens.

MINCED: Used just about everywhere: in sauces, vinaigrettes, most of our salads, and with sautéed vegetables like our cucumbers with dill, butter, and shallots.

chiles

Chiles appear throughout the year at Lark. Fresh serranos and jalapeños brighten the Geoduck Ceviche (page 177). The hot Tuscan controne pepper, used dry and ground, shows up often in our pastas and braises. Goat Horn, Hatch, Rio de Oro, or habanero from Alvarez Organic Farms in the Yakima Valley all find homes; they are charred, stuffed, and pickled every year during the season of Bounty.

Chiles and peppers should be washed carefully, cored, and seeded, and then can be cut depending on their use. Toasting in a pan changes the flavor profile considerably. For very hot peppers, use gloves when handling, and remember, your knives and cutting board will absorb some of the oils from the peppers, so wash them well before moving on to the next task.

A NOTE ON DRY SPICES

Dry spices should be bought often and in small quantities, preferably in whole or seed form. Toast in a dry pan, cool to room temperature, and grind in a spice grinder or clean coffee grinder before using. Tired, years-old spices will contribute very little to your cooking other than a dusty staleness. See Sources on page 277 for our favorite suppliers.

This is a very adaptable dish that can be served any time of year and falls into a family of rice dishes that I call "soupy." This Evergreen version features first-of-the-season English peas. Black venere rice is a Chinese varietal now grown in the Po Valley of Piedmont, Italy. We use house-made pancetta or guanciale most of the time, but the end piece of a good prosciutto works nicely too.

black venere rice

WITH SQUID, PANCETTA, PEAS, AND PARSLEY

MAKES 4 SERVINGS

1   Open the squid tubes by inserting a knife into the tube and slicing down one side of the tube. Open up the squid tube so that the inside is facing up. Using a sharp knife, score the inside of the tube in a crisscross pattern. When scoring the squid, be sure not to cut all the way through the flesh.

2   Heat 2 tablespoons of the oil in a large sauté pan over medium-high heat. Sear the squid quickly for 30 to 45 seconds, tubes first, and in batches if they won't all fit in the pan in a single layer. Set aside. Add the pancetta and the remaining 1 tablespoon oil to the pan. Once the pancetta is cooked about three-quarters of the way through, add the shallot and cook for 1 minute. Add the garlic and cook for another minute. Add the rice and stir to incorporate and coat it with fat. Add the wine and simmer until it has reduced by half. Season with about the salt and pepper. Add the stock and water. Simmer until the rice is tender, 35 to 45 minutes, adding more water if the pan starts to dry out before the rice is cooked. The consistency should be thick and soupy. Add the peas and cook for about 2 minutes. Stir in the squid to warm through. Add a pinch of hot pepper. Add the lemon juice and stir to incorporate. Adjust seasoning to taste.

3   To serve, divide the squid and rice among four plates and sprinkle a little of the parsley on top of each serving.

CHEF'S NOTE: Bomba or carnaroli rice can be substituted in this recipe. (I know, they're all kind of hard to find.)

1 pound squid tentacles and tubes, cleaned

3 tablespoons extra-virgin olive oil, divided

4 ounces pancetta, cut into 1-by-¼-inch strips

2 tablespoons minced shallot

2 teaspoons minced garlic

1 cup black venere rice

⅓ cup dry white wine

2 teaspoons kosher salt, plus more for seasoning

½ teaspoons freshly ground black pepper, plus more for seasoning

1 cup chicken stock

1 cup water, plus more as needed

1 cup freshly shelled English peas

Ground controne hot pepper

2 teaspoons freshly squeezed lemon juice

1 tablespoon thinly sliced (chiffonade) Italian parsley leaves

Sweetbreads are the thymus gland of lamb or veal. I serve both during the year, but particularly enjoy lamb sweetbreads. They have an almost briny taste that is more pronounced than that of veal, though both are very rich, fatty, and concentrated proteins. Try them lightly floured or breaded and then pan-fried until crispy. I have fond memories eating sweetbreads in Argentina, where they are grilled and served with bread, kosher salt, and a generous squeeze of lemon as part of an asador (barbecue).

lamb sweetbreads

WITH ARTICHOKE HEARTS, WHITE BEANS, AND GREEN GARLIC

MAKES 4 SERVINGS

FOR THE WHITE BEANS

1 cup dry cannellini or great northern beans

4 unpeeled cloves garlic, cracked

2 sprigs thyme

1 bay leaf

2 teaspoons kosher salt

FOR THE ARTICHOKES

1 lemon, halved

1   To prepare the white beans, cover the dry beans with cold water by at least 2 inches and soak them overnight.

2   Drain the beans and place them in a medium saucepan over medium heat. Cover them with cold water and add the garlic, thyme sprigs, and bay leaf. Simmer for 1 to 1½ hours, or until the beans are tender. In the last few minutes of cooking, add the salt.

3   Drain the beans and cool them in a single layer on a baking tray. Once cooled, pick out and discard the garlic, thyme sprigs, and bay leaf. If not using right away, the beans will keep in an airtight container in the refrigerator for up to 2 days.

4   To prepare the artichokes, fill a mixing bowl with water and squeeze the juice from the lemon into the water. Add the lemon halves.

5   Peel the outer leaves from the artichokes. Using a paring knife, trim the artichokes until just the heart remains. Using a spoon, scoop out the inner furry choke. After trimming, cut each artichoke into quarters through the stem. Place them in the lemon water until ready to cook. (This will help prevent oxidation.)

6   In a saucepan large enough to fit the artichoke quarters in 1 or 2 layers, melt the butter over medium heat. Add the garlic and sauté until softened but not browned, about 2 minutes. Add the artichoke hearts, wine, and water, and season to taste with salt and pepper. Add more water as needed so that the artichokes are completely covered.

7   Cut out a round of parchment paper that will just fit inside the rim of the saucepan. Reserve the parchment paper lid (known as a cartouche).

8   Bring the water to a simmer and cover the pan with the cartouche. Cook until the artichokes are just barely tender when tested with the tip of a knife, 30 to 40 minutes. Remove the pan from the heat and allow the artichokes to cool in the cooking liquid until it reaches room temperature. You can store the artichokes in the liquid until you are ready to use them. Otherwise, remove them from the liquid, store in an airtight container, and refrigerate for up to 3 days.

9   To prepare the sweetbreads, cover the sweetbreads in cold water and soak them in the refrigerator overnight. Remove the sweetbreads and discard the water.

10   Combine the sweetbreads, onion, celery, carrot, garlic, thyme sprigs, and bay leaf in a large saucepan. Add enough water to cover everything and bring it to just under a simmer over medium heat. Poach gently for just 3 to 5 minutes.

11   Remove the sweetbreads from the poaching liquid and place on a plate lined with a clean kitchen towel, letting half the towel hang off the plate. Fold that half of the kitchen towel over the top of the sweetbreads and place another plate on top. Put moderate weight, 2 to 3 pounds, on top of the plate and place in the refrigerator overnight.

(CONTINUED)

2 artichokes

1 tablespoon unsalted butter

4 cloves garlic, thinly sliced

¼ cup dry white wine

1 cup water or chicken stock

Kosher salt and freshly ground black pepper

FOR THE SWEETBREADS

12 ounces lamb sweetbreads

½ onion, cut into large dice

½ celery rib, cut into large dice

1 small carrot, cut into large dice

2 cloves garlic

3 sprigs thyme

1 bay leaf

Kosher salt and freshly ground black pepper

2 tablespoons extra-virgin olive oil

2 tablespoons chopped green garlic

¼ cup dry white wine

½ cup chicken or lamb stock

Leaves from 3 sprigs thyme, chopped

1 tablespoon unsalted butter

12   Remove the sweetbreads from the refrigerator and peel off the outer membranes. When you peel them, the sweetbreads will separate into smaller pieces. Pat them dry and season with salt and pepper.

13   Heat the oil in a medium sauté pan over medium-high heat. Add the sweetbreads to the pan and cook them on each side until golden brown, 3 to 4 minutes per side. Remove from the pan and set aside. Add the green garlic to the pan and sauté for about 2 minutes. Add the wine and reduce slightly. Add the stock, cooked white beans, artichoke quarters, and the thyme leaves. Simmer until the mixture has reduced slightly and resembles a ragout.

14   Add the butter and sweetbreads. Simmer together for 1 minute to reheat the sweetbreads thoroughly. Adjust seasoning to taste.

15   To serve, leave the sweetbreads in the pan while you spoon out the artichokes and beans into a mound on each of four plates. Place the sweetbreads on top. Spoon the extra sauce around each plate.

CHEF'S NOTE: The sweetbreads need to soak in cold water for 24 hours before cooking, and so do the beans. Also, once the sweetbreads have been poached, they will need to press in the refrigerator overnight. Be sure to keep this in mind when planning the dish.
  If you don't want to cook the beans from scratch, you can substitute canned. If using canned, buy the best, one small can will do, and rinse before adding them.

Pork belly has become almost synonymous with Lark. It's much more common now, but when we first opened, it was a rare sight outside of an Asian restaurant. After all, who would want all that fat? Julia Child said "fat equals flavor," and I've been an adherent to her philosophy for years. I buy a superb Tamworth/Hampshire cross from Nick and Sara at Jones Family Farms on Lopez Island. Once you try the meat from a heritage-breed hog, you'll never go back to commodity pork. We change the pork belly accompaniments many times throughout the year, and this combination is a perennial favorite.

pork belly

WITH ENGLISH PEAS, PEA VINES, AND WHOLE GRAIN MUSTARD SAUCE

1   Place the pork belly in a pan or container large enough to hold it. Cover it completely with the brine. Place plastic wrap directly onto the brine and set a plate or other weight on the plastic wrap to hold the pork belly down below the liquid. Refrigerate for 24 hours.

2   Preheat the oven to 325 degrees F.

3   Remove the pork belly from the brine and, without rinsing it, place it in a large, deep ovenproof pot with sides at least 4 inches high. Add the carrot, onion, celery, garlic, bay leaves,

(CONTINUED)

MAKES 4 SERVINGS

2 pounds pork belly, skin removed

½ gallon Basic Brine (see recipe on page 120)

1 carrot, peeled and cut into large dice

½ onion, cut into large dice

1 celery rib, cut into large dice

4 unpeeled cloves garlic,
   cracked

2 bay leaves

1 tablespoon whole black
   peppercorns

1 cup dry white wine

2 quarts chicken or
   pork stock

FOR THE ENGLISH PEAS
AND PEA VINES

1 cup English peas, shucked

1 tablespoon unsalted butter

8 spring or cipollini onions,
   quartered lengthwise

2 cups young pea vines,
   washed, trimmed, and
   torn into bite-size pieces

Kosher salt and freshly
   ground black pepper

FOR THE WHOLE GRAIN
MUSTARD SAUCE

1 tablespoon plus 1 tea-
   spoon cold unsalted
   butter, divided

1 tablespoon minced shallot

2 tablespoons dry
   white wine

1 cup chicken stock

1 tablespoon Dijon mustard

1 tablespoon whole
   grain mustard

½ tablespoon very finely
   chopped chives

Kosher salt

Fleur de sel, for finishing

and peppercorns. Add the wine, stock, and enough water to cover the pork belly. Place the pot over a medium-high heat until it comes just to a simmer. Skim off any foam that accumulates.

4   Place a round of parchment paper directly onto the pork belly. Set an ovenproof plate on top of the parchment to keep the pork belly completely submerged. Cover the pot tightly with a lid or aluminum foil.

5   Place the pot in the oven and cook for 3 to 3½ hours, or until the pork is fork-tender. It may take even longer—be patient and don't remove it from the oven until it is fork-tender. Remove the pot from the oven, uncover (lid, plate, and parchment), and cool to room temperature.

6   Once it has cooled, remove the pork belly from the braising liquid and place it on a baking tray or large plate. Remove any aromatics that may be stuck to the pork. Cover the pork with a piece of parchment paper. Strain the braising liquid and reserve for another use, if desired. (See page 30 for more on making and using stocks.)

7   Place another baking tray or large plate on top of the pork belly and add a 2-pound weight (such as a can or a box of salt). Place it in the refrigerator and chill for at least 4 hours or overnight for best results.

8   Set the pressed pork belly on a board with the fat side facing up. Cut crisscrossed lines about ⅛ inch deep and ¼ inch apart into the fat. This allows for a crispier top when searing. Trim the edges so that you have straight sides. (Save the trimmings for another use.) Cut the pork belly into equal portions of about 4 ounces each, or into pieces about 2 by 3 inches. At this point, you can wrap the pork belly blocks in plastic wrap and refrigerate them until you are ready to sear them. They will keep for about 4 days.

9   Preheat the oven to 400 degrees F.

10   Heat a cast-iron skillet over medium heat. Place the pork belly pieces in the hot pan, fat side down, then put the pan in the oven for 10 minutes. The scored, fatty side should be golden brown and crispy; if it is not, return the pan to the oven for a few more minutes.

11 Turn the pieces over and drain some of the excess fat from the pan. Be careful; the rendered fat has a tendency to spit. Place the pan back in the oven for another 2 to 3 minutes. Remove the pork from the pan and blot on a paper towel.

12 To prepare the English peas and pea vines, in a large saucepan, bring about 2 quarts salted water to a boil. Prepare an ice bath. Blanch the peas in the boiling water until just cooked, 2 to 4 minutes. Drain and shock the peas in the ice bath. Drain and set aside.

13 In a medium sauté pan over medium heat, melt the butter. Add the spring onions and sauté until translucent and just tender, 7 to 8 minutes. Stir in the pea vines and cook for 2 minutes, or just until wilted. Add the peas and season to taste with salt and pepper. Cook until the peas are just warmed through.

14 To make the whole grain mustard sauce, in a small saucepan over medium heat, melt 1 teaspoon of the butter. Add the shallot and cook until softened but not browned, 2 to 3 minutes. Add the wine to deglaze the pan. Simmer until the pan is almost dry. Add the chicken stock and simmer until it is reduced to ¼ cup. Whisk in both of the mustards and the remaining 1 tablespoon butter. Add the chives and season with salt if necessary. Keep warm until ready to serve.

15 To serve, spoon the warm pea mixture around each of four plates. Place the pork belly, crispy side up, in the center. Sprinkle each piece with fleur de sel. Drizzle the mustard sauce around the plate.

CHEF'S NOTE: Brining, braising, and pressing the pork belly is a 2-day process, so allow yourself plenty of time. On the other hand, once it has been braised and pressed, it can last up to 4 days in the refrigerator until you are ready for the final step of crisping the top. The amount of brine produced by the Basic Brine recipe is more than you'll need for this recipe. You can either cut the amount in half or save the leftover brine for another use.

In many of our homes, roasted chicken is a mainstay in the colder months. This method takes just minutes longer in prep time than a traditional chicken that's just buttered before roasting. We use a rotisserie at Lark to cook these, with the pan of potatoes placed underneath to catch those delicious drippings. If you have a rotisserie attachment for your grill, I suggest giving it a try—it's a showstopper.

mustard-roasted chicken

WITH DRIPPINGS POTATOES, SAUTÉED CHARD, AND LEMON

1   Preheat the oven to 450 degrees F.

2   In a small mixing bowl, whisk together the wine, mustards, and 2 tablespoons of the shallot. Add the thyme and 1 tablespoon of the oil.

3   Truss the chicken with kitchen string (see instructions on page 119).

4   Reserve ¼ cup of the mustard marinade and rub the rest evenly all over the chicken. The chicken can be roasted right away or refrigerated until ready to cook. If chilled, be sure to leave it out at room temperature for about 30 minutes before roasting. Season the chicken with salt and pepper.

5   In a large cast-iron skillet, toss the potatoes with the remaining 2 tablespoons oil. Season to taste with salt and pepper. Arrange the potatoes in the pan so that they slightly overlap, like shingles. Place the chicken on top of the potatoes and put the skillet in the oven. Roast for about 30 minutes, then brush the reserved marinade onto the chicken. Continue to roast the chicken for about another 30 minutes or until the juices run clear. Insert a meat thermometer at the thickest part of the thigh; the chicken is ready when it reads 180 degrees F. Remove the pan from the oven and let the chicken rest for 10 to 15 minutes before serving.

6   Meanwhile, prepare the chard. In a large sauté pan over medium-high heat, melt the butter. Add the remaining 1 tablespoon shallot and cook for 1 to 2 minutes, or until softened and just golden. Add the chard and sauté until lightly wilted. Season to taste with salt and pepper. Squeeze a little lemon juice over the chard and toss to incorporate. Adjust seasoning to taste.

7   To serve, spoon the chard onto a serving platter. Using a microplane, zest the lemon half over the chard. Carve the chicken and serve it with the drippings potatoes.

MAKES 4 SERVINGS

½ cup dry white wine

¼ cup Dijon mustard

¼ cup whole grain mustard

3 tablespoons minced shallot, divided

Leaves from 3 sprigs thyme

3 tablespoons extra-virgin olive oil, divided

1 whole chicken (3½ pounds), giblets removed, rinsed and patted dry

Kosher salt and freshly ground black pepper

6 large Yukon Gold potatoes, cut into ¼-inch-thick slices

1 tablespoon unsalted butter

1 bunch rainbow chard, washed, stemmed, and leaves cut into 3-inch-wide strips

½ lemon

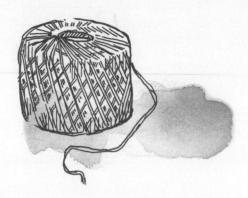

BRINING AND CURING

Almost any meat that we slow cook or confit at Lark is brined or cured first. Curing is simply sprinkling with salt, adding aromatics, and chilling overnight. It's like marinating but not quite as elaborate: no wine, oil, chiles, or sugar as a rule. You'll be enhancing the natural flavors without changing them too much. This type of curing differs from the long curing used to make pancetta or other charcuterie items. We cure lamb shanks and necks, beef short ribs, pork shoulders, duck legs, and rabbit thighs, just to name a few.

For example, I will start with a couple pounds of thick-cut beef short ribs, pat them dry, and sprinkle them lightly with kosher salt all over. I put them in a pan with eight unpeeled cloves garlic (cracked with the side of a knife), a dozen whole peppercorns, two bay leaves, and six thyme sprigs, and refrigerate overnight. When I braise the ribs the next day, I add the aromatics in and remove them after cooking.

We brine pork bellies, trotters, chickens, guinea fowl, briskets, and fish that will be smoked. With brining, you'll find that the meat turns out feeling a bit more dense but still very juicy.

The following brine recipe (page 120) is a good starting place. Play around with how long you leave things in the brine: 3 hours for a whole chicken, 2 to 3 days for a whole beef brisket, 1 day for a pork loin, 1 hour for a trout for smoking. Go ahead—make the recipe your own. Toss some cracked garlic cloves in. Add a bit of spice with some chopped serrano chiles. Hate juniper? Leave it out. You get the idea.

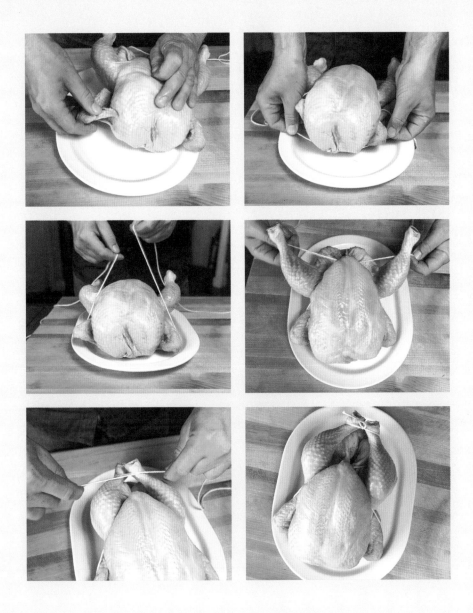

how to truss a chicken

Trussing a chicken serves several purposes. The bird will cook more evenly, it will be easier to carve, and it will be more attractive in presentation. When cooking a chicken on a rotisserie, it keeps the legs and wings from flopping around and burning as it turns on the spit. An untrussed bird will also throw the balance off of the turning spit; a neat, tight package works more effectively. After the bird has been fully cooked and rests, trim the string off with kitchen shears. You may need to cut the string in a few places to be able to untruss the bird more easily, but make sure to remove every last bit—you don't want to send any string out to the dinner table.

(CONTINUED)

1   Rinse a whole chicken with cold water inside and out, then thoroughly pat dry.

2   Place the chicken on a cutting board in front of you, with the legs pointing toward you. Shape it by compressing the legs in toward the body, and try to make the bird round and compact. Tuck and fold the wings under the body to secure them.

3   Pass a 24- to 30-inch-long piece of kitchen string under the body and legs. With the string ends in each hand, bring both sides up and cross over the top of the tail.

4   Wrap each end of string around the bone end of a drumstick, cross them again, and pull to tighten the string (this should pull the ends of the drumsticks together).

basic brine

If the meat you are brining will not require so much liquid to submerge it, cut the recipe in half. Do not reuse the brine.

MAKES 1½ GALLONS

1½ gallons water

2 cups granulated sugar

2 cups kosher salt

10 whole juniper berries

10 whole cloves

10 whole black peppercorns

4 bay leaves

1   Combine all the ingredients in a large stockpot and bring to a boil. Remove the pot from the heat and let the brine cool to room temperature. Transfer the brine to an airtight container and store in the refrigerator for up to 3 days.

Morels, rabbit, and cream are a winning combination, and the addition of fava beans and this subtle emmer pappardelle make it truly spectacular. Fresh morels are ideal, but this is a recipe where dried mushrooms can be used: just soak them in the cooking wine for 30 to 60 minutes, then slice them, reserving the wine for the sauce.

rabbit

WITH MORELS, FAVA BEANS, AND EMMER PAPPARDELLE

1   To make the emmer pappardelle, combine both flours and the salt in a mixing bowl and whisk thoroughly. Put the flour mixture on a clean, dry counter or board and mound it up, making a well in the center. In a small bowl, whisk together the eggs and water. Pour the mixture to the well and use a fork to gradually mix the egg into the flour until it forms a crumbly dough. Using your hands, bring the dough together into a rough ball. Knead it for about 10 minutes, or until it is smooth and elastic. Cover the dough with plastic wrap and let it rest for 30 minutes at room temperature.

2   Remove the plastic wrap and cut the dough into slabs about ½ inch thick. Using a pasta roller, starting at its widest setting, roll the dough through the machine. Fold the dough into thirds and run it through the machine at its widest setting again.

(CONTINUED)

MAKES 4 SERVINGS

FOR THE EMMER
PAPPARDELLE

1 cup all-purpose flour

1 cup Bluebird Grain Farms
   organic emmer flour, plus
   more for sprinkling

½ teaspoon kosher salt

4 large eggs

1 tablespoon water

FOR THE RABBIT

1 fryer rabbit, cut into loin
   and hind legs (save the
   forelegs for another use)

3 tablespoons extra-virgin
  olive oil, divided

1 tablespoon minced garlic

Leaves from 6 sprigs thyme,
  chopped

Kosher salt and freshly
  ground black pepper

FOR THE MOREL SAUCE

1 tablespoon unsalted butter

1 teaspoon minced garlic

1 tablespoon minced shallot

1 cup morel mushrooms,
  washed and thinly sliced

¼ cup dry white wine

½ cup chicken stock

½ cup heavy cream

½ cup fava beans, blanched,
  shocked, and peeled

Leaves from 2 sprigs thyme,
  chopped

Kosher salt and freshly
  ground black pepper

Fleur de sel, for finishing

Repeat this 8 to 10 times. Continue to roll the dough through
the machine, adjusting the setting to make it smaller each time.
Roll twice on each setting before moving on to the next.

3   Once you have rolled out the dough to the desired thickness, cut the sheet into 2-inch-wide strips. Sprinkle the strips
with a little emmer flour and loosely coil them on a baking
tray or plate. Set aside at room temperature until you are ready
to proceed.

4   Bring a large pot of salted water to a boil. Cook the
pappardelle until it is tender but al dente, 4 to 5 minutes.
Remove the pasta from the pot and drain, reserving some of
the cooking liquid.

5   To prepare the rabbit, marinate the rabbit pieces in 2 tablespoons of the oil, the garlic, and thyme and refrigerate overnight.

6   Preheat the oven to 375 degree F.

7   Remove the rabbit from the refrigerator and wipe off the
garlic. Season each rabbit piece with salt and pepper.

8   Heat a large ovenproof sauté pan over medium-high heat.
Add the remaining 1 tablespoon oil and sauté the rabbit pieces
for 3 to 4 minutes, or until crispy and golden. Turn them over
and cook on the other side for a few more minutes.

9   Remove the loins from pan and set aside on a large plate to rest. Place the pan still containing the hind legs in the oven for 8 to 10 minutes to finish cooking. Place the legs on the plate and let them legs rest for 4 to 5 minutes. Return the loins to the pan and put in the oven for about 1 minute, just to heat them through, and then slice each loin into 5 or 6 pieces.

10   To make the morel sauce, heat a medium sauté pan over medium-high heat and add the butter, garlic, and shallot. Sauté until golden and cooked through. Add the morels and cook for 1 to 2 minutes, or until they have softened a little. Add the wine and reduce it slightly. Add the stock and cream and let the sauce simmer until it thickens a bit. Add the fava beans and thyme. Season to taste with salt and pepper.

11   To serve, add the pasta to the sauté pan with the morel sauce. If the sauce seems a little thick, add a couple spoonfuls of reserved cooking liquid and swirl the pan to mix it in. Spoon onto four serving plates and arrange the rabbit pieces over the top. Sprinkle with a little fleur de sel.

> CHEF'S NOTE: Emmer flour pasta dough will resemble whole wheat pasta dough and has a great texture when it is cooked. It can be made up to 1 day ahead of time. Toss it with a little flour to prevent sticking, or lay the strips of pappardelle out on the counter to dry slightly before refrigerating, which also helps prevent sticking. Keep the pasta in the refrigerator covered with a kitchen towel.

Fresh porcini mushrooms are a real treat, and when they're available you should use them in everything, with abandon! Even dried or frozen porcinis will contribute a rich and unique flavor to a dish, especially when infused into a stock or with cream. We're lucky in the Northwest to get porcinis twice a year, in May or June and then again in October.

hanger steak
WITH PORCINI BUTTER AND MIZUNA SALAD

1   Preheat the grill and rub each steak with ½ tablespoon of the oil. Season the steaks generously on all sides with salt and pepper.

2   Drizzle the porcini slices with 2 tablespoons of the oil and season to taste with salt and pepper. Grill the porcinis on each side for 2 to 3 minutes. Set aside.

3   Grill the steaks for about 2 minutes on each side, or until the internal temperature reaches 125 degrees F. Set the steaks on a large plate and set them aside to rest for at least 5 minutes.

4   In a mixing bowl, combine the mizuna, parsley, chives, and shallot. Add the lemon juice and the remaining 1 tablespoon oil and toss well to combine. Season to taste with salt and pepper.

5   To make the porcini butter, using your hands, mash the butter up in a bowl so that it is pliable. Add the porcini, chives, and garlic to the butter and mix with a fork to combine. Season with salt and pepper. Shape the butter into a disk or loaf and wrap in parchment or plastic wrap.

6   To serve, rewarm the steaks and porcinis on the grill for about 1 minute. Slice the steaks against the grain into ¼-inch-thick slices and arrange them on four plates. Lay the porcinis against the steak slices and top them with a generous dollop of the porcini butter. Divide the mizuna salad among the plates. Sprinkle each steak with fleur de sel.

> CHEF'S NOTE: The porcini butter can be made ahead of time and stored in an airtight container in the refrigerator for up to 3 days. Pull it out a little beforehand to let it soften slightly before using.

MAKES 4 SERVINGS

20 ounces hanger steak, divided into 5-ounce portions

5 tablespoons extra-virgin olive oil, divided

Kosher salt and freshly ground black pepper

4 fresh medium porcini mushrooms, cleaned and thickly sliced

1 bunch mizuna or arugula, washed, dried, and stemmed

¼ cup whole parsley leaves

1 tablespoon minced chives

1 tablespoon minced shallot

1 teaspoon freshly squeezed lemon juice

FOR THE PORCINI BUTTER

½ cup (1 stick) unsalted butter, at room temperature

1 fresh medium porcini mushroom, cleaned and cut into ¼ dice

1 tablespoon minced chives

1 teaspoon minced garlic

Kosher salt and freshly ground black pepper

Fleur de sel, for finishing

Asparagus is so versatile and easy to work with that from late April to June it will be on the menu in several places. At home I love it cooked in a cast-iron pan or grilled, then tossed in a salad or showered with grated pecorino. This recipe is just one of many ways to enjoy asparagus. I also recommend trying this dish with chopped toasted hazelnuts or toasted pecan halves sprinkled on top.

yakima asparagus
WITH LEMON BROWN BUTTER

MAKES 4 SERVINGS

1 bunch asparagus, woody ends trimmed

2 tablespoons unsalted butter

½ teaspoon freshly squeezed lemon juice

Kosher salt and freshly ground black pepper

1   Peel the asparagus from about 2 inches below the tip to the end.

2   Prepare an ice bath. In a large pot of boiling salted water, blanch the asparagus until just cooked and tender, 2 to 4 minutes depending on thickness. Shock the asparagus in the ice bath to stop cooking. Drain the asparagus and set it aside on a plate to dry, or pat dry with a paper towel.

3   Heat the butter in a medium sauté pan over medium heat until it is golden brown and has a nutty aroma. It will be quite foamy as it browns. Add the asparagus to the browned butter and toss to coat. Cook it just long enough to warm through, about 1 minute. Add the lemon juice and season to taste with salt and pepper. Toss to incorporate.

4   Transfer the asparagus to a serving platter and drizzle the extra brown butter over the top. Serve warm.

This quick and easy recipe is great by itself as a warm salad or as a side for roasted lamb or halibut. Green chickpeas are available for a few weeks each spring and are very different from dried chickpeas: they're light, fresh, and more like a pea. Black garlic originally hails from Korea but it's now produced in California. These heads of garlic have been fermented and slowly dried, resulting in a sweet, smoky, caramelized, tender clove of garlic that is unlike anything else.

green chickpeas

WITH BLACK GARLIC AND CONTRONE PEPPER

1   Prepare an ice bath. In a medium pot of boiling salted water, blanch the chickpeas until they are just cooked through. They should be tender but still have some texture. Shock them in the ice bath and drain.

2   Heat the oil in a medium sauté pan over medium heat. Add the chickpeas and a pinch of salt and sauté for 2 minutes, or just to heat them through. Add the black garlic and sauté for about 1 minute before stirring to combine it with the chickpeas. Add the parsley and hot pepper. Toss to mix them with the chickpeas. Adjust seasoning to taste. Serve warm.

MAKES 2 SERVINGS

1 cup fresh green chickpeas, shucked

1 tablespoon extra-virgin olive oil

Kosher salt

2 cloves black garlic, thinly sliced

1 tablespoon thinly sliced (chiffonade) Italian parsley leaves, for finishing

Ground controne hot pepper or crushed red chile flakes, for finishing

The first time I had gnudi was at April Bloomfield's The Spotted Pig in New York City's West Village. I was entranced and vowed right then to figure out how to make them as well as she did. It took months of testing and trials, but we finally figured them out. Gnudi are very delicate once cooked, so handle them gently; they will fall apart if overcooked.

ricotta gnudi

WITH NETTLES, PINE NUTS, AND PARMIGIANO-REGGIANO BRODO

MAKES 4 SERVINGS

FOR THE PARMIGIANO-REGGIANO BRODO

1 quart water or chicken stock (use stock for richer brodo)

4 ounces Parmigiano-Reggiano rinds

2 celery ribs, cut into large dice

1 carrot, peeled and cut into large dice

½ onion, sliced

4 unpeeled cloves garlic, cracked

1 bay leaf

10 whole black peppercorns

1   To make the Parmigiano-Reggiano brodo, in a large saucepan over high heat, combine all of the brodo ingredients. Bring to a boil, then turn the heat down to maintain a simmer for 2 hours. Strain the brodo through a fine mesh strainer and chill until ready to use.

2   To make the ricotta gnudi, place the ricotta in a few layers of cheesecloth and squeeze out as much moisture as possible.

3   In a large bowl, whisk the eggs. Add the ricotta and use your hands to thoroughly incorporate. Add the flours and Parmigiano-Reggiano to the bowl and stir to thoroughly incorporate. Add the salt and season to taste with pepper.

4   Scoop out 1 to 1½ tablespoons of the ricotta mixture and gently hand-shape it into a slightly oval-shaped ball. It should

resemble a small egg. Gently roll each gnudi piece in semolina flour and place on a baking tray or large plate. Repeat with the remaining mixture until the tray is full. Loosely cover with plastic wrap and chill the gnudi for at least 1 hour before cooking, preferably longer. Don't boil the gnudi until immediately before serving.

5   To make the nettle sauce, wearing gloves to protect yourself from the nettles, pick the leaves off the stalks (as you would pick basil off the stem). Rinse in water to clean the nettles.

6   Heat the oil and garlic in a large saucepan over medium heat. Sauté gently until the garlic has softened and turns light golden. Using tongs, add the nettles and stir to combine with the garlic. Cook until the nettles wilt slightly, about 1 minute. Add 1 cup of the brodo to the pan and bring to a simmer. Add the butter and season to taste with salt and pepper. Stir until the butter is incorporated, then reduce the heat to low to keep the sauce warm. Adjust seasoning to taste.

7   To serve, bring a pot of salted water to a gentle boil. Add three or four gnudi per person (about sixteen pieces total) to the water and boil gently for about 4 minutes, or until the gnudi have risen to the surface. Do not overcook! Use a slotted spoon to remove the gnudi from the water and transfer them directly into the saucepan with the nettle sauce. Gently coat the gnudi with the sauce. Be very gentle with them as they are delicate and will break easily.

8   Spoon the gnudi evenly among four serving bowls. Spoon some of the nettles and sauce over the gnudi and sprinkle with the Parmigiano-Reggiano and pine nuts. Drizzle a little oil into each bowl and serve immediately.

CHEF'S NOTE: Parmigiano-Reggiano or Grana Padano rinds work great for flavoring broths. Store them in the freezer in a ziplock bag until you have enough to make brodo (Italian for "broth"). It is worth buying real Parmigiano-Reggiano—it's expensive, but you'll use less because the flavor is so much richer than domestic brands, and if you save the rinds like we do, you'll be able to use every scrap so there's no waste.

FOR THE RICOTTA GNUDI

1¾ pounds dry ricotta cheese (ricotta varies in moisture, so choose the driest one possible)

2 large eggs

⅓ cup semolina flour, plus more for rolling

2 tablespoons all-purpose flour

4 ounces finely grated Parmigiano-Reggiano

1 teaspoon kosher salt

Freshly ground black pepper

FOR THE NETTLE SAUCE

4 cups stinging nettles

1 tablespoon extra-virgin olive oil

1 tablespoon slivered garlic

1 tablespoon unsalted butter

Kosher salt and freshly ground black pepper

2 tablespoons finely grated Parmigiano-Reggiano, for finishing

2 tablespoons toasted pine nuts, for finishing

1 tablespoon extra-virgin olive oil, for finishing

One of the great pleasures of the Northwest is the local asparagus season. The Yakima Valley and Walla Walla areas are known for producing superior asparagus. When the season gets going, you'll find it on our menu in several places: an easy appetizer like this recipe, part of a salmon or halibut dish, made into soup, or nestled alongside a juicy ribeye steak. White asparagus is such an elegant option, and it is a bit milder without the chlorophyll.

Bagna càuda means "hot bath" in Italian and is a specialty of Piedmont in the north. Modern versions are often made without milk, but I like the depth and complexity it adds. If you have extra, it also makes a great dip for raw vegetables.

white asparagus bagna càuda

WITH POACHED EGGS

MAKES 4 SERVINGS

1 cup whole milk

12 salt- or oil-packed anchovy fillets

4 cloves garlic, thinly sliced

Ground controne hot pepper or cayenne pepper

1 cup extra-virgin olive oil

¼ teaspoon freshly ground black pepper

1   To make the bagna càuda, in a small saucepan, combine the milk, anchovies, garlic, and hot pepper. Whisk in the oil and black pepper. Set the saucepan over medium heat and bring the bagna càuda to a simmer. Turn the heat down to low and maintain a gentle simmer for about 1 hour. Keep warm until ready to serve.

2   Carefully peel the asparagus with a vegetable peeler to remove the stringy outer layer.

3   Prepare an ice bath. In a medium saucepan over high heat, bring 2 quarts water, 2 tablespoons of the salt, and the sugar to a boil. Add the asparagus and simmer for 3 to 5 minutes, or until tender. Remove the asparagus from the water and shock in the ice bath. Drain and pat dry. Set aside.

4   In the same pan, bring another 2 quarts water to a boil over high heat, then turn it down to maintain a simmer. Add the remaining 1 tablespoon salt and the vinegar. Swirl the water with a spoon and gently pour the eggs into the water one at a time. Poach the eggs for 3 to 4 minutes, or until the whites are set but the yolks are runny. Using a slotted spoon, remove the eggs from the water and drain on a paper towel.

5   Meanwhile, preheat the oven to 400 degrees F.

6   Warm the asparagus in the oven for 4 to 5 minutes. Divide the warm asparagus among four plates and top each with a poached egg. Dress each plate generously with bagna càuda, stirring each time it is spooned. Sprinkle with the parsley.

1 bunch Yakima white asparagus or other good-quality white asparagus, woody ends trimmed

3 tablespoons kosher salt, divided

2 tablespoons granulated sugar

1 teaspoon white vinegar

4 large local, organic eggs, cracked into 4 ramekins

Leaves from ¼ bunch Italian parsley, for finishing

CHEF'S NOTE: White asparagus is the same species as green asparagus, but it is grown in the dark or completely underground so that the green pigment doesn't develop. It has a somewhat different taste from green asparagus and can be a little bitter, which is why we add sugar to the blanching water. To keep white asparagus from becoming too woody, be sure to keep it chilled, and use it quickly. Always peel white asparagus, because the skin is tough and stringy.

When an egg is one of the stars of the dish, it is worth paying top dollar for the best you can find. Don't skimp here; you'll notice the difference.

Sunchokes (or Jerusalem artichokes) are one of the first vegetables we planted in our back-yard garden at Lark. I love the earthy, nutty flavor, especially with brown butter. They're also delicious roasted with diced apple. Extremely versatile, they can be served raw, pickled, boiled, roasted, caramelized, and more. I prefer to leave the peel on, as it adds great color in this soup, as well as depth of flavor. Just scrub them very well . . . lots of nooks and crannies!

sunchoke soup
WITH TRUFFLED SUNCHOKE CHIPS

1   To make the truffled sunchoke chips, in a medium saucepan, heat the canola oil to 350 degrees F. In small batches, add the sliced sunchokes and fry them until golden brown. Using a slotted spoon or skimmer, transfer the sunchokes from the pan into a mixing bowl. Toss them with a sprinkling of truffle salt right away while still glossy with oil. Sprinkle the chips with a little truffle oil and cool to room temperature in a single layer on paper towels. Store the chips in an airtight container at room temperature until ready to serve. The chips will keep for up to 1 day.

2   To make the sunchoke soup, in a large saucepan over medium heat, melt the butter. Add the onion and a generous pinch of salt and cook slowly until the onion is caramelized and golden brown, about 10 minutes. Add the sunchokes, salt, and water to the pan and bring to a simmer. Cook until the sunchokes are very tender, about 30 minutes.

3   Transfer the mixture to a blender in batches, and blend until very smooth. (Be careful when blending hot liquids.) Pass the mixture through a fine mesh strainer so that the soup is smooth but still has some body. Discard the solids. Add salt and pepper to taste. If the soup is too thick, adjust the consistency using water.

4   Divide the soup into four bowls. Drizzle each bowl with a little truffle oil and garnish with chives. Serve warm with a pile of sunchoke chips on the side.

MAKES 4 SERVINGS

FOR THE TRUFFLED SUNCHOKE CHIPS

2 cups canola or vegetable oil

1 cup sunchokes, scrubbed and very thinly sliced

½ teaspoon truffle salt

½ teaspoon white or black truffle oil

FOR THE SUNCHOKE SOUP

¼ cup (½ stick) unsalted butter

1 yellow onion, sliced

1 teaspoon kosher salt, plus more for seasoning

4 cups sunchokes, scrubbed and chopped into walnut-size pieces

4 cups water

Freshly ground black pepper

½ teaspoon white or black truffle oil, for finishing

½ teaspoon minced chives, for finishing

Bloomsdale long-standing spinach is a somewhat-hearty variety that survives our fairly mild winters and is great sautéed because it doesn't lose its volume as much as the grocery varieties. It's sweet, crunchy, tangy, and wonderful raw as well as cooked. If you're using regular or baby spinach, it's best double the quantity so you'll have enough. The fragrant Meyer lemon butter can be used for a number of dishes aside from this one: tossed with other vegetables, over fish, or as a dip for crab.

bloomsdale spinach

WITH MEYER LEMON BUTTER

MAKES 4 SERVINGS

2 tablespoons water

3 tablespoons cold unsalted butter, cut into cubes, divided

Kosher salt and freshly ground black pepper

1 to 2 teaspoons freshly squeezed Meyer lemon juice (regular lemons will also work, just use less)

1 tablespoon minced shallot

2 bunches Bloomsdale spinach, washed and spun dry

Zest from 1 Meyer lemon

1   In a small nonreactive saucepan, bring the water to a simmer. Turn the heat to the lowest setting possible and whisk in 2 tablespoons of the butter until it has emulsified. Season to taste with salt and pepper. Add the lemon juice to taste. Set aside in a warm place until ready to serve.

2   Heat a large sauté pan over medium heat. Add the remaining 1 tablespoon butter and shallot and cook until soft, about 1 minute. Add the spinach, season to taste with salt and pepper, and toss. Once the spinach has wilted slightly, transfer it to a serving dish. Spoon the lemon butter over the spinach, sprinkle with the lemon zest, and serve.

Pork rillettes is an easy appetizer to have handy year-round. All it takes is a little planning, quick prep, and then some time left alone, first to cook, then to chill and deepen in flavor. When the first radishes of late spring show up in the market, we slice them up and serve the rillettes with good butter sprinkled with fleur de sel on walnut crostini. In autumn they're great with ripe pears or a slow-cooked fruit chutney like our Mostarda d'Uva (see recipe on page 145).

pork rillettes

LARK
CLASSIC WITH FRENCH BREAKFAST RADISHES AND FLEUR DE SEL BUTTER

**MAKES ABOUT
36 OUNCES (FOR
12 SERVINGS)**

2½ pounds boneless pork
   shoulder, cut into
   2-inch pieces

¼ cup kosher salt

5 unpeeled cloves garlic,
   cracked

¼ bunch thyme

4 bay leaves

1 tablespoon whole black
   peppercorns

1   In a roasting pan, arrange the pork pieces in a single layer. Sprinkle half the salt evenly over the pork. Turn the pieces over and sprinkle with the remaining salt. Add the garlic, thyme, bay leaves, and peppercorns to the pan. Arrange the pork so that the aromatics are evenly scattered throughout the meat. Cover the pan with plastic wrap and chill for 24 hours.

2   Remove the pan from the refrigerator and set it aside at room temperature for 1 hour. Preheat the oven to 300 degrees F.

3   Remove the plastic wrap and cover the pork with the luke-warm fat. Cover the pan tightly with foil or a lid. Place the pan

in the oven and cook the pork until it's very tender and shreds easily, 2 to 3 hours. Remove the pan from the oven, uncover it, and allow the pork to cool to room temperature, about 1 hour.

4   Separate the meat from the fat and strain the fat through a fine mesh strainer. Let the fat cool, reserving a little to top off the rillettes, and save the rest for another use.

5   Using your hands, gently pull the meat apart until it is very finely shredded. Add salt and pepper to taste. If the pork seems too dry, add a little of the cooled fat back into the meat until the desired richness is achieved.

6   Fill four 8-ounce glass jars or dishes with the pork rillettes to ½ inch from the top, packing it down as you go. Chill the jars for 30 minutes and then smooth the top. Cover with ⅛ inch of the reserved fat to "seal" each jar, lid each jar, and chill until you are ready to serve. Once sealed with fat, the rillettes will keep in the refrigerator for up to 1 week. Set the rillettes out at room temperature for 30 minutes before serving.

7   To serve, place each jar of rillettes in the middle of a large plate. Serve with the radishes, walnut bread, and a generous spoonful of butter. Sprinkle the butter with fleur de sel.

2½ pounds rendered pork or duck fat, lukewarm

Freshly ground black pepper

1 bunch French Breakfast radishes, halved lengthwise

Walnut bread or baguette slices, toasted

2 tablespoons high-quality unsalted butter (the best you can get)

Fleur de sel, for finishing

CHEF'S NOTE: The pork rillettes take a little planning because the pork cures overnight and then is slow cooked the next day. Once it is slow cooked, it has to chill for quite a long time before it is ready. I recommend giving yourself at least 2 days to prepare this recipe; I assure you it's worth the wait.

If you don't have canning jars on hand, you can pack the rillettes into a small loaf pan. Simply slice off a thick piece and serve.

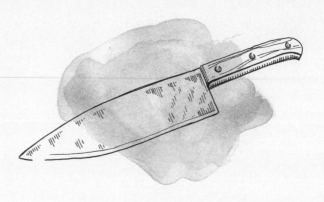

BALANCING A DISH

Many elements come together to make a recipe delicious: quality ingredients, careful preparation, attentive application of heat (or cold), and seasoning. Managing the interplay of ingredients and how they are treated is a chef's primary role. Understanding flavor and when to do what to a dish is our biggest challenge. Our palates can identify sweet, salty, bitter, umami (savory or meaty), and sour.

Sour is the taste that detects acidity. Acidity plays a huge role in the kitchen. Nearly every dish needs some acid—vinegar, citrus, or wine—for balance. Imagine radicchio with just a drizzle of olive oil. Salt and freshly ground pepper would improve the flavor, but it's still too simple. But add a bit of brisk sherry vinegar, and it's a salad. Or make a crab roll with Dungeness crab, mayonnaise, and herbs. It's good but plain. Add a big squeeze of lemon juice, and it is complete. Call it magic or chemistry, but don't forget this important facet of flavor.

Lemon and vinegar are the most common choices, but there are many other sources that affect flavor. Timing makes a difference as well. My general rule for seasoning (salt, aromatics, spices, and acids) is to go lightly, but at several intervals: early in a preparation, partway through, and always just before serving. It's hard to go back if you overdo the vinegar or lime juice in a dish, so take it easy and use just a little at a time.

At Lark we frequently use fresh lemon juice or vinegar to correct the balance in a dish. If I taste a sauce and it's a bit too rich or cloying, a few drops of lemon juice or sherry vinegar just before serving is often just the thing to bring it back into alignment. I have to imagine someone not just having one bite of a dish, but several, and I want each one to be great. It's the same approach we take to salting food. Something highly salted might actually taste really good if you just have one bite. But if you have a dozen bites, your palate will be worn out and shredded.

Wine can be used as a flavoring, a cooking liquid, and a marinade, and it generally adds the least acidity. As such you can use more of it, and earlier in the cooking process. Add a reduction of red wine to flavor a stock-based sauce, or pour a bottle in your beef stew to add a bit of sweetness or bitterness depending on the qualities of that wine. The varietal used will influence the flavor quite a bit—think of how distinct and nutty sherry wine is compared to Riesling or dry sauvignon blanc. Red wine will affect a finished dish more than white wine, and it might taste like acidity, but it's more likely the tannins asserting themselves. Wine has an acidity of about 0.5 to 0.85 percent.

Lemon, lime, and sometimes bitter orange juice are used as flavoring, a cooking medium (think ceviche), and in marinades. Citrus juices contribute tanginess, brightness, and contrast. Lemon juice isn't right for a traditional stew, but orange juice can be wonderful in moderation there. The floral, fruity Meyer lemon is lower in acidity than regular grocery store varieties. Fresh lemon juice is 2 to 3 percent citric acid.

Vinegar has myriad uses in the kitchen. Sherry vinegar is a real workhorse in the Lark kitchen; it's used in vinaigrettes, for pickling, and as a balancing agent in many sauces and stews. Garnacha vinegar is Spanish red wine vinegar that's been aged in wooden barrels; it's very intense and one of my personal favorites. Balsamic vinegar has a rich tradition surrounding its production and varies greatly in intensity, sweetness, viscosity, and overall quality. In general, you get what you pay for; think of the more artisanal brands as "finishing vinegars," adding just a few drops once a dish is completed. Fruit vinegars, such as the Acetoria brand apple or cherry vinegars from Italy, can be amazing and will give a pronounced boost to a dish using those same fruits. And let's not forget the basic: good red wine vinegar, white wine vinegar, champagne vinegar, and apple cider vinegar. Vinegar will usually be around 5 percent acidity.

Vinegar's other main use is in pickling. Pickled foods add tremendous variety, flavor, and completeness to a dish. In the United States, a pickle almost always refers to a pickled cucumber, but with the rise in awareness of international flavors and food culture, pickle varieties abound. At Lark we pickle our own ramps, spring onions, asparagus, green peaches, green strawberries, green beans, cherries, huckleberries, peppers, squash, and mushrooms.

(CONTINUED)

THE ANATOMY OF A BALANCED DISH

Raw Beets
Bright, bitter

Roasted Beets
Earthy, sweet

**Mt. Townsend Creamery
Seastack Cheese**
Creamy, smooth, nutty

Thyme
Herbal, fragrant

Aged Balsamic Vinegar
Woody, sweet, acidic

Extra-Virgin Olive Oil
Spicy, grassy

We're very lucky to have Theo Chocolate in Seattle, with its organic bean-to-bar production line and magical Wonka-like brick factory. Fernet-Branca is an Italian amaro made with lots of herbs and spices; it's pretty medicinal in flavor. In this ice cream recipe, the medicinal qualities are balanced out nicely by the custard. I've been serving this with the chocolate pavé as a homage to my favorite of the Girl Scout cookies: Thin Mints.

Each of the components take a bit of time. It's OK to spread this recipe out over a couple of days, as they all hold quite well.

theo chocolate pavé

WITH FERNET ICE CREAM AND DOUBLE CHOCOLATE COOKIE CRUMBLE

1   To make the chocolate pavé, butter all the sides of a small terrine mold or loaf pan. Cut parchment paper pieces so that they will fit the sides and bottom of the mold. This will help remove the pavé from the mold once it's chilled.

2   Place the chocolate in a heatproof bowl and set it over a saucepan of just-simmering water to create a double boiler. Stir occasionally until the chocolate is completely melted. Remove from the heat.

3   In a medium saucepan over medium heat, combine the milk and cream and bring just to a simmer. Remove the bowl of melted chocolate from the double boiler and set on a kitchen towel on the counter. Immediately pour the heated milk over the chocolate and whisk to combine. Add the yolks, coffee, and butter and whisk to combine. Pour the mixture into the

(CONTINUED)

MAKES 6 TO 8 SERVINGS

FOR THE CHOCOLATE PAVÉ

12 ounces Theo Pure
    70 percent dark
    chocolate, chopped

1¼ cups whole milk

1 cup heavy cream

8 egg yolks

½ cup strong brewed coffee
    or espresso

1 tablespoon unsalted but-
    ter, at room temperature,
    plus more for greasing

FOR THE FERNET ICE CREAM

2 cups whole milk

¾ cup heavy cream

8 egg yolks

½ cup granulated sugar

3 tablespoons Fernet
    Brancamenta

3 tablespoons Fernet-Branca

½ teaspoon kosher salt

FOR THE COOKIE CRUMBLE

1 cup (1 sticks) unsalted but-
    ter, at room temperature

1½ cups granulated sugar

2 large eggs

2 teaspoons pure
    vanilla extract

2 cups all-purpose flour

⅔ cup cocoa powder

¾ teaspoon baking soda

¼ teaspoon kosher salt

1 cup chopped Theo Pure
    70 percent dark chocolate

parchment-lined mold. Gently tap the whole mold a couple of times on the counter to remove any air bubbles.

4   Prepare a water bath: Choose a pan large enough to fit the mold. Place the mold into the larger pan and fill the pan with water so that it comes two-thirds up the sides of the mold. Set the water bath on the stovetop and bring it just to a simmer. Watch it carefully to make sure the water doesn't come to a boil. Reduce the heat to low and keep it just under a simmer. Cook the pavé in the water bath until the chocolate is just firm when the mold is jiggled, about 1 hour. Remove the mold from the water bath and allow it to come to room temperature for 30 minutes, then transfer it to the refrigerator and chill for at least 4 hours or overnight.

5   To remove the pavé from the mold, fill a large container with hot tap water and dip the bottom of the mold into the hot water for about 30 seconds. Be careful no water gets into the pavé. Run a paring knife around the inside edge of the mold. Invert the mold over a cutting board or baking tray lined with parchment paper. Tap the mold to loosen the pavé. If it doesn't come loose, tap again. Sometimes it takes two tries.

6   Remove the parchment paper clinging to the pavé, and using a large knife dipped in hot water, cut the pavé into ⅜-inch-thick slices. Place each slice separately on parchment paper and keep chilled until ready to serve.

7   To make the Fernet ice cream, in a medium heavy-bottomed saucepan over medium-high heat, combine the milk and cream. Bring the mixture just to a simmer. Remove from the heat.

8   Meanwhile, prepare an ice bath.

9   In a large bowl, thoroughly beat together the egg yolks and sugar. While whisking the egg mixture, add ½ cup of the hot milk mixture to the bowl to gently temper the eggs. Whisk-ing constantly, add in another ½ cup of the hot milk mixture. (Continuous whisking prevents the eggs from scrambling.)

10   Now begin whisking the milk mixture in the saucepan and slowly pour in the tempered egg mixture. Place the saucepan over medium heat and stir constantly with a wooden spoon or heatproof spatula. Continue stirring until the mixture has reached a temperature of 180 degrees F and is thick enough to coat the back of a spoon.

11   Strain the custard through a fine mesh strainer into a metal bowl or container. Whisk in the Fernets and salt and

immediately place the metal bowl into the ice bath. Stir occasionally until the custard cools to room temperature. Place the custard in the refrigerator to chill completely, at least 4 hours and preferably overnight.

12   Process the custard in an ice cream maker according to manufacturer's instructions. Transfer the ice cream to a lidded container and freeze for at least 8 hours before serving.

13   To make the cookie crumble, using an electric mixer on medium speed, cream together the butter and sugar. Add the eggs and vanilla and mix thoroughly.

14   In a separate bowl, sift together the flour, cocoa powder, baking soda, and salt. Add the dry ingredients to the butter mixture and mix just until incorporated. Add the chocolate and stir by hand to incorporate. Flatten the dough into a disk and wrap it in plastic wrap. Refrigerate for at least 2 hours.

15   Preheat the oven to 350 degrees F.

16   On a lightly floured surface or between two sheets of parchment paper, roll the dough out to ¼ inch thick. If you want to reserve any dough for another use, it can be refrigerated for up to 2 days or frozen for up to 4 weeks.

17   Transfer the rolled dough to a baking tray and bake for 10 minutes. Remove from the oven and cool completely to room temperature, but leave the oven on.

18   Flip the cookie over, and using your hands, break it up into smaller pieces. Return the smaller pieces to the oven for 4 to 5 more minutes to crisp. Remove from the oven and cool completely to room temperature.

19   Transfer the cookie pieces to a food processor and pulse them to a crumble, or transfer to a bag and crush with a rolling pin. Place the crumble in an airtight container and store it at room temperature for up to 2 days.

20   To serve, place a slice of the pavé on each dessert plate and sprinkle with some cookie crumble. Form a quenelle (an egg- or football-shaped spoonful) of ice cream and place it on top.

CHEF'S NOTE: The double chocolate cookie crumble makes delicious cookies too. After making and chilling the dough, roll into walnut-size balls, flatten them, and bake for 10 to 12 minutes. You will have plenty of dough left over to try them; you can also freeze it to bake on another day.

Read through Ice Cream and Sorbet on page 78 for some general rules of thumb before proceeding with this recipe.

Mostarda d'uva, or Cugnà as it's known in the Piedmont region of Italy, is a wonderful harvest chutney. It is perfect with cheese and salumi or cured meats. Mostarda d'uva is made with nebbiolo grape must, nuts, and very ripe harvest fruit of every sort. It has served as a multipurpose condiment and even as dessert on top of fresh snow for many generations of Piedmontese. I used to buy a brand called Il Mongetto, which is from Vignale Monferrato, a little hill town. Now I make my own batch every autumn, using our own Northwest bounty. If I'm lucky I'll get a basket of wine grapes from vintner friends, though Concords work well too. And don't worry, it cooks for a long while and gets mashed, so those grape seeds just disappear.

salumi coppa
WITH SESAME CIABATTA AND MOSTARDA D'UVA

1   To make the mostarda d'uva, in a large heavy-bottomed saucepan over medium heat, combine the grapes, apple, pear, quince, and pumpkin. Add the walnuts, hazelnuts, wine, and water to the pan. Season with the salt and pepper and bring to a simmer. Turn the heat down to low and cook slowly, partially covered, for 3 to 4 hours. Stir often to prevent scorching, adding a little water if necessary. The mixture will darken as it cooks and the nuts will soften. Mash the fruit and nuts with a spoon or pulse a couple of times with an immersion blender to break down the solids a little. The mostarda should have a coarse rustic texture that is not too smooth.

2   Remove the pan from the heat and let cool to room temperature. Transfer the mostarda d'uva to an airtight container and refrigerate for up to 2 weeks or freeze for up to 3 months.

3   Drizzle the bread with the oil and toast it on a grill or in a large sauté pan until golden and crispy. Slather each piece of ciabatta with mostarda d'uva and top with the coppa. Serve immediately.

MAKES 4 SERVINGS

FOR THE MOSTARDA D'UVA

1 cup Syrah or nebbiolo grapes, stemmed and halved

½ cup diced Granny Smith or other tart apple

½ cup diced ripe Bartlett or Bosc pear

½ cup peeled, cored, diced quince

½ cup peeled, diced pumpkin

½ cup lightly toasted walnut pieces

½ cup hazelnuts, toasted, peeled, and chopped

½ cup red wine

1 cup water

1 teaspoon kosher salt

Freshly ground black pepper

4 thick slices sesame or ciabatta bread

1 teaspoon extra-virgin olive oil

16 coppa slices

This dish is not for the squeamish, as it requires brining, cooking, and picking the meat from a whole pig's head. The resulting "headcheese" is the greatest cold cut around. Ramps are wild leeks with a strong garlicky punch. They don't grow in the Northwest, but are special enough that I usually buy them for a few weeks in spring. When they're young and tender, we sauté them, grill them, and use them in soups and sauces. Once they get bigger, we pickle the bulbs to use on dishes like this.

tête de cochon

WITH PICKLED RAMPS AND MUSTARD

MAKES 8 TO 10 SERVINGS

1 pig's head (with or without skin), split and brain removed

1 gallon cold Basic Brine (see recipe on page 120)

2 onions, cut into large dice

2 carrots, peeled and cut into large dice

2 celery ribs, cut into large dice

6 cloves garlic, crushed

4 sprigs thyme

2 bay leaves

1 tablespoon whole black peppercorns

Kosher salt and freshly ground black pepper

1 teaspoon whole grain mustard

1 teaspoon Dijon mustard

1 teaspoon minced shallot

1 tablespoon champagne vinegar or white wine vinegar

1   Wash and dry the pig's head. Put the head in a large non-reactive container that fits in your refrigerator. Add the brine and make sure the pig's head is completely submerged. If it floats, place a plate with weight on top to submerge it fully. Leave the head in the brine in the refrigerator for 2 to 3 days.

2   Rinse the pig's head under cold water and discard the brine.

3   Place the pig's head in a large stockpot over high heat and fill with enough water so that it is completely submerged. Add the onion, carrots, celery, garlic, thyme, bay leaves, and peppercorns to the pot. Once the water comes to a simmer, turn the heat down to maintain just a light simmer. Cook until the meat is fork-tender, 3 to 4 hours. If the head still has the skin and ears on it, the skin should be very tender. If it is not, keep simmering until it is.

4   Remove the head from the pot and set aside to cool to room temperature on a baking tray or roasting pan so that any liquid is collected. It will be dripping with very hot water, so be careful. Discard the cooking liquid and solids.

5   Once the head is cool enough to handle, remove the meat from the bones. Remove any skin and ears and keep them with

the meat. Run through the meat with your hands to make sure you don't also have any unwanted cartilage, small bones, or teeth. Tear the meat (and skin) so that it is somewhat shredded. Season to taste with salt and pepper.

6   Sprinkle a few drops of water onto the counter (this keeps the plastic wrap from slipping). Unroll a large piece of plastic wrap about 1 foot wide and 2 feet long, but do not cut it off the roll. Place it on the counter with the loose end facing you and the attached box pushed away directly ahead lengthwise.

7   To form the meat into a log, place about 2 cups of the meat on the plastic wrap, centered on the front edge. Using your hands, form the meat into a log 2 to 3 inches thick and about

3 tablespoons extra-virgin olive oil

2 bunches watercress

2 tablespoons thinly sliced pickled ramps or pickled pearl onions

Fleur de sel, for finishing

1 loaf Lark Country Bread (page 253), sliced

(CONTINUED)

6 inches long. Roll the loose end of the plastic wrap forward over the meat to help shape the log. Roll the meat log in the plastic wrap toward the box and twist the excess plastic wrap on each side of the log to help shape it. Once the log has been rolled close to the box, cut the plastic wrap.

8   Holding the excess plastic on each end of the log, keep twisting it until it is tight and compacted. Knot the excess plastic wrap at each end of the log right up against the meat or tie it with string; it will resemble a large candy wrapper. This process takes a little practice and patience. If you have problems with it, just start again with a new piece of plastic wrap.

9   Repeat this shaping and rolling process until you have used all the meat. The number of logs you will make will depend on how much meat the pig's head yielded. Refrigerate the logs overnight so that the meat cools and sets.

10   To make the mustard vinaigrette, in a small mixing bowl, stir together the mustards and shallot. Add the champagne vinegar and whisk to combine. While whisking, slowly drizzle in the olive oil. Season to taste with salt and pepper.

11   Set aside until ready to use, whisking again to incorporate the ingredients before serving if they have separated. The mustard vinaigrette will keep in the refrigerator for up to 2 days.

12   In a medium bowl, combine the watercress and ramps and toss them with just enough of the mustard vinaigrette to coat. Adjust seasoning to taste.

13   Unwrap the chilled meat and cut each log into slices ⅜ to ½ inch thick. Place a slice of headcheese on an appetizer plate and top it with some of the dressed salad. Sprinkle a little fleur de sel on each piece of headcheese. Drizzle a little mustard vinaigrette around the plate. Serve with Lark Country Bread.

CHEF'S NOTE: Cooking the head of a pig is quite a long process that takes a couple of days; some stages can be rather time-consuming, especially the first time. Your pig's head may or may not come with a tongue. If it does, you can either simmer the tongue with the head, or braise it on its own. Once the tongue has simmered until it is tender, remove it from the liquid and peel off the outer membrane. At that point, add the tongue meat to the meat from the rest of the head and continue with the recipe.

As a kid my favorite ice cream–truck treat was a Creamsicle—that magic combination of vanilla ice cream wrapped in orange sherbet. As a grown up I've expanded my range to include cherry sorbet with vanilla ice cream, blood orange sorbet with lemon ice cream, goat cheese sorbet with port poached figs, and more. The contrast of sweet and creamy with tart or tangy is the best.

berry float

WITH BUTTERMILK ICE CREAM, STRAWBERRY SORBET, AND CHAMPAGNE

1   To make the buttermilk ice cream, in a medium heavy-bottomed saucepan over medium-high heat, bring the cream just to a simmer. Remove from the heat.

2   Meanwhile, prepare an ice bath.

3   In a large bowl, thoroughly beat together the egg yolks and sugar. While whisking the egg mixture, add ½ cup of the hot cream to the bowl to gently temper the eggs. Whisking constantly, add in another ½ cup of the hot cream. (Continuous whisking prevents the eggs from scrambling.)

(CONTINUED)

MAKES 8 TO 10 SERVINGS

FOR THE BUTTERMILK ICE CREAM

2 cups heavy cream

12 egg yolks

1 cup granulated sugar

2 cups buttermilk

1 teaspoon pure vanilla extract

½ teaspoon kosher salt

FOR THE STRAWBERRY SORBET

1¼ cups granulated sugar, divided

1 cup water

4 cups fresh strawberries, cored and quartered

1 whole egg, shell washed

FOR THE BERRY COMPOTE

1 cup fresh strawberries, cored

1 cup fresh raspberries

½ cup granulated sugar

1 teaspoon freshly squeezed lemon juice

FOR THE BERRY FLOAT

1 cup fresh strawberries, cored

1 cup fresh raspberries

1 bottle chilled dry sparkling wine, such as Blanquette de Limoux

4   Now begin whisking the cream in the saucepan and slowly pour in the tempered egg mixture. Place the saucepan over medium heat and stir constantly with a wooden spoon or heat-proof spatula. Continue stirring until the mixture has reached a temperature of 180 degrees F and is thick enough to coat the back of a spoon.

5   Strain the custard through a fine mesh strainer into a metal bowl or container. Stir in the buttermilk, vanilla, and salt. Immediately place the metal bowl into the ice bath. Stir occasionally until the custard cools to room temperature. Place the custard in the refrigerator to chill completely, at least 4 hours and preferably overnight.

6   Process the custard in an ice cream maker according to manufacturer's instructions. Transfer the ice cream to a lidded container and freeze for at least 8 hours before serving.

7   To make the strawberry sorbet, make a simple syrup by combining 1 cup of the sugar and the water in a small saucepan over high heat. Bring to a boil, then turn off the heat and let the syrup cool completely.

8   In a large saucepan over medium-high heat, place the strawberries and remaining ¼ cup sugar. Bring the strawberries just to a simmer and cook, stirring frequently, for about

10 minutes. Remove the pan from the heat and let the strawberries cool to room temperature.

9 Blend the strawberries in a blender or food processor and strain through a fine mesh sieve to remove the seeds.

10 Combine the strawberries with ¾ cup of the simple syrup in an airtight container. To make sure that there is the right amount of sugar in the mixture for freezing, complete the "egg test" described on page 79. When it passes the test, place the mixture in the refrigerator and chill for at least 1 hour.

11 Process the mixture in an ice cream maker according to manufacturer's instructions. Transfer the sorbet to a lidded container and freeze for at least 8 hours before serving.

12 To make the berry compote, in a small saucepan over medium-high heat, combine the berries and sugar. Once the juices start to simmer, turn the heat down and cook until thickened, 25 to 30 minutes. Stir in the lemon juice. Transfer to an airtight container and allow to cool to room temperature for 30 minutes, then chill the compote in the refrigerator until ready to use.

13 To make the berry float, place a spoonful of the berry compote in the bottom of a tumbler glass. Put one scoop each of buttermilk ice cream and strawberry sorbet on top of the compote. Place the fresh berries on top of and around the ice cream and sorbet. Top with the sparkling wine, filling the glass to ¼ inch from the top. Serve immediately.

CHEF'S NOTE: Read through Ice Cream and Sorbet on page 78 for some general rules of thumb before proceeding with this recipe.

I first met Ruth and Lori Babcock of Tieton Farm and Creamery as customers at Lark. They would come in to eat a few times per year with a group of friends and make their way thoughtfully through the menu. At some point they asked if I would like some eggs that their hens had just laid. Of course I said yes! We carried on this tradition for a while, trading eggs for dinner. One thing led to the next, and a few years later they bought some land in Tieton, Washington, a hotbed of arts, crafts, and artisan food. They now make several delicious cheeses; have fresh pork, lamb, ducks, and chickens for sale; and of course still offer those fantastic duck and chicken eggs.

tieton creamery chèvre
WITH FAVA BEANS AND MINT

1   Prepare an ice bath. In a large pot of boiling salted water, blanch the shucked fava beans until just tender, 2 to 3 minutes depending on the size. Shock them in the ice bath. Peel the outer membrane off the beans and discard.

2   In a medium mixing bowl, combine the fava beans, mint, and shallot. Toss with the olive oil and season to taste with salt and pepper.

3   Place the whole wheel of chèvre on a serving plate. Spoon the fava beans on and around the cheese and serve.

CHEF'S NOTE: Most cheeses are at their best when served at room temperature. Take the cheese out of the refrigerator about 45 minutes before you plan to serve it.

MAKES 2 SERVINGS

1½ cups fresh fava beans, shucked

1 tablespoon thinly sliced (chiffonade) mint leaves

1 teaspoon minced shallot

1 tablespoon extra-virgin olive oil

Kosher salt and freshly ground black pepper

4 ounces Tieton chèvre or other fresh goat cheese, at room temperature

Many aged sheep's milk cheeses are produced in Europe, so I often choose one of them for this salad-like dish. The Ferme Kukulu version is delicious. Some of my other favorites: Fiore Sardo, U Taravu, and Scoparolo. We've got some great examples made closer to home now too. Black Sheep Creamery's Baasque and St. Helens cheese are both just lovely on a cheese board or shaved into a salad or pasta.

kukulu sheep's milk cheese

WITH RAW ASPARAGUS AND TRUFFLE VINAIGRETTE

MAKES 4 SERVINGS

1 bunch green asparagus, woody ends trimmed

1 tablespoon extra-virgin olive oil

1 teaspoon white or black truffle oil

1 teaspoon freshly squeezed lemon juice

Kosher salt and freshly ground black pepper

6 ounces Kukulu cheese

1   Peel the asparagus from about 2 inches below the top down to the base. Halve each asparagus spear and cut each half lengthwise into thin strips.

2   In a medium mixing bowl, combine the asparagus with the oil and toss gently. Add the truffle oil and lemon juice and season to taste with salt and pepper.

3   Using a sharp knife, cut the Kukulu into thin slices.

4   Arrange the Kukulu and asparagus in alternating layers on a serving platter. Drizzle a little of the extra vinaigrette around the plate.

CHEF'S NOTE: The asparagus in this dish is eaten raw, so make sure to use only crisp asparagus of medium thickness.

I've always been a fan of malt, starting with Whoppers and Ovaltine as a kid, and now of malty beers as well. My wife, JM, is an even bigger fan, and it was Horlicks that she drank as a kid. For the first year and half at Lark, we hand-churned this ice cream in a White Mountain ice cream maker (which we still use at home). Eventually we got too busy to keep up with demand and bought an electric machine. Saul Perez, the Yoda of prep cooks, never looked back!

 # malt ice cream

LARK
CLASSIC WITH ALMOND CROQUANT

MAKES 4 SERVINGS

2 cups whole milk

¾ cup heavy cream

8 egg yolks

½ cup granulated sugar

¾ cup Horlicks or Carna-
tion malted milk powder
(Ovaltine works great too)

1 teaspoon pure vanilla
extract

Pinch of kosher salt

1 In a medium heavy-bottomed saucepan over medium-high heat, combine the milk and cream. Bring the mixture just to a simmer. Remove from the heat.

2 Meanwhile, prepare an ice bath.

3 In a large bowl, thoroughly beat together the egg yolks and sugar. While whisking the egg mixture, add ½ cup of the hot milk mixture to the bowl to gently temper the eggs. Whisking constantly, add in another ½ cup of the hot milk mixture. (Continuous whisking prevents the eggs from scrambling.)

4   Now begin whisking the milk mixture in the saucepan and slowly pour in the tempered egg mixture. Place the saucepan over medium heat and stir constantly with a wooden spoon or heatproof spatula. Continue stirring until the mixture has reached a temperature of 180 degrees F and is thick enough to coat the back of a spoon.

5   Strain the custard through a fine mesh strainer into a metal bowl or container. Whisk in the malt powder and strain through a fine mesh strainer again. Whisk in the vanilla and salt and immediately place the metal bowl into the ice bath. Stir occasionally until the custard cools to room temperature. Place the custard in the refrigerator to chill completely, at least 4 hours and preferably overnight.

6   Process the custard in an ice cream maker according to manufacturer's instructions. Transfer the ice cream to a lidded container and freeze for at least 8 hours before serving.

7   To make the almond croquant, preheat the oven to 350 degrees F. Butter a baking tray or line with a nonstick baking mat.

8   In a medium bowl, whisk the egg white until it's foamy and then whisk in the sugar. Add the almonds and salt and stir to combine.

9   Spread the mixture thinly onto the baking tray. Bake until golden brown all over and crispy on the edges, about 8 to 10 minutes. Cool completely to room temperature, break into smaller pieces, and store in an airtight container at room temperature for up to 2 to 3 days.

10   To serve, place a generous scoop of ice cream into a chilled bowl and garnish with pieces of the almond croquant.

CHEF'S NOTE: Read through Ice Cream and Sorbet on page 78 for some general rules of thumb before proceeding with this recipe.

FOR THE ALMOND CROQUANT

1 tablespoon unsalted butter, for buttering

1 egg white

2½ tablespoons granulated sugar

4 ounces sliced raw almonds

Pinch of kosher salt

Rhubarb is one of those true indications that spring is on the way. Here in the Northwest, we usually see hothouse-grown rhubarb in March or April, followed by field-grown in May and June. Hazelnuts are a great pairing, but almonds, pecans, or even no nuts would be delicious in this topping. Another great variation: substitute half of the rhubarb with quartered strawberries. Wait for your farmers' market run; it'll be worth it.

rhubarb hazelnut crisp

MAKES 6 SERVINGS

FOR THE TOPPING

1½ cups all-purpose flour

½ cup hazelnuts, toasted, peeled, and roughly chopped

¼ cup granulated sugar

¼ cup light brown sugar

½ teaspoon ground cinnamon

¼ teaspoon freshly ground nutmeg

½ cup (1 stick) unsalted butter, melted

FOR THE FILLING

2 pounds rhubarb, cut on the bias into ⅜-inch-thick coins

1¼ cups granulated sugar

¼ cup cornstarch

½ cup dry white wine

½ teaspoon pure vanilla extract

Ice cream or whipped cream, for finishing (optional)

1   To make the topping, in a mixing bowl, stir together the flour, hazelnuts, sugars, cinnamon, and nutmeg. Drizzle in the butter and mix until incorporated and crumbly. Set aside.

2   To make the filling, place the rhubarb in a large mixing bowl. Add the sugar and cornstarch and mix well. Add the wine and vanilla and set aside to macerate for 30 minutes.

3   Meanwhile, preheat the oven to 350 degrees F.

4   Fill individual crocks or pans (1 to 1½ cups in size) with the filling. (Alternatively, you can make one big crisp.) Pack the rhubarb down and drizzle the extra syrup from the bowl over the rhubarb. Divide the topping evenly among the crocks. Bake for 30 to 35 minutes, or until the rhubarb is cooked and syrupy and the topping is golden brown.

5   Serve warm, topped with a scoop of ice cream.

CHEF'S NOTE: This can be baked in advance on the same day and held at room temperature until you are ready to serve. Just pop it back in the oven to reheat. Our Buttermilk Ice Cream recipe on page 149 would be great with this.

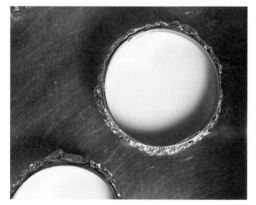

This is a lighter yet still richer and silkier cheesecake than you've probably had before. The dish is assembled just before serving, which allows the crushed graham crackers to stay nice and crisp and makes for a wonderful contrast to the cheesecake. It's very adaptable—try it with this rhubarb compote in April, fresh cherries or berries in July, or with caramelized apples in October.

mascarpone cheesecake
WITH GRAHAM CRACKER CRUMBS AND RHUBARB COMPOTE

1   To make the graham cracker crumbs, in the bowl of a stand mixer fitted with the paddle attachment, combine the flour, brown sugar, baking soda, and salt and mix well. Add the butter and mix until the mixture is coarse and resembles bread crumbs. Add the honey, milk, and vanilla and mix on low until just combined.

2   Place a large piece of plastic wrap on the counter. Scrape the dough onto the plastic wrap and pat it together to form a rectangle. Wrap the dough in the plastic and chill for at least 1 hour.

3   Preheat the oven to 325 degrees F.

4   On a nonstick baking mat or lightly floured surface, roll the dough out to ¼ inch thick. Bake the dough until it is golden brown, about 20 minutes.

5   Remove from the oven and cool to room temperature, but leave the oven on. Break the cookie up into 2- to 3-inch pieces, turn them over, and bake again for another 10 minutes.

(CONTINUED)

MAKES ABOUT 6 MINI CHEESECAKES

FOR THE GRAHAM CRACKER CRUMBS

1¼ cups whole wheat flour or graham flour (flour that still contains the bran)

½ cup brown sugar

½ teaspoon baking soda

½ teaspoon kosher salt

3½ tablespoons cold unsalted butter, cut into ½-inch dice

¼ cup honey

2½ tablespoons whole milk

1 tablespoon pure vanilla extract

FOR THE RHUBARB COMPOTE

1 cup finely diced rhubarb

½ cup granulated sugar

1 tablespoon freshly squeezed lemon juice

1½ cups chilled cream
   cheese

½ cup granulated sugar

2 egg yolks

1 whole egg

3 tablespoons crème fraîche

2 tablespoons heavy cream

Finely grated zest from
   1 lemon

1 cup mascarpone

Whipped cream,
   for finishing

6   Remove from the oven and cool to room temperature. Put the graham crackers in a food processor and pulse until they resemble fine crumbs. Store in an airtight container at room temperature for up to 2 days.

7   To make the rhubarb compote, in a small saucepan over medium-high heat, combine the rhubarb, sugar, and lemon juice and bring to a simmer. Turn the heat down to low and let the mixture cook slowly until it resembles a jam, about 30 minutes.

8   Remove the pan from the heat and let the compote cool to room temperature. If not using immediately, it will keep in an airtight container in the refrigerator for up to 3 days.

9   To make the mascarpone cheesecake, preheat the oven to 325 degrees F.

10   Wrap the bottom of six ring molds with plastic wrap. Make sure to pull it tight by twisting the excess plastic wrap to seal the bottom so the cheesecake doesn't leak out while baking. To help make the mold waterproof, place a piece of aluminum foil tightly over the plastic wrap and make sure it comes most of the way up the sides of the mold.

11   In the bowl of a stand mixer fitted with the paddle attachment, combine the cream cheese and sugar. Start the mixer on a low speed and then increase to a medium speed to thoroughly cream them together until light and fluffy. Turn the mixer back down to low and add the egg yolks and whole egg. Scrape down the sides of the bowl often while incorporating the eggs into the batter. Add the crème fraîche, cream, and lemon zest, mixing to incorporate. Add the mascarpone and continue to mix, scraping down the sides periodically.

12   Strain the mixture through a fine mesh strainer. Some zest will be left behind.

13   Pour the batter into the individually wrapped ring molds until each one is about three-quarters full. Place the molds into a roasting pan that is at least 3 inches deep. Fill the pan with just enough hot water to reach halfway up the sides of the molds. Bake for 25 to 30 minutes, or until there is very little jiggle left in the center of the cheesecakes.

14   Very carefully remove the roasting pan from the oven so that no water splashes into the cheesecakes. Remove the cheesecakes from the water bath, let them cool at room temperature for 20 minutes, then chill in the refrigerator for at least 2 hours.

15   To serve, spoon some of the compote onto each plate. Remove the foil and plastic wrap from the ring mold and place the cheesecake onto the plate. Run a paring knife around the outside of the cheesecake to release it from the ring mold and lift it off. Top with some graham cracker crumbs and a generous spoonful of whipped cream.

CHEF'S NOTE: We like to serve this cheesecake with the graham cracker crumbs loosely placed on top of the cheesecake. Because they have no crust, we cook the cheesecake portions individually in 2- to 3-inch ring molds so that they are smaller and easier to handle.

   The cheesecakes are baked in a water bath because it is a gentle process. It is very important that the ring molds are waterproof so that no water gets into the cake while it is baking.

bounty

AUGUST TO OCTOBER

We Northwesterners have been known to complain about the weather, frankly. Summer can be brief, and it always arrives later than we expect (though we keep our hopes low). We wait, trying to be patient. Awarded heat and sunshine, we don our sunglasses and become lighter, effervescent versions of ourselves in the season of Bounty. The market stalls are brimming with fantastic produce, and we head to the beaches with our picnics to swim, kayak, sip rosé, and graze.

Bounty is our fastest season—availability changes week to week, and we take great pleasure in keeping up with which stand has the sweetest cherries or the most perfect lettuce. The walk-in cooler is brimming with good things, shelves of inspiration that direct me in creating specials each day.

During this warm season, I sometimes sneak away on my scooter over Capitol Hill to nearby farmers' markets, catching glimpses of the Olympic mountain range with the Elliott Bay glistening nearby. These weekly trips allow me to wander the tables, connecting with friends and suppliers, finding out what produce they're excited about.

At Lark, we have a kitchen garden with a variety of berries, herbs, cardoons, and tomatoes. Some years we are more inspired than others, but it always reminds us of the importance of growing food and having the freshest produce at our fingertips. We tend it diligently until mid-summer when local farms make us rich with corn, tomatoes, green beans, and melons, and we completely forget to water our own plants. This neglect is great for the herbs and the golden raspberries, which often produce into October when the apples are being crunched, simmered, and juiced in Lark's kitchen.

Then the kids go back to school (I feel bad for them because September is always one of the most beautiful times of the year here), and the Asian pears, winter squash, and root crops arrive. We wait as long as possible to add them to the menu, but as the nights get cooler and the frost seems certain, we embrace the grapes, quince, pumpkin, and wild mushrooms. The best kind of tired follows the frantic pace of Bounty, and we settle in for changing of seasons once more.

This is a quick one-pot meal, best served with some toasted Lark Country Bread (page 253) rubbed with garlic and drizzled with good olive oil. It's extra special with Hama Hama baby clams if you can get your hands on some. Mama Lil's peppers are pickled and soaked in olive oil and are fantastic in a sandwich, with eggs, or paired with a simple cheese. Have a jar on hand for use here, or substitute a minced fresh Thai red chile or good-quality crushed red chile flakes.

manila clams

WITH CHISTORRA CHORIZO, HOT PEPPERS, AND PARSLEY

1   In a wide saucepan with a lid over medium heat, combine the oil, chorizo, and shallot. Cook until most of the fat has rendered and the chorizo is crispy. Add the garlic and cook until tender, about 1 minute. Add the clams and stir to coat. Add the wine, peppers, and a little salt and pepper.

2   Cover and cook for 3 to 6 minutes, or until all of the clams open and the sauce is slightly reduced. You will hear the clams start popping open. Discard any clams that don't open. Adjust seasoning to taste and add the parsley.

3   Serve in the pan or a large bowl with the bread on the side.

> CHEF'S NOTE: Wash the clams under running water to remove any sand or dirt from the shells. Discard any clams that do not close or are cracked or damaged. Store them in a pan or bowl covered with a wet towel. Do not submerge them in water.

MAKES 2 SERVINGS

2 tablespoons pure olive oil

4 ounces chistorra chorizo, cut into ⅛-inch-thick slices

2 tablespoons sliced shallot

4 cloves garlic, thinly sliced

2 pounds Manila clams, washed

2 tablespoons dry white wine

2 tablespoons Mama Lil's Mildly Spicy Peppers, chopped

Kosher salt and freshly ground black pepper

2 tablespoons thinly sliced (chiffonade) Italian parsley

Toasted Lark Country Bread (page 253)

Dungeness crab is one of the distinctive seafoods available on the Pacific Coast, ranging from central California to Alaska. This salad is crisp, cool, creamy, and succulent—perfect as a light but memorable meal. This is an earth-meets-ocean combination that I played around with while at the restaurant of the same name. The combination of mild celery and the tart, lightly sweet apple play very nicely with the crab.

dungeness crab salad
WITH GREEN APPLE AND CELERY

MAKES 4 SERVINGS

1   To make the apple mayonnaise, in a medium bowl, whisk the egg yolks and lemon juice for 2 to 3 minutes, or until pale yellow and thickened. While whisking, slowly drizzle in the canola oil until it's emulsified and fully incorporated. Season to taste with salt and pepper. Fold the apple and celery into the mayonnaise and adjust seasoning to taste.

2   To make the crab salad, in a medium bowl, combine the crabmeat and chives. Add ½ cup apple mayonnaise and mix gently. Season to taste with salt and pepper.

3   To serve, swipe each plate with a dollop of apple mayonnaise. Place a mound of the crab salad on the plate. Top with the julienned apple and celery leaves.

FOR THE APPLE
MAYONNAISE

2 egg yolks

1 teaspoon freshly squeezed
lemon juice

⅓ cup canola oil

Kosher salt and freshly
ground black pepper

1 tablespoon very finely
diced skin-on Granny
Smith apple

1 tablespoon very finely
diced celery rib

FOR THE CRAB SALAD

1 pound Dungeness crab-
meat, picked through

1 teaspoon minced chives

Kosher salt and freshly
ground black pepper

¼ cup julienned skin-on
Granny Smith apple,
for finishing

1 tablespoon celery heart
leaves, for finishing

This recipe is the epitome of the season of Bounty for me, featuring a combination of ripe corn and wild lobster mushrooms, which are both best in August and September. Sockeye salmon tend to run later in the summer and are full-flavored but not quite as fatty as Chinook. Any type of salmon would be delicious in this recipe as long as it's Pacific and wild caught.

wild sockeye salmon

WITH CORN, BACON, AND LOBSTER MUSHROOM RAGOUT

MAKES 4 SERVINGS

FOR THE CORN BROTH

½ gallon water

3 corncobs, kernels removed (reserve the kernels for the ragout)

1 onion, cut into large dice

2 sprigs thyme

1 bay leaf

1 tablespoon whole black peppercorns

FOR THE CORN, BACON, AND MUSHROOM RAGOUT

4 ounces bacon, cut into ¼-inch lardons

6 spring onions, halved lengthwise (quartered if large)

1 To make the corn broth, fill a saucepan large enough to hold all of the broth ingredients with the water and place over medium-high heat. Add the corncobs, onion, thyme, bay leaf, and peppercorns. Once the mixture has reached a boil, turn it down to low heat to just maintain a simmer for about 1 hour. Strain the broth and let cool to room temperature. The broth will keep in an airtight container in the refrigerator for about 3 days.

2 To make the corn, bacon, and mushroom ragout, heat a large sauté pan over medium-high heat, add the bacon, and cook for 2 to 3 minutes to render it. Add the onions and cook for 2 to 3 minutes, or until they are starting to wilt a little. Add the corn kernels and mushrooms. Cook for another 2 to 3 minutes, or until the mushrooms become tender. Add ½ cup corn broth and bring the mixture to a simmer. Cook for another 2 to 3 minutes, or until the corn broth has reduced by half. Add the

butter, chives, and tarragon and stir to incorporate. Season to taste with salt and pepper.

3   To prepare the salmon, heat the olive oil in a medium sauté pan over high heat. Season the salmon on both sides with salt and pepper.

4   Sauté the salmon, skin side down, until the skin is crispy, 2 to 3 minutes. You can peek at the skin during cooking to make sure it is getting crispy and not burning, but leave it in one place so that it will cook evenly. Flip the salmon over and add the butter to the pan. As the butter melts and foams, use a spoon to baste the salmon. (Be careful, the butter will be very hot.) Cook the salmon until it is medium-rare to medium, 2 to 3 more minutes, then transfer it from the pan to a plate. Let it rest for about 2 minutes before serving.

5   To serve, place a couple of spoonfuls of the ragout onto each plate. Place a piece of the salmon on top of the ragout and sprinkle with a little fleur de sel.

> CHEF'S NOTE: The corn broth recipe makes more than you will need for the ragout. The leftover broth makes a great base for a corn soup.

Kernels from 3 ears corn (reserve the cobs for the corn broth)

4 ounces lobster mushrooms (oyster mushrooms or chanterelles also work), cleaned and cut into about ¼-inch-thick slices

1 tablespoon unsalted butter

1 tablespoon minced chives

1 tablespoon minced tarragon

Kosher salt and freshly ground black pepper

FOR THE SALMON

1 tablespoon extra-virgin olive oil

24 ounces skin-on wild sockeye salmon, scaled and deboned, cut into 6-ounce portions

Kosher salt and freshly ground black pepper

1 tablespoon unsalted butter

Fleur de sel, for finishing

Fill this Nicoise salad with crisp lettuce, summer vegetables, new potatoes, tomatoes, and anything else that inspires you that day. Splurge on really great olive oil–packed tuna—it makes a world of difference. Fishing Vessel St. Jude's canned tuna is excellent and the fish are solely troll-caught, which is the sustainable method recommended by the Monterey Bay Aquarium's Seafood Watch. Ventresca is the extra-rich fatty belly of a tuna.

albacore ventresca

WITH GREEN BEANS, SWEET PEPPERS, QUAIL EGGS, AND NICOISE OLIVES

1   To make the aioli, in a medium bowl, combine the egg yolks, lemon juice, and garlic. Whisk together for 2 to 3 minutes, or until pale yellow and thickened. While whisking, slowly drizzle in the olive oil until it's emulsified and fully incorporated. Season to taste with the salt and pepper. Store the aioli in an airtight container in the refrigerator for up to 3 days.

2   To make the salad, begin by arranging an assortment of vegetables around the edge of a serving platter. What follows is how we do it at Lark, but feel free to arrange them as you like. Arrange the potatoes and green beans on either corner of the platter. Place a few tomato wedges around the edge. Next, add the anchovies. Gently break up the tuna and add it to the platter.

3   In a medium bowl, whisk together the olive oil and vinegar. Season to taste with salt and pepper. Gently toss the lettuce with the vinaigrette. Adjust seasoning to taste. Place the tossed lettuce in the center of the platter.

4   Gently position dollops of the aioli and the olives around the platter. Place the quail eggs around the greens. Sprinkle a little fleur de sel on the tuna and eggs.

CHEF'S NOTE: To hard-boil the quail eggs, place them in a small saucepan and cover them with cold water by 1 inch. Bring to a boil, and then remove the pan from the heat and cover. After 5 minutes, place the eggs into an ice bath in order to prevent them from overcooking. Once they have cooled, they are ready to peel.

MAKES 4 SERVINGS

FOR THE AIOLI

2 egg yolks

1 teaspoon freshly squeezed lemon juice

½ teaspoon finely minced garlic

½ cup extra-virgin olive oil

Kosher salt and freshly ground black pepper

FOR THE SALAD

2 medium red potatoes, just cooked through, thickly sliced

1 cup green beans, stems trimmed, blanched, and shocked

2 medium heirloom tomatoes, cut into wedges

6 oil-packed anchovy fillets

1 (6- to 8-ounce) jar or can very high-quality tuna

1 tablespoon extra-virgin olive oil

1 teaspoon Garnacha or red wine vinegar

Kosher salt and freshly ground black pepper

1 head speckled lettuce, leaves separated, washed, and spun dry

½ cup whole Nicoise olives

3 quail eggs, hard-boiled, peeled, and halved

Fleur de sel, for finishing

The geoduck clam is one of the iconic Northwest species: elusive, mysterious, startling, and ultimately so delicious. The name comes from the native Nisqually language, g'ideq, or gweduc, though they have nothing to do with ducks, but that's how these things go. Geoducks are one of the world's largest, longest-lived, most highly prized, and most expensive clams. Try this recipe for a rare summertime treat.

geoduck ceviche

WITH CHERRY TOMATOES, CHILES, AND MINT

1   In a medium mixing bowl, combine the tomatoes, geoduck, and chiles. Add the lime juice and stir gently to incorporate. Season with the salt. Add the oil and mix gently with a spoon. Transfer to the refrigerator to chill and marinate for 30 minutes.

2   Just before serving, stir the parsley into the ceviche. Add salt and pepper to taste. Divide the ceviche among two chilled glasses or bowls. Garnish each serving with the mint leaves and a little drizzle of olive oil.

> CHEF'S NOTE: Most fishmongers will clean your geoduck for you if you ask.

MAKES 2 SERVINGS

1 pint cherry tomatoes, halved (quartered if large)

4 ounces geoduck clam, cleaned and very thinly sliced

1 tablespoon seeded and minced serrano chile

1 tablespoon seeded and minced red jalapeño or Thai red chile

Juice from 2 limes

½ teaspoon kosher salt

1 tablespoon extra-virgin olive oil, plus more for finishing

2 tablespoons thinly sliced (chiffonade) Italian parsley leaves

Freshly groun black pepper

6 mint leaves, for finishing

I usually have this salad when Little Gem lettuce comes into season. We begin serving it with shaved radishes and Dungeness crab, and when tomato season starts, we switch to cherry tomatoes, avocado, and chilled spot prawns (Maine lobster works great too).

little gem lettuce

WITH GREEN GODDESS DRESSING,
CHERRY TOMATOES, AVOCADO, AND SPOT PRAWNS

1   In a medium saucepan, combine 2 cups water, the wine, salt, and bay leaf. Squeeze in lemon juice and then add the lemon halves to the pan. Bring the mixture to a boil and then turn the heat down so that it is just below a simmer. Add the prawns and poach just to cook through, about 2 minutes, or until just opaque and slightly firm. Be careful not to overcook them.

2   Using a slotted spoon, remove the prawns from the pan and transfer them to a plate. Refrigerate until they are completely chilled, then gently peel off the shells. Slice the back of each prawn and remove the vein. Chill again until ready to serve.

3   To make the green goddess dressing, in a food processor, combine the anchovies, green onions, tarragon, parsley, shallot, and garlic. Pulse a few times to distribute evenly. Add the aioli, buttermilk, vinegar, salt, and pepper. Process the mixture until it is pureed, well combined, and pale green. Adjust seasoning to taste.

4   In a mixing bowl, toss the lettuce with just enough dressing to coat. Add the shallot and chives and gently toss to coat. Transfer the salad to a large serving platter, or divide it among individual plates.

5   In the same mixing bowl, dress the prawns with a little dressing and a sprinkle of fleur de sel. Place the prawns in and around the salad, being careful not to weigh down the greens. Dot the salad with the avocado slices and cherry tomatoes and serve.

CHEF'S NOTE: The prawns can be poached and deveined up to 1 day ahead of time. The dressing can be made up to 2 days ahead of time and stored in an airtight container in the refrigerator.

MAKES 4 TO 6 SERVINGS

1 cup dry white wine

1 teaspoon kosher salt

1 bay leaf

1 lemon, halved

16 shell-on spot prawns

FOR THE GREEN
GODDESS DRESSING

2 anchovy fillets, chopped

3 tablespoons chopped green onion (green part only)

2 tablespoons chopped tarragon

2 tablespoons chopped Italian parsley

2 teaspoons minced shallot

1 teaspoon minced garlic

½ cup aioli (see recipe on page 175)

¼ cup buttermilk

2 tablespoons champagne vinegar

1 teaspoon kosher salt

½ teaspoon freshly ground black pepper

6 to 8 Little Gem lettuce heads or baby speckled lettuce (whatever delicate lettuce is available), torn into sections, washed, and spun dry

2 teaspoons minced shallot

1 teaspoon minced chives

Fleur de sel, for finishing

1 avocado, sliced

½ cup cherry tomatoes, halved

LOCAL VERSUS ELSEWHERE

Months before opening Lark, I began thinking about the best sources for ingredients. At the time, Seattle already had a great network of small organic farms within a hundred miles supplying area restaurants. No problem there; I had a half dozen in mind that went on to form the core group who still supply Lark today. Nowadays, I meet new farmers every year, and I just can't help it, I strike up a conversation and the next thing you know I'm ordering a few bunches of spigarello greens from my new pals! In the summer, it's pretty easy to go mostly local and organic with produce.

When it came time to source cheeses, it wasn't so easy to go local at first. There were a few pioneers of Washington's artisanal cheese movement: Rick and Lora Lea of Quillisascut, Joan and Pierre-Louis of Monteillet Fromagerie, and of course Sally Jackson, all bringing their cheeses to Seattle each month. Many years later, we have dozens of local cheeses, in many different styles, from sheep's and goat's milk (like halloumi, which was inspired by the Eastern Mediterranean and produced in Tieton, Washington) to Kurtwood Farms' rich cow's milk Camembert from Vashon Island, just twelve miles away as the crow flies (and did I mention it's made on an island?).

We have great and reliable local sources for most of the pork, beef, and lamb we use at Lark. I can't rave enough about natural and organic meats from smaller producers; the flavor is nearly always superior to any grocery store options. It often means you'll pay more, but to cut back a bit on the meat portion sizes and increase your grains and vegetables—isn't that what the doctor ordered anyway?

Washington wines are among the best, produced by an award-winning and growing farming community that keeps us happy. We've been over to Chinook Wines in Prosser to help with the crush and never cease to be inspired by their dedication and their attention to product. They grow some of their grapes and oversee every cluster that they crush and make into wine. When Kelly, my business partner and wine director, adds new wine to our list, she always chooses ones that will pair well with my menus while keeping a range of choices available.

I admit it, we also love the elsewhere: Italy, France, Spain. Even California. Buying local is the ideal, but I can't see ignoring some of the great products I can get from all over the world. Our wine list is international by choice; in season I buy game from Scotland; and I have a weakness for jamón Ibérico. Aged balsamic vinegars and extra-virgin olive oil from Italy and argan oil from Morocco will always be welcome in the Lark kitchen. And what would we do without Meyer lemons, Black Mission figs, and pineapples? Balance is important. I always choose local when it's as good or better. Our coffee and chocolate? Roasted here in Seattle. And when we must reach out farther for our needs, we find ourselves choosing smaller producers even when they're thousands of miles away—it just seems more neighborly.

Hanger steak has long been called the butcher's steak. I think since there's only one per cow, it must not have been seen as practical to sell, so the butcher took it home. After all, it's much easier to portion out a New York strip into steaks. But now the secret's out and this juicy, flavorful cut has been making the rounds for a few years. In a French bistro it might be called onglet, *in Mexico,* arrachera. *I call it* delicious!

hanger steak

WITH HEIRLOOM TOMATOES, ARUGULA, AND TOASTED GARLIC SAUCE

MAKES 4 SERVINGS

FOR THE TOASTED GARLIC SAUCE

1 tablespoon extra-virgin olive oil

2 tablespoons thinly sliced garlic

1 tablespoon dry white wine

1 teaspoon freshly squeezed lemon juice

3 tablespoons cold unsalted butter

1 To make the toasted garlic sauce, heat the olive oil in a small nonreactive saucepan over medium heat. Add the garlic and fry until light golden and crispy. Add the wine and lemon juice to deglaze the pan. Bring the liquid to a simmer. Immediately remove the pan from the heat and whisk in the butter, 1 tablespoon at a time, until emulsified. Season to taste with salt and pepper. Set the pan aside in a warm place until you are ready to use the sauce. Fold in the parsley just before serving.

2 Season each hanger steak generously on all sides with salt and pepper.

3   Heat the olive oil until very hot in a large sauté pan over medium-high heat. Add the steaks to the pan and sear on until crispy and brown, 2 to 3 minutes per side. Add the butter to the pan and as it melts and foams, use a spoon to baste the steaks. When the internal temperature of each steak reaches 125 degrees F, transfer the steaks to a plate and let them rest for about 5 minutes. After resting, the steaks will reach medium-rare doneness.

4   Drain most of the fat from the steak pan and set the pan over medium heat. Arrange the bread slices in the pan (in batches if needed) and toast each side until golden and crispy. Set aside.

5   Preheat the oven to 400 degrees F.

6   Place the steaks in the oven to reheat for 1 to 2 minutes. Cut each steak into ¼-inch slices.

7   Meanwhile, in a large mixing bowl, whisk together the olive oil and lemon juice to make a vinaigrette. Add the arugula, shallot, a pinch of salt, and a few grinds of pepper and toss to coat. Adjust seasoning to taste.

8   Arrange the tomatoes on a platter or four plates. Place a slice of toasted bread beside the tomatoes. Place sliced steak on top of the bread and lightly sprinkle with fleur de sel. Spoon the warm toasted garlic sauce around each steak. Divide the salad among the plates and serve.

CHEF'S NOTE: When cooking steaks in a sauté pan, it is important not to cook too many at once as it will prevent a caramelized crust from forming. I recommend leaving 2 to 3 inches between each steak, and if they won't all fit in the pan, just cook them in batches. It is also very important to let the steaks rest afterward. This will allow them to continue cooking from the residual heat and let the juices redistribute evenly throughout the steak.

Kosher salt and freshly ground black pepper

1 tablespoon chopped Italian parsley leaves

20 ounces hanger steak, cut into 5-ounce portions

Kosher salt and freshly ground black pepper

1 tablespoon extra-virgin olive oil

1 tablespoon unsalted butter

4 slices Lark Country Bread (page 253), cut ⅓ inch thick

1 tablespoon extra-virgin olive oil

1 teaspoon freshly squeezed lemon juice

1 bunch arugula, trimmed, washed, and spun dry

1 tablespoon minced shallot

½ pound heirloom tomatoes, cored and sliced

Fleur de sel, for finishing

Squabs are underappreciated in America these days, but I love the rich, succulent, rosy meat. Several generations ago, when our diets were far more diverse than they are today, squabs were abundant on many farms throughout the country. At that time squab served as a reliable source of protein alongside beef, pork, and chicken. I'm lucky to have two Washington suppliers at hand: the Mad Hatcher Farm, with its focus on poultry and rabbits, and Sunleaf Farms, which sells primarily to the Chinese restaurant community.

squab

WITH GUANCIALE-ROASTED FIGS, SPECKLED LETTUCE, AND MALETTI BALSAMIC

MAKES 2 SERVINGS

6 Black Mission figs

12 paper-thin slices guanciale

2 whole squabs

Kosher salt and freshly ground black pepper

2 tablespoons extra-virgin olive oil

2 tablespoons unsalted butter

4 sprigs thyme

1 tablespoon minced shallot

1 head speckled lettuce, leaves separated, washed, and spun dry

1 Preheat the oven to 400 degrees F.

2 Wrap each fig all the way around with two slices of guanciale. Place the figs in an ovenproof pan and cook until the guanciale is a little crispy and the figs are soft, 10 to 15 minutes.

3 Meanwhile, butcher the squabs. Remove any internal organs. Cut off the wing tips. Cut each squab in half, keeping the breast, leg, and thigh from each side together as one piece. Season the squabs all over with salt and pepper.

4 Heat the olive oil in a large sauté pan over high heat. Place the squabs in the pan, skin side down. Cook until the skin is crispy, 2 to 3 minutes. Turn the squabs over and add the butter and thyme sprigs to the pan. Once the butter melts and foams,

use a spoon to baste the squab breast skin, continuing to cook for another 2 to 3 minutes.

5   Transfer the squabs from the pan to a large plate to rest. After 4 to 5 minutes, separate the legs from the breasts and slice the breasts into 3 equal pieces.

6   Remove the thyme from the pan and drain all but about 1 tablespoon of the fat. Set the pan over medium heat and add the shallot, letting it sweat for a minute. Place the lettuce in the pan and gently toss, just wilting it slightly and coating with shallot. Transfer the lettuce to a platter or plate.

7   Keeping the pan off the heat, add the balsamic vinegar and swirl it with the oil and shallots that remain.

8   To serve, place the roasted figs in and around the lettuce. Place the squab breasts and legs in and around the lettuce. Drizzle the balsamic mixture over the lettuce and around the plate. Sprinkle the squab with a little fleur de sel.

1 tablespoon very good-quality balsamic vinegar (with a high viscosity)

Fleur de sel, for finishing

CHEF'S NOTE: Butchering a squab is the same as butchering a chicken, it's just a smaller body. In this recipe the breast, leg, and thigh from each side of the bird are kept in one piece so they cook more gently.

This is definitely a dish to cook when you have some time and energy to devote to a dinner party or an anniversary meal. It goes pretty quickly once you've done the prep for the pavé, and you'll be heartily rewarded for your efforts once you tuck in! It works well with dried cherries if you want to try it in colder weather, but it's especially good with firm, ripe Bing or Rainier cherries.

pork duo:
TENDERLOIN AND SHOULDER PAVÉ WITH CHERRIES AND TREVISO

1 To make the pork pavé, arrange the pork strips in a single layer in a roasting pan. Sprinkle half the salt evenly over the pork. Turn the pieces over and sprinkle with the remaining salt. Add the garlic, thyme, bay leaves, and peppercorns to the pan. Arrange the pork so that the aromatics are evenly scattered throughout the meat. Cover the pan with plastic wrap and chill for 24 hours.

2 Remove the pan from the refrigerator and set it aside at room temperature for 1 hour. Preheat the oven to 300 degrees F.

3 Remove the plastic wrap and cover the pork with the luke-warm fat. Cover the pan tightly with foil or a lid. Place the pan in the oven and cook the pork until it's very tender and shreds easily, 2 to 3 hours. Remove the pan from the oven, uncover it, and allow the pork to cool to room temperature, about 1 hour.

4 Separate the meat from the fat and strain the fat through a fine mesh strainer. Let the fat cool, reserving a little to top off the pavé, and save the rest for another use.

5 Using your hands, gently pull the meat apart until it is very finely shredded. Adjust seasoning to taste. If the pork seems too dry, add a little of the cooled fat back into the meat until the desired richness is achieved.

6 Line a terrine mold or loaf pan with plastic wrap or parchment paper. Press the shredded pork onto the plastic wrap and smooth it to an even layer about 1 inch thick. Place another piece of plastic wrap on top of the pork and press down with another pan directly on top of the plastic wrap. Press to make it flat and smooth (the bottom of a glass works well for smaller molds). Chill overnight.

(CONTINUED)

MAKES 4 SERVINGS

FOR THE PORK PAVÉ

½ pound boneless pork shoulder, cut into 2-inch strips

1 tablespoon kosher salt

2 unpeeled cloves garlic, cracked

2 sprigs thyme

2 bay leaves

½ teaspoon whole black peppercorns

1 pound rendered pork or duck fat, lukewarm

2 tablespoons extra-virgin olive oil or canola oil

Freshly ground black pepper

½ cup all-purpose flour

FOR THE PORK TENDERLOIN

1 pound pork tenderloin, cut into 4-ounce portions

4 tablespoons extra-virgin olive oil, divided

1 tablespoon chopped garlic

1 tablespoon chopped thyme leaves

1 tablespoon chopped rose-mary leaves

Kosher salt and freshly ground black pepper

FOR THE TREVISO SALAD

1 tablespoon extra-virgin olive oil

2 teaspoons minced shallot

1 tablespoon aged
   balsamic vinegar

1 head Treviso radicchio,
   leaves separated, washed,
   spun dry, and torn into
   bite-size pieces

1 cup cherries, stemmed
   and pitted

Fleur de sel

Freshly ground
   black pepper

Fleur de sel, for finishing

7   Remove the pork from the mold or pan and discard the plastic wrap. Cut the pork into 2-inch squares.

8   Heat the olive oil in a large sauté pan over medium heat. Season the pavé squares with salt and pepper. Lightly dust them with flour and shake off any excess (reseason after shaking if necessary). Sauté the pavé squares until they are crispy and golden brown on each side. Drain the pavé on paper towels and set aside.

9   To prepare the pork tenderloin, combine the tenderloin with 3 tablespoons of the oil and the garlic, thyme, and rosemary. Cover and marinate overnight.

10   Remove the pork from the marinade and wipe off any garlic. Season to taste with salt and pepper.

11   Heat the remaining 1 tablespoon oil in a large sauté pan over medium-high heat. Sauté the tenderloin on all sides until crispy and golden and an internal temperature of about 150 degrees F is reached. If the pieces are thick, finish cooking them in a 400-degree-F oven. Transfer the pork from the pan to a plate and let rest for 4 to 5 minutes.

12   To make the Treviso salad, in a large mixing bowl, combine the oil and shallot. Whisk in the balsamic vinegar. Add the Treviso and cherries. Season with a pinch of fleur de sel and pepper. Gently toss with the dressing to coat lightly. Adjust seasoning to taste.

13 To serve, divide the pork pavé among four plates. Cut each
piece of tenderloin into four slices. Sprinkle with a little fleur de
sel. Fan the tenderloin slices beside the pavé. Divide the Treviso
salad among the plates and drizzle a little balsamic vinaigrette
around the plate. Sprinkle with a little more fleur de sel.

CHEF'S NOTE: The pork tenderloin should marinate overnight. The
pork pavé recipe is a 2-day process; it is first marinated overnight,
then cooked, and finally pressed overnight. The pork shoulder can
be cooked up to 1 week in advance as long as it is refrigerated and
completely submerged in the fat. You can store it that way until
you are ready to shred the meat and continue making the pavé.
This is the same process as that for Pork Rillettes (see recipe on
page 136) and you could even use the same meat for both recipes.

I'm a big fan of looking beyond the basics when we think about dinner. Quail fits right into that niche when you're looking for a quick-cooking yet mild-tasting change from chicken or turkey. Wrapping quail in bacon adds a smoky richness to the meat, and the mustard sauce adds a contrasting piquant flavor. The vegetable portion of this dish, a Northwest riff on succotash, is also delicious alone or served alongside grilled beef or pork.

bacon-wrapped quail
WITH CHANTERELLES, CORN, AND GREEN BEANS

1 Preheat the grill.

2 Rinse each quail and pat dry with paper towels. Remove the wing tips. Cut a slit in one of the lower pieces of the leg and thread the other leg through the slit to cross the legs. Season the quails on both sides with salt and pepper. Lay two pieces of the bacon parallel to each other and slightly overlapping on each quail. Wrap the bacon strips tightly around the quail so that the seams are on the bottom. Set aside.

3 In a large sauté pan over medium-high heat, melt the butter. Add the chanterelles, season to taste with salt and pepper, and cook for 3 to 4 minutes, or until soft. Add the corn, green beans, and thyme. Season with salt and pepper and stir. Cook for 3 to 4 minutes, or until all the vegetables are hot. Adjust seasoning to taste.

4 Meanwhile, place the quails, breast side down, on the hot grill. Grill on one side for 2 to 3 minutes, then flip over and grill the other side for another 1 to 2 minutes. The bacon should be crispy and the quails just cooked through. Transfer the quails from the grill to a large platter and let rest for 1 to 2 minutes.

5 To make the mustard sauce, in a medium sauté pan over medium-high heat, melt 1 tablespoon of the butter. Add the shallot and garlic and sweat them until soft. Stir in the wine and cook until reduced by half. Stir in the stock and cook until reduced by half. Stir in the mustards and thyme to incorporate. Stir in the remaining 1 tablespoon butter. Season to taste with salt and pepper. Keep the sauce warm until ready to use.

6 To serve, spoon some of the chanterelle mixture onto a plate. Place one or two quails on top. Spoon some of the mustard sauce around the plate.

MAKES 4 SERVINGS

8 semi-boneless quail

Kosher salt and freshly ground black pepper

16 thin bacon slices

2 tablespoons unsalted butter

8 ounces chanterelles, cleaned and cut into bite-size pieces

Kernels from 2 ears corn

1½ cups green beans, blanched, shocked, and cut into ½- to ¾-inch pieces

1 teaspoon chopped thyme leaves

FOR THE MUSTARD SAUCE

2 tablespoons unsalted butter, divided

1 tablespoon minced shallot

1 tablespoon thinly sliced garlic

¼ cup dry white wine

1 cup chicken stock

1 tablespoon Dijon mustard

1 tablespoon whole grain mustard

1 teaspoon chopped thyme leaves

Kosher salt and freshly ground black pepper

I buy beautiful lamb several times throughout the year from Linda Neunzig of Ninety Farms and Jeff Rogers of Snoqualmie Valley Lamb. They are both pros and raise some of the tastiest lamb I've ever had. We always buy them whole and portion them into chops and loins to grill, legs to roast, and shanks and necks to braise.

lamb chops

WITH LAVENDER SALT, HONEY-GLAZED CARROTS, AND ROASTED POTATOES

MAKES 4 SERVINGS

1 tablespoon fleur de sel

½ teaspoon dried English lavender blossoms

5 tablespoons extra-virgin olive oil, divided, plus more as needed

1 tablespoon chopped garlic

1 tablespoon chopped thyme leaves

1 tablespoon chopped rosemary leaves

12 lamb chops (2 ounces each)

Kosher salt and freshly ground black pepper

1 pound fingerling potatoes, scrubbed and halved lengthwise

16 baby rainbow carrots

2 tablespoons unsalted butter

2 teaspoons local honey

1   First, make the lavender salt. Put the fleur de sel in a small jar with lid. Crush the lavender over the salt by rubbing it between your fingers. Stir and cover with the lid. The lavender salt will keep at room temperature for a few weeks.

2   Next, marinate the lamb. In a small bowl, whisk together 2 tablespoons of the oil, the garlic, thyme, and rosemary to form a marinade. Rub the marinade all over the lamb chops, cover, and refrigerate overnight.

3   Preheat a large sauté pan or a grill over medium-high heat.

4   Wipe any garlic off the lamb chops and season generously with salt and pepper. You may need to cook the lamb in batches. To sauté the first batch, add about 1 tablespoon oil to the pan and then add a few chops, being careful not to crowd them. Cook the lamb until medium-rare, about 3 minutes on each side. Repeat with the rest of the lamb chops. To grill, place the chops directly on the grill and cook until medium-rare, about 3 minutes per side. Transfer the lamb chops from the pan

or grill to a large platter and let rest for 4 to 5 minutes. Warm them again briefly in a hot oven or on the grill before serving.

5   Preheat the oven to 375 degrees F. Preheat a heavy roasting pan or cast-iron skillet in the oven for about 10 minutes.

6   In a medium mixing bowl, combine the potatoes and the remaining 2 tablespoons oil, tossing to coat. Season to taste with salt and pepper. Transfer the potatoes to the hot pan in a single layer, cut side down.

7   Return the pan to the oven and roast the potatoes for about 15 minutes, or until they begin to crisp and brown on the cut side. Use a spatula to flip the potatoes over. They shouldn't stick to the pan if they are browned enough. Return the pan to the oven and roast the potatoes for another 5 to 8 minutes, or until cooked through. Serve hot.

8   Meanwhile, cook the honey-glazed carrots. First, prepare an ice bath. Then bring a large saucepan of salted water to a boil. Boil the carrots for 2 to 3 minutes, or until just tender. Strain the carrots and immediately dunk them in the ice bath. Remove the carrot peels by gently rubbing them off with a kitchen towel. (They should rub off quite easily.) Cut the carrots in half lengthwise.

9   Heat a medium sauté pan over medium-high heat. Add the butter and honey to the pan and melt them together. Add the carrots and toss to coat. Season to taste with salt. Cook until the carrots are heated through and the honey-butter forms a sticky glaze. Adjust seasoning to taste. Serve hot.

10   To serve, arrange the honey-glazed carrots and roasted potatoes on a large platter. Add the lamb chops and sprinkle with a pinch of lavender salt. Drizzle some honey butter glaze around the plate.

CHEF'S NOTE: Be sure to allow time to marinate the lamb chops overnight.

This risotto is pure decadence. There are usually a couple of weeks in autumn when all three of these mushroom varieties intersect: chanterelle, lobster, and porcini (of course any one of them alone is great, but the combination is out of this world). Don't skimp on the Parmigiano-Reggiano; it's expensive, but a little goes a long way.

wild mushroom risotto

MAKES 4 SERVINGS

FOR THE MUSHROOM STOCK

1 onion, diced

2 celery stalks, diced

½ carrot, peeled and sliced

2 cloves garlic

½ cup dry white wine

1 pound mushrooms (wild, cremini, or button), including any wild mushroom trimmings you might have

2 sprigs thyme

3 parsley stems (without leaves)

1 tablespoon kosher salt

½ teaspoon whole black peppercorns

1   To make the mushroom stock, in a large pan over medium heat, sweat the onion, celery, carrot, and garlic. Deglaze the pan with the wine. Add the mushrooms, thyme, parsley stems, salt, and peppercorns and cover with water. Bring just to a boil and maintain a simmer for about 1 hour. If the water level dips below the vegetables, top off with more water so they stay submerged. Turn off the heat and let the stock steep at room temperature for about 1 hour. Strain the stock through a fine mesh strainer, cover, and refrigerate if not using right away. The mushroom stock will keep in an airtight container in the refrigerator for about 3 days.

2   To make the risotto, heat a medium sauté pan over high heat. Add about 1 tablespoon of the butter, the chanterelles, and one-third of the minced garlic. Season to taste with salt and pepper. Toss and cook until golden brown and cooked through. Transfer the chanterelles to a plate to cool. Repeat with the lobster mushrooms (plus ½ tablespoon of the butter

and another third of the garlic) and with the porcinis (again, with ½ tablespoon of the butter and the remaining garlic), until all the mushrooms are cooked and set aside to cool.

3   In a medium pot over medium heat, warm 1 to 2 quarts of the mushroom stock.

4   Heat the olive oil in a large, wide sauté pan over a medium-high heat. Add the onion and sauté for 2 to 3 minutes, or until just golden brown. Stir in the carnaroli rice to coat with the oil. Stirring continuously, cook the rice for 1 to 2 minutes, or until the outside of the grains look slightly translucent. Deglaze the pan with the wine and season with about 1 tablespoon salt. Stir constantly until the wine has been absorbed by the rice.

5   Pour a ladleful or two of mushroom stock at a time into the pan, repeating as the stock is absorbed, and continue to stir until the rice is cooked but still has a little bite to it (al dente), 15 to 20 minutes total. Turn off the heat and let the risotto sit, untouched, for just about 1 minute. Stir in the reserved mushrooms and any juices that have collected on the plate.

6   Stir in the remaining 4 tablespoons butter, the rosemary, and Parmigiano-Reggiano until completely incorporated. Adjust the risotto consistency, if needed, by adding a little more of the mushroom stock. The risotto should be creamy and slightly loose, not thick and gloppy. Adjust seasoning to taste.

7   To serve, divide the risotto among four bowls. Top with more Parmigiano-Reggiano. Drizzle each serving with ½ teaspoon truffle oil and sprinkle with ½ teaspoon parsley.

CHEF'S NOTE: This delicious vegetarian risotto can also be made with the Parmigiano-Reggiano brodo (broth) that we use with our Ricotta Gnudi on page 128, or you can substitute chicken stock.

FOR THE RISOTTO

- 6 tablespoons unsalted butter, divided
- 3 ounces chanterelle mushrooms, brushed and trimmed
- 2 cloves garlic, minced, divided
- Kosher salt and freshly ground black pepper
- 3 ounces lobster mushrooms, brushed and trimmed
- 3 ounces porcini mushrooms, brushed and trimmed
- 1 tablespoon extra-virgin olive oil
- 1 yellow onion, cut into small dice
- 1½ cups carnaroli rice
- ½ cup dry white wine
- 1 tablespoon chopped rosemary leaves
- 1¼ ounces grated Parmigiano-Reggiano, plus more for finishing
- 2 teaspoons white truffle oil, for finishing (optional)
- 2 teaspoons thinly sliced (chiffonade) Italian parsley, for finishing

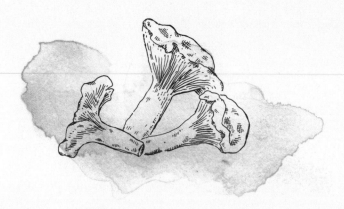

BRINGING THE WILD INTO THE KITCHEN

Seattle restaurants have long been supporting local foragers. This rogues' gallery of colorful characters—some grandmothers, some not very grand at all—would bring intriguing ingredients to our kitchens. Wild mushrooms were the first thing I noticed; I looked up at the back door to find my boss and a guy with a box full of beautiful piney matsutakes. Tasting huckleberries and salmonberries for the first time was astonishing. They were both familiar and unique at once.

It took a few years before I started getting out into the woods myself to hunt for berries or mushrooms, but now an afternoon hike with my family turns into a fun search for potential edibles. It's a wonderful pursuit, but one that requires training or a good mentor—seek out your local mycological society for ways to get started. Always have a professional inspect and approve anything you forage before consuming it, and be sensitive to local regulations and property rights before starting out.

It's rare these days to see Jeremy Faber, the founder of Foraged and Found Edibles. He has helpers now to make the restaurant rounds so he can stay in the woods more and more. Once in a while he'll show up with the most perfect box of morels from a secret patch near Blewett Pass or a strange new plant (goosefoot, anyone?) to try out. Whenever I spend time with Jeremy, or *Fat of the Land* author Langdon Cook, I gain a deeper understanding of their craft. It makes me want to get outside, and it makes me want to cook.

Every year at the beginning of the season of Mist, I start to introduce wild game meats onto the menu. This is the traditional time when hunters would go out and begin their quest for venison, boar, hare, and wild fowl. In the United States, unless you're a hunter yourself, true wild game is difficult to find, even with a chef's extensive suppliers. Most of what we call wild is actually semi-wild, or a species that we think of as wild, that's actually farm-raised. The wild boar that I serve is from Texas and ranges over thousands of acres, living wild and off the land. When it's time for field-harvest, the boar is shot from long range, with the idea being a low-stress death. They are then processed in mobile facilities, under USDA inspection, before being shipped around the country.

The Roosevelt elk I use is free-ranged over large areas in Western Oregon, and is rich, tender, and has a medium-level gamey taste. New Zealand venison and elk are farm-raised with regulated feed, and have substantially milder taste. I purchase a variety of Scottish game for our Wild Beast dinner in November; rare and expensive blue hare, grouse, wood pigeons, and partridge are fairly gamey in flavor and very delicious when cooked with great care.

Wild ingredients are definitely a trend among chefs trying to differentiate themselves, but the real joy in using them is their freshness. Some forager went out on Wednesday morning and by Thursday afternoon he's hawking his goods. Featuring these treasures is a way to connect to the earth, to get in touch with our inner hunter-gatherers. My guests may never go digging for razor clams or try their hand at foraging chanterelles, but I hope they are inspired to eat wild. Pairing wild ingredients with something more familiar (and often well-loved) is a great way to introduce new and maybe strange-sounding foods to skeptical diners, thus: Neah Bay Halibut with Creamed Nettles and Morels (see recipe on page 97) or raw yellowtail with cherry tomatoes and pickled sea beans.

AN INCOMPLETE LIST (WE'RE STILL LEARNING), OF GOOD THINGS FROM THE FOREST:

MIST (NOVEMBER-MARCH): Hedgehog mushrooms, black trumpet mushrooms, Yellowfoot chanterelles, local black truffles, local white truffles, green alder cones

EVERGREEN (APRIL-JULY): Stinging nettles, wild watercress, miner's lettuce, wood violets, wood sorrel, sheep's sorrel, cherry blossoms, maple blossoms, spruce buds, porcini mushrooms, morel mushrooms

BOUNTY (AUGUST-OCTOBER): Sea beans, licorice root, red huckleberries, blue huckleberries, native blackberries, Blackcap raspberries, salmonberries, chanterelle mushrooms, lobster mushrooms, matsutake mushrooms, lion's mane mushrooms, cauliflower mushrooms

---

Our guests have loved the beauty and simplicity of our sautéed mushrooms since opening night. We prefer to use all wild mushrooms like morels, chanterelles, porcini, lobster, hedgehog, or black trumpets. Sometimes we can only serve one variety at a time, and in the winter months when wild mushrooms are scarce, we do a mixture of wild and cultivated mushrooms such as cremini, shiitake, or oyster.

wild mushrooms

WITH GARLIC, OLIVE OIL, AND SEA SALT

1   Clean the mushrooms as needed, then trim and slice into bite-size pieces.

2   Heat the oil in a large sauté pan over high heat until very hot. Add the mushrooms and spread them out in a single layer. Let them cook for a minute or two before stirring. Toss the mushrooms a couple of times and season to taste with salt and pepper. Continue cooking until the mushrooms are golden brown and juicy but not wet. If the mushrooms are wet, you will need to let them go a little longer to cook off excess moisture. Once the mushrooms are almost done, add the garlic and toss. Cook for 1 or 2 more minutes. Adjust seasoning to taste.

3   To serve, spoon the mushrooms into a warm serving dish. Sprinkle with the chives.

MAKES 4 SERVINGS

½ pound wild and cultivated mushrooms, depending on the season

1 teaspoon extra-virgin olive oil

Kosher salt and freshly ground black pepper

1 teaspoon slivered garlic

1 teaspoon minced chives, for finishing

CHEF'S NOTE: When cleaning mushrooms, it is best to use a brush or towel to gently remove the dirt. Some mushrooms, like black trumpets and morels, can be especially dirty and hard to clean completely with a brush. Often they need to be washed in water. It is important not to soak them, though; dunk in the water and toss around briefly, then dry them immediately in a salad spinner before laying them out on paper towels.

This is my one of my favorite summer side dishes, and when the beans are "on" there are so many varieties to choose from: green, yellow wax, Dragon Tongue, and Romano, just to name a few. Use one type or a combination of several; just blanch and shock them separately as the variation in size and shape will affect the cooking time.

green beans
WITH BACON AND ROASTED-TOMATO VINAIGRETTE

1   Preheat the oven to 400 degrees F.

2   To make the roasted-tomato vinaigrette, toss together the tomatoes, 1 tablespoon of the oil, and the garlic in a casserole dish. Season with a generous amount of salt and pepper. Roast in the oven for 30 to 40 minutes, or until the tomato and garlic skins have blistered and darkened and the garlic is roasted. Remove the dish from the oven and let cool to room temperature. When cool enough to handle, peel the skins from the tomatoes and garlic.

3   Place the tomatoes, roasted garlic, and any juice accumulated in the dish into a food processor. Pulse a couple of times to make a coarse puree. Transfer the puree to a medium mixing bowl and stir in the sherry vinegar and remaining 2 tablespoons oil. Adjust seasoning to taste. Set aside.

4   Prepare an ice bath. Then bring a large pot of salted water to a boil. Blanch the green beans until just cooked, 4 to 6 minutes depending on thickness. Using a slotted spoon, immediately transfer the beans to the ice bath to stop cooking. Drain the beans and set on a plate to dry, or pat with paper towels.

5   Heat a large sauté pan over medium heat and add the bacon, cooking it until crispy, about 8 to 10 minutes. Drain off excess fat, leaving 1 to 2 tablespoons in the pan. Add the shallot to the bacon and cook until softened, about 1 minute. Add the beans and thyme and sprinkle with a little salt and pepper. Heat through and adjust seasoning to taste.

6   Loosely pile some beans onto each of four plates. Spoon a generous amount of the tomato vinaigrette over the top and serve.

MAKES 4 SERVINGS

3 beefsteak tomatoes, cored

3 tablespoons extra-virgin olive oil, divided

3 unpeeled cloves garlic, cracked

Kosher salt and freshly ground black pepper

1 tablespoon sherry vinegar

2 cups green, yellow wax, or Dragon Tongue beans (or a mixture), stem ends trimmed

¼ cup bacon, cut into ⅓-inch lardons

½ tablespoon minced shallot

½ teaspoon chopped thyme leaves

At some point every summer, you'll go to the grocery store or farmers' market and buy a little bit of everything because all of the produce is so tempting. This is the meal for that week. Add or subtract vegetables until you come up with your favorite combination. A play on the classic Tuscan bread and vegetable soup, I've made this into a hearty vegetable stew.

summer ribollita

WITH WHITE BEANS, CHARD, TOMATOES, SQUASH, AND BASIL

MAKES 4 SERVINGS

FOR THE CANNELLINI BEANS

1 cup dry cannellini or great
   northern beans

4 cloves garlic, crushed

2 sprigs thyme

1 bay leaf

FOR THE PISTOU SAUCE

1 cup stemmed basil leaves

¼ cup chopped tomatoes

2 cloves garlic, minced

1 tablespoon pine nuts,
   lightly toasted

¼ cup extra-virgin olive oil

1   To prepare the cannellini beans, cover the beans by at least 2 inches with cold water and soak them overnight in the refrigerator.

2   Drain the beans and place them in a medium saucepan over medium-high heat. Cover the beans with at least 2 inches of cold water and add the garlic, thyme, and bay leaf. Bring just to a boil, then turn the heat down to low to maintain a bare simmer. Cook the beans until tender, 1 to 1½ hours.

3   Drain the beans and spread in a single layer on a baking tray to cool. Pick out and discard the garlic, thyme, and bay leaf. The ribollita uses ½ cup of the beans; reserve the extra beans for another use. They will keep in an airtight container in the refrigerator for up to 2 days.

4   To make the pistou sauce, in a food processor, combine the basil, tomatoes, garlic, and pine nuts. Pulse to chop, scraping down the sides of the bowl occasionally. Once all of the ingredients are evenly chopped, run the processor and drizzle in the olive oil in a slow stream. Stop when all of the oil is incorporated. You should have an emulsified sauce. Season to taste with salt and pepper. The pistou sauce will keep in an airtight container in the refrigerator for up to 2 days.

5   To make the ribollita, heat the olive oil in a large saucepan over medium heat. Add the onion and a pinch of salt. Cook until light golden, 7 to 8 minutes. Add the garlic and cook until softened but not browned. Add the wine and bring to a boil. Turn the heat down to maintain a simmer and let the wine reduce slightly, 1 to 2 minutes. Add the summer squash, all tomatoes, and green beans. Stir in the bread pieces, chard, and ½ cup of the cannellini beans.

6   Add the Parmigiano-Reggiano brodo and season to taste with salt and pepper.

7   Bring the ribollita to a boil, and then turn the heat down to maintain a simmer. Add the summer savory and continue to simmer until the vegetables are tender, 10 to 15 minutes.

8   To serve, stir 3 tablespoons of the pistou sauce into the ribollita and immediately ladle it into four serving bowls. Sprinkle the basil evenly over the ribollita right before serving. Top each bowl with a sprinkle of fleur de sel and serve the remaining ½ cup pistou sauce on the side.

CHEF'S NOTE: This dish takes a little planning because the beans will need to soak overnight before they can be cooked. Alternatively, you can use 1 (8-ounce) can rinsed cannellinis in a pinch. This recipe is a great way to use up day-old bread.

Kosher salt and freshly ground black pepper

FOR THE RIBOLLITA

2 tablespoons extra-virgin olive oil

1 cup yellow onion, cut into ¼ inch slices

Kosher salt

1 tablespoon slivered garlic

¼ cup dry white wine

1 cup summer squash, cut into ½-inch dice

1 cup tomatoes, cored and cut into ½-inch dice

¼ cup cherry tomatoes, halved

¼ cup green beans, cut into ½-inch pieces

2 slices day-old bread, lightly toasted and torn into bite-size pieces

1 cup Swiss chard, stems removed, leaves cut into 2-inch strips

4 cups Parmigiano-Reggiano brodo (see recipe on page 128)

Freshly ground black pepper

1½ teaspoons chopped summer savory leaves

2 tablespoons torn basil leaves, for finishing

Fleur de sel, for finishing

This is a great way to use up ripe tomatoes when you have an overabundance. The soup is not cooked at all, so make sure the tomatoes are washed very well and are ripe but not damaged. I love it with Taxi tomatoes, a deep yellow-orange variety that is very sweet, but any flavorful variety will work. Picked Dungeness crabmeat also makes a delicious finishing touch instead of the yogurt.

yellow taxi tomato soup
WITH GOAT'S MILK YOGURT AND SHISO

1   In a large nonreactive bowl, combine the tomatoes, garlic, and salt. Toss together to combine well. Cover and set aside to marinate for 30 to 60 minutes.

2   Pass the tomatoes through a food mill with a fine mesh plate, or push them through a fine mesh strainer. This will remove most of the skin and seeds.

3   In a large bowl with lid, combine the strained tomatoes and champagne vinegar. Season to taste with salt and pepper. Stir in the olive oil and taste for seasoning and balance. Add more salt, pepper, oil, or vinegar as needed.

4   Chill the soup thoroughly, in the freezer if possible, for 1 to 2 hours.

5   Stir yogurt in a small bowl or in its container, and season to taste with salt and pepper.

6   Divide the yogurt among four chilled serving bowls and sprinkle shiso around the yogurt. Spoon chilled soup around the yogurt. Garnish with the parsley and serve.

MAKES 4 SERVINGS

2¾ pounds ripe Taxi tomatoes (or other yellow variety), cored and roughly chopped

3 cloves garlic, minced

2 teaspoons kosher salt, plus more as needed

¼ cup champagne vinegar, plus more as needed

Freshly ground black pepper

¼ cup extra-virgin olive oil

½ cup goat's milk yogurt

1 shiso leaf, thinly sliced (chiffonade)

1 teaspoon thinly sliced (chiffonade) Italian parsley leaves, for finishing

On a trip through northern Italy a few years ago, I made it a personal goal to try as much lardo as possible. All in, I tasted no fewer than fifteen types in half as many days in Piedmont, Lombardy, and the Veneto. In Colonnata, lardo is usually rubbed with rosemary or cinnamon after curing and aged in large Carrara marble basins. It was always served cold in Italy, and we often do the same at Lark. However, warming it slightly as we do in this preparation is a great treat and good for the beginner. We make our own lardo at Lark, or we buy it from Salumi or Tails and Trotters. Slice lardo like this carefully by hand, or ask your butcher to thinly slice it with a meat slicer.

lardo on toast

WITH TOMATO-LAVENDER CHUTNEY AND MARCONA ALMONDS

MAKES 4 SERVINGS

2 beefsteak tomatoes

4 teaspoons extra-virgin olive oil, divided

1 tablespoon sliced garlic

2 teaspoons sherry vinegar

1 tablespoon local honey

1 teaspoon chopped thyme leaves

1 teaspoon fresh crumbled lavender

Kosher salt

4 slices ciabatta or Lark Country Bread (page 253)

4 ounces lardo, thinly sliced

¼ cup Marcona almonds

1   First, make the tomato-lavender chutney. Prepare an ice bath. Then fill a medium saucepan two-thirds full with water and bring it to a boil.

2   Cut an *X* into the stem end of each tomato about ⅛ inch deep. Place the tomatoes in the boiling water for just about 15 seconds. Using a slotted spoon, transfer the tomatoes to the ice bath. (This makes it much easier to remove the skins without actually cooking the tomatoes.) Drain the tomatoes and peel off the skins. Cut each tomato lengthwise into quarters and remove the seeds. Roughly chop the tomatoes.

3   In a small saucepan over medium-high heat, combine 2 teaspoons of the olive oil and the garlic. Cook the garlic until slightly golden brown. Add the tomatoes, lower the heat, and let them simmer. Cook for about 45 minutes, or until the tomatoes have broken down and thickened to the consistency of a jam or chutney. Stir in the sherry vinegar. Stir in the honey, thyme, lavender, and a pinch of salt. Adjust seasoning to taste.

4   Remove the pan from the heat and let the chutney cool to room temperature. It can be stored in an airtight container in the refrigerator for up to 3 days.

5   Heat the remaining 2 teaspoons olive oil in a large sauté pan over medium-high heat. Arrange the bread slices in the pan and toast on both sides for a few minutes. Drape the lardo slices to cover the entire piece of toast and dot with the chutney. Place Marcona almonds on top. Cut each slice of bread into bite-size pieces and serve.

ON THE SIDE:
CONDIMENTS, PRESERVES, DRESSINGS,
AND SAUCES

I add extra elements to the plate for many reasons: to provide contrasting
flavors or textures, to bring forward a flavor that's subtle when I want to high-
light it, or to add interest and variety. These are a few of our favorites.

slightly sweet

HONEYCOMB (see Dinah's Cheese on page 74): There's no recipe for honeycomb, but ever since I was a kid I've loved it, chewing on the wax to extract
every bit of golden sweetness, gum in its purest form. Since opening, we've
served our cheeses at Lark with a hunk of honeycomb on the side. On occasion we'll move to artisan flavors like wild heather, acacia, tupelo, blackberry,
thyme blossom, chestnut, and sometimes even bitter varieties like cardoon
or Corbezzolo.

ARMAGNAC PRUNES (see Chicken Liver Parfait on page 63): Again, this
is a very simple condiment but so right on many occasions. I keep a supply
of these on hand for celebrating. Take a pound of good-quality pitted prunes,
place in a jar or tub, and cover with Armagnac or some good-quality brandy.
Cover tightly with a lid and refrigerate for at least two weeks, turning or
stirring every couple of days to make sure that all of the prunes are getting a
chance to soak up some goodness. If they seem to dry out at any point, just
add more Armagnac. The prunes will then be ready to serve with cheeses,
pâtés, or salamis, or to enjoy just as they are. They're exceptional stuffed with
a little foie gras mousse on Christmas Day . . . trust me, I know.

QUINCE PRESERVE (*membrillo* in Spanish): This is one of my all-
time favorites, perfect with just about any cheese or cured meat. I've
even served pork belly tartines with a smear of quince preserve and it's

impossibly delicious. I've been fortunate to get to know the Buck family, who have a small farm on Shaw Island (one of the San Juans), and every year I buy all of their quince, anywhere from twenty to one hundred pounds, which we use to make our own quince preserve and serve poached with Seared Foie Gras (see recipe on page 40).

chutneys and marmalades

I think of a chutney as any combination of sweet (fruit) and savory (vegetable), usually cooked and spiced in some way. Jam and preserves are similar, made of cooked, smashed fruit and syrup. A conserve is the same as a preserve, but made with whole fruit. A marmalade is a sweet citrus preserve, often made with a gelling agent. I use all of these terms somewhat interchangeably depending on what I think sounds the most appropriate, with no rhyme or reason other than my own aesthetic.

TWELFTH-CENTURY CHUTNEY (see Goose Prosciutto on page 61): Normally served with prosciutto, this is also excellent with Chicken Liver Parfait (page 63) and aged sheep's milk cheeses.

MOSTARDA D'UVA (see Salumi Coppa on page 145): This chutney is a fantastic amalgam of the harvest. I'm pretty sure it originated as a way to use overripe or damaged fruits and squash. As with many recipes of thrifty, humble origins, long, careful cooking resulted in an exceptional condiment that deserves a place in your repertoire.

TOMATO-LAVENDER CHUTNEY (see Lardo on Toast on page 206): This is a great all-around condiment that we use throughout tomato season with cheeses, charcuterie, and grilled or roasted fish.

salad dressings

GREEN GODDESS DRESSING (see Little Gem Lettuce on page 179): The tangy, creamy, and savory combination of buttermilk, mayonnaise, anchovies, garlic, and tender herbs is unbeatable. Our grandmothers knew of its versatility first: this is an easy dip, a salad dressing, and a great sauce on a roast beef and arugula sandwich.

AIOLI (see Albacore Ventresca on page 175): You see aioli in many forms and flavors these days, but at its heart, aioli is an emulsified sauce of garlic and olive oil, usually egg yolks, and often mustard and lemon juice. At Lark, we

(CONTINUED)

make aioli by hand every day for our steak tartare. Once you have the basic version down, you can flavor it by adding an extra ingredient or two depending on what you're serving it with. Some smoked paprika and a pinch of chile make a delicious zesty sauce for a fish stew or a roast pork sandwich. Some extra lemon juice, tarragon, and chives turn it into a sauce to complement chilled peel-and-eat prawns.

TRUFFLE AIOLI (see Crispy Pork Trotters on page 37): In this luxurious aioli, I lighten up on the garlic and add a generous amount of truffle oil, truffle salt, and freshly grated black truffle. Try it on a steak sandwich or with potato chips.

BAGNA CÀUDA (see White Asparagus on page 130): We use this warm garlic, anchovy, and olive oil–based sauce throughout the year as a dressing on a range of salads (try it on radicchio) and vegetables (it's especially great with the Brassica family: broccoli, cauliflower, and Romanesco). And I often dip chunks of crusty bread into it as an end-of-shift snack.

dessert sauces

RED WINE-POACHED CHERRIES: Wash and pit Bing cherries (we leave the stems in—it's tricky but it's possible, and I like the way they look), poach in red wine, sugar, a sachet of black peppercorns, cloves, and a cinnamon stick until tender. Cool and store in the red wine syrup. These are lovely spooned over ice cream or almond cake, or add a splash of good red wine vinegar to them and serve alongside country pâté or with sliced coppa.

RED WINE HUCKLEBERRIES: Use the same ingredients and preparation as for the poached cherries. These can also be used in desserts (the sweet version) or savory dishes (the version with vinegar). I usually freeze twenty to thirty pounds of wild huckleberries in September when they are perfectly ripe for use in the colder, leaner months. These are delicious worked into a quick pan sauce to serve over a bit of elk loin or a couple of thin pork chops.

VANILLA KUMQUAT PRESERVE (see Foie Gras Terrine on page 73): This is a play on orange marmalade, which I've never liked that much. The tartness and intensity, as well as the finer texture of the thinly sliced kumquats make this version much more intriguing to me, and the vanilla bean adds just the right balance to the sweet and sour. Use it in both dessert and savory dishes—add a spoonful to your usual vinaigrette for a salad dressing that will please everyone.

THEO DARK CHOCOLATE SAUCE (see Chocolate Madeleines on page 82): We use this barely sweet sauce primarily as a dip for the chocolate madeleines, but it's also great spooned over ice cream or served with a slice of cake.

CARAMEL SAUCE (see Black Fig Tarte Tatins on page 220 and Lacquered Peaches on page 227): What's not to love about caramel sauce? We flavor our base sauce with grappa, Calvados, single-barrel rum, and bourbon throughout the year for various desserts, and we always add just a bit of sea salt for balance.

CUSTARD SAUCE (see Cherry Clafouti on page 224): This is a rich, sweet, egg yolk–thickened sauce also known as crème Anglaise. Most ice cream bases are a variation of custard sauce.

The La Quercia brand is a relative newcomer to the prosciutto-making scene, but they have quickly distinguished themselves as the best in the United States, rivaling some of the premier hams from Italy and Spain. Earthy, buttery, and nutty all at once, this salt-cured ham is perfect on its own (but I couldn't include a recipe with only one ingredient). We make our own truffled green nectarines every spring when the young fruits are just setting on the branches but the pit hasn't fully developed. If you can't find any, marinated Lucques or Picholine olives substitute nicely.

la quercia prosciutto
WITH TRUFFLED GREEN NECTARINES AND PARMIGIANO-REGGIANO

1   Lay the prosciutto on four individual plates or a large platter so that the slices are a little ruffled. Using a peeler, thinly slice the Parmigiano-Reggiano onto the prosciutto. Cut the flesh of the nectarines away from the pit into ¼-inch-thick slices. Arrange the nectarine slices around the plate. Drizzle the olive oil over the plate. Sprinkle with the chives and serve.

MAKES 4 SERVINGS

- 16 paper-thin slices of La Quercia prosciutto
- 4 ounces Parmigiano-Reggiano
- 4 truffled green nectarines or your favorite large green olive
- 1 tablespoon extra-virgin olive oil
- 1 teaspoon minced chives

Burrata is a lovely fresh cow's milk cheese originally from Puglia, Italy. Burrata means "buttered" in Italian, I'm certain a reference to the creamy, rich interior. Fresh mozzarella is stretched into a pouch and filled with a mixture of unstretched mozzarella curd and cream. Then the top is twisted into a topknot to seal it. It is best eaten very fresh, certainly within days of being made. I serve it several ways throughout the year: with roasted cipollini onions and aged balsamic vinegar, with marinated artichokes and black olives, and of course, with great tomatoes.

burrata

WITH HEIRLOOM TOMATOES, ARUGULA, AND OLIVE OIL CROUTONS

MAKES 4 SERVINGS

FOR THE TOMATO COULIS

1 tablespoon extra-virgin olive oil

1 tablespoon minced shallot

4 ripe heirloom tomatoes, cored and roughly chopped

Kosher salt

¼ cup lovage leaves (or a combination of celery and parsley leaves), cut into wide strips

1   To make the tomato coulis, heat the olive oil in a saucepan over medium heat. Add the shallot and let it sweat for about 2 minutes. Add the tomatoes and a pinch of salt to the saucepan and simmer for about 25 minutes. Stir in the lovage and cook for about 5 minutes. Remove the saucepan from the heat and let cool for 10 minutes.

2   Transfer the tomato mixture to a food processor and puree. Strain the puree through a mesh sieve small enough to strain out the skins and seeds but still allow the pulp to pass through. You might have to push the pulp with a spoon or spatula. Adjust seasoning to taste.

3   Chill the coulis in the refrigerator for at least 30 minutes. It
can be stored in an airtight container in the refrigerator for up
to 4 days.

4   To make the olive oil croutons, trim the crust off of the
bread. Tear the bread into rough bite-size pieces.

5   In a medium saucepan with high sides, heat the olive oil
to 320 degrees F. In small batches, carefully fry the bread until
golden brown and crispy all the way through. Using a slotted
spoon or skimmer, remove the croutons from the oil and drain
on paper towels. Immediately sprinkle with the salt. Cool to
room temperature. The croutons will keep in an airtight container for up to 2 days.

6   In a large mixing bowl, combine the arugula, shallot, olive
oil, and lemon juice and gently toss to coat. Adjust seasoning
to taste.

7   To serve, spread some tomato coulis on a serving platter
and arrange the burrata slices over the top. Place the sliced
tomatoes next to and around the burrata. Sprinkle both with a
little fleur de sel and pepper. Arrange the arugula and croutons
around the burrata and tomato slices.

FOR THE OLIVE OIL
CROUTONS

1 cup ciabatta or other white
   country bread

1 cup extra-virgin olive oil

½ teaspoon kosher salt

1 bunch arugula, trimmed,
   washed, and spun dry

1 tablespoon minced shallot

1 tablespoon extra-virgin
   olive oil

1 teaspoon freshly squeezed
   lemon juice

½ pound burrata cheese,
   thickly sliced

½ pound ripe heirloom
   tomatoes, cored and
   sliced

Fleur de sel, for finishing

Freshly ground black
   pepper

The Mt. Townsend Creamery in Port Townsend, Washington, has quickly established itself as a pillar of the artisan cheese movement here in the Northwest. Just a few years ago they started out with the Camembert–like Cirrus and now they have ten cheeses on the market. Seastack is their homage to the great French Chaource.

mt. townsend creamery seastack cheese

WITH MARINATED BABY BEETS

1   Remove the Seastack from the refrigerator about 1 hour before serving and cut it into six wedges.

2   Using a mandoline, slice the raw beets thinly, about $\frac{1}{16}$ inch thick, and then cut them into matchsticks. Place in a medium bowl with ½ tablespoon of the olive oil and ½ teaspoon of the thyme. Toss well to coat and set aside to marinate.

3   Place the roasted beets into another bowl with the remaining 2 tablespoons olive oil and ½ teaspoon thyme. Season to taste with salt and pepper. Toss well to coat and set aside to marinate. (If you are using a combination of red and other colored beets, marinate separately because the red will bleed onto the other beets.)

4   Place a wedge of Seastack cheese on each of six plates. Spoon a small pile of roasted beets and a small pile of raw beets onto the plate. Drizzle some olive oil and balsamic vinegar over the beets and serve.

MAKES 6 SERVINGS

1 wheel of Mt. Townsend Creamery Seastack cheese (or a soft, creamy cow's milk cheese like Camembert)

½ cup small raw Chioggia beets, peeled

2½ tablespoons extra-virgin olive oil, divided, plus more for finishing

1 teaspoon fresh thyme leaves, divided

½ cup small beets, roasted, peeled, and cut into ½-inch dice (see page 57 for instructions for roasting beets)

Kosher salt and freshly ground black pepper

1 tablespoon aged balsamic vinegar

This is more of an idea for a quick party appetizer than a recipe. It's a fun late-summer project to clean, roast, and stuff a couple of jars of cherry or baby bell peppers when they're available at the farmers' market.

chorizo

WITH ANCHOVY-STUFFED CHERRY PEPPERS

MAKES 4 SERVINGS

16 bite-size cherry peppers or baby bell peppers

2 tablespoons extra-virgin olive oil, divided, plus more for storing the peppers

Kosher salt

½ cup minced celery

2 tablespoons chopped anchovies

2 tablespoons capers

1 tablespoon minced garlic

½ cup white wine

Freshly ground black pepper

8 ounces cured chorizo

Fleur de sel, for finishing

2 tablespoons celery leaves (yellow leaves only, from the center of a celery head)

1   Preheat the oven to 350 degrees F.

2   To make the stuffed cherry peppers, first wash the peppers and pat them dry. Remove the stems with a paring knife by slicing around the top. Scoop out the seeds with the tip of the knife or a small spoon. Toss the peppers with 1 tablespoon of the oil and season lightly with salt. Arrange the peppers on a baking tray, cut side up. Roast for 10 to 12 minutes, or until just barely starting to color and soften. Transfer the peppers to a plate and let cool to room temperature.

3   Meanwhile, heat the remaining 1 tablespoon oil in a medium sauté pan over medium heat. Add the celery and sauté for 5 to 6 minutes, or until tender. Add the anchovies, capers, and garlic and cook for 2 to 3 minutes. Deglaze the pan with the wine and simmer until the wine has been absorbed. Season to taste with salt and pepper. Remove the pan from the heat and let cool to room temperature.

4   Stuff each pepper with about 1 teaspoon of the celery mixture. If not serving right away, pack the peppers in a single layer in an airtight container, cover the peppers completely with a layer of oil, and store in the refrigerator for up to 2 weeks.

5   Peel the outer casing off the chorizo if necessary. Thinly slice the chorizo on the bias. Fan it out onto serving plate and sprinkle with a little fleur de sel. Arrange four of the stuffed cherry peppers on the plate and drizzle a little of the oil from the container around the plate. Scatter the celery leaves on the plate and serve.

We always serve a tarte tatin at Lark, changing the fruit throughout the year to reflect the season: apple, pear, quince, pineapple, apricot, nectarine, and peach all see a bit of time on the menu. But the fig tatin that we usually serve in August and September seems to be the favorite. The combination of goat cheese sorbet, grappa caramel, and fig is unbeatable.

black fig tarte tatins

WITH GOAT CHEESE SORBET AND GRAPPA CARAMEL SAUCE

MAKES 6 SERVINGS

FOR THE GOAT CHEESE
SORBET

1½ cups granulated sugar

1 cup water

1 cup goat cheese

1 cup crème fraîche

1 tablespoon freshly
squeezed lemon juice

½ teaspoon kosher salt

FOR THE GRAPPA CARAMEL
SAUCE

1 cup granulated sugar

¼ cup light corn syrup

¼ cup water

3 tablespoons unsalted
butter, cubed

1   To make the goat cheese sorbet, first make a simple syrup by combining the sugar and water in a small saucepan over high heat. Bring to a boil, then turn off the heat and let the syrup cool completely.

2   In a large bowl, whisk together the simple syrup, goat cheese, crème fraîche, lemon juice, and salt until smooth. To make sure that there is the right amount of sugar in the mixture for freezing, complete the "egg test" described on page 79. When it passes the test, place the mixture in the refrigerator and chill for at least 1 hour.

3   Process the mixture in an ice cream maker according to manufacturer's instructions. Transfer the sorbet to a lidded container and freeze for at least 8 hours before serving.

4   To make the grappa caramel sauce, in a medium saucepan over medium-high heat, combine the sugar, corn syrup, and ¼ cup water. Stirring frequently, cook the mixture until it

becomes a golden-brown caramel. Remove the pan from the heat and very carefully whisk in the butter a little at a time. While whisking, slowly drizzle in the cream until it is incorporated. Be careful because the caramel will sputter. Let the caramel cool until it reaches room temperature, about 30 minutes. Whisk in the grappa and salt.

5   Chill the caramel sauce until ready to use. It will keep in an airtight container in the refrigerator for up to 1 week. Before serving, gently rewarm the sauce in a small saucepan until it pours easily.

6   To make the fig tarte tatins, preheat the oven to 425 degrees F.

7   Place a nonstick baking mat on a baking tray large enough to accommodate all the puff pastry squares. Dot the mat with 2 teaspoons of the caramel sauce for each tatin, spacing them out so you can get six tatins on the tray.

8   Cut four deep slices into each fig (six if they are large), keeping the figs intact at the stem end so that the slices can be fanned out but will stay joined.

9   Arrange three figs (depending on size) fanned out in a circle over each dot of caramel. Arrange them so that the stem ends are at the center and the fanned slices create the outside of the circle.

10   Remove the puff pastry squares from the freezer. Do not allow them to thaw or droop (they will puff up better if still slightly frozen). Place one square on top of each fig circle. Brush each puff pastry square with just enough of the egg to coat it. Bake for 8 to 10 minutes, or until puffed, golden brown, and lightly caramelized around the edges. Let the tartins cool to room temperature on the pan until you are ready to serve.

11   To serve, if necessary, reheat the tatins in a 400-degree-F oven until warm, 1 to 2 minutes. Using a spatula, carefully lift each tatin and flip it over onto a serving plate. Drizzle with a little of the warm caramel sauce. Sprinkle with some confectioners' sugar and top with a scoop of goat cheese sorbet.

CHEF'S NOTE: The sorbet needs time to freeze, so it is best to prepare it at least a day ahead. The caramel needs to cool before you can use it to make the tarte tatin, so it's also best made the day before.
   Many store-bought puff pastry sheets come folded. Defrost the sheet, unfold it, cut it into 4-inch squares, and then refreeze until ready to use.

½ cup heavy cream

2 tablespoons grappa (or rum)

½ teaspoon kosher salt

FOR THE FIG TARTE TATINS

18 just-ripe Black Mission figs, stemmed

6 frozen puff pastry squares (4 by 4 inches)

1 large egg, beaten

2 teaspoons confectioners' sugar

No other place has berry season quite like the Pacific Northwest. With so many varieties in such plenitude, you really must have a handful of recipes and ideas ready—there comes a point when you can't resist picking or purchasing more than you can possibly eat. Blackcap raspberries and the tiny, native wild blackberries are my favorites.

English summer pudding goes way back as a thrifty way to use day-old bread and the bounty of the season. Traditionally the berries would be stewed with sugar and the pudding made several hours or a day ahead and then unmolded. My version is a bit fresher, and we toss the toasted brioche cubes with the berries and berry sauce just before serving so it still has a hint of a crunch. If you're short on berries, no one will complain if you slice up some cherries and add them to the mix.

summer pudding

WITH BRIOCHE AND BERRIES

MAKES 4 SERVINGS

1   Preheat the oven to 250 degrees F.

2   Place the brioche onto a baking tray in a single layer and toast in the oven until dried out and just starting to turn brown, about 5 to 7 minutes. Set aside.

3   In a medium saucepan over medium-low heat, place ½ cup each of the raspberries, strawberries, blueberries, and sugar. Once the mixture starts to bubble, turn the heat down to low and let simmer for 20 to 25 minutes. Remove the pan from the heat and let cool to room temperature.

4   Transfer the berry mixture to a food processor and process until smooth. If you prefer to remove the seeds, press the mixture through a medium mesh sieve.

5   In a large bowl, combine the toasted brioche with the berry mixture and mix well. Fold in the remaining ½ cup each of the berries.

6   In a mixing bowl (or in an electric mixer fitted with the whisk attachment), combine the cream and remaining 1 tablespoon sugar. Whip the cream until medium-stiff peaks form.

7   To serve, place a generous spoonful of the pudding onto a plate. Garnish with a dollop of the whipped cream.

- 4 cups brioche bread, crusts trimmed and cut into ½-inch dice
- 1 cup red raspberries, divided
- 1 cup strawberries, cored, divided
- 1 cup blueberries, divided
- ½ cup plus 1 tablespoon granulated sugar, divided
- 1 cup heavy cream

Every June I daydream about sneaking over to Prosser in the Yakima Valley to pick up a case or two of wine at Kay Simon and Clay Mackey's place, Chinook Wines. Their wines are gorgeous, and with luck I can pop out to their cherry orchard for some of Washington's best cherries as well. Use very ripe, just-picked cherries for this recipe. We like to follow tradition and leave the cherries unpitted so their almond flavor will be infused as they are baked.

cherry clafouti
WITH LEMON VERBENA CUSTARD SAUCE

MAKES 6 TO 8 SERVINGS

FOR THE LEMON VERBENA CUSTARD SAUCE

3 cups whole milk

1 cup heavy cream

8 lemon verbena leaves, crushed

12 egg yolks

1¼ cups granulated sugar

1½ teaspoons pure vanilla extract

Zest and juice from 2 lemons

¼ teaspoon kosher salt

1   To make the lemon verbena custard sauce, first prepare an ice bath.

2   In a medium saucepan over medium heat, heat the milk, cream, and lemon verbena leaves until almost boiling.

3   In a heatproof mixing bowl, beat the egg yolks and sugar. While whisking the egg mixture, very slowly pour in half of the hot milk mixture to temper the eggs.

4   Return the pan to the stove. While whisking the hot milk in the saucepan, slowly pour the egg mixture into the pan. Cook slowly, stirring constantly, over medium heat until the custard is thick enough to easily coat the back of a spoon and reaches a temperature of about 180 degrees F.

5   Strain the custard through a fine mesh strainer into a bowl set in the ice bath. Add the vanilla, lemon zest and juice, and salt, stirring to incorporate. Store in the refrigerator until ready to use, up to 5 days.

6   To make the cherry clafouti, in a food processor, combine the almonds, sugar, flour, and salt. Process to grind the almonds and thoroughly combine the ingredients. Add the cream, egg yolks, whole eggs, and almond extract. Process until very smooth. Transfer the batter to an airtight container and chill in the refrigerator for at least 4 hours.

7   Preheat the oven to 350 degrees F.

8   Butter an 8-by-12-inch glass or ceramic baking dish, or individual pans. Place a layer of the cherries in the baking dish. Stir the batter and then spoon it around the cherries so that it comes halfway up the fruit. Bake for 45 to 50 minutes, or until the batter is golden brown and just firm in the center.

9   Serve the clafouti immediately. Dust with the powdered sugar and serve the custard sauce on the side in a small serving pitcher or glass. Pour a little of the custard sauce onto the clafouti just before eating.

CHEF'S NOTE: Make and chill the lemon custard sauce first, up to 2 days ahead. The clafouti should be served directly out of the oven.

FOR THE CHERRY CLAFOUTI

1 cup slivered almonds

1 cup granulated sugar

1 cup all-purpose flour

¼ teaspoon kosher salt

2 cups heavy cream

6 egg yolks

4 whole eggs

2 tablespoons almond extract

1 tablespoon unsalted butter

30 very ripe cherries, stemmed but unpitted

2 teaspoons powdered sugar

This combination of butter and sugar–roasted peaches, rum caramel, and almond ice cream is otherworldly and is my favorite dessert of the season . . . I think. Almonds and most stone fruit are botanically related (if you crack the pit open of a cherry, apricot, or peach, you'll find a very small almond-like center) and are very complementary to each other. Use just-ripe (not overripe) peaches for this recipe, as they'll roast for a total of about twenty minutes.

lacquered peaches

WITH RUM CARAMEL SAUCE AND ALMOND ICE CREAM

1   To make the almond ice cream, in a medium heavy-bottomed saucepan over medium-high heat, combine the milk, cream, and almonds and bring just to a simmer. Turn off the heat and let the almonds steep in the milk for about 30 minutes. Strain the almonds and discard. Return the milk mixture to the saucepan and bring to a simmer over medium heat.

2   Meanwhile, prepare an ice bath.

3   In a large bowl, thoroughly beat together the egg yolks and sugar. While whisking the egg mixture, add ½ cup of the hot milk mixture to the bowl to gently temper the eggs. Whisking constantly, add in another ½ cup of the hot milk mixture. (Continuous whisking prevents the eggs from scrambling.)

4   Now begin whisking the milk mixture in the saucepan and slowly pour in the tempered egg mixture. Place the saucepan over medium heat and stir constantly with a wooden spoon or heatproof spatula. Continue stirring until the mixture has reached a temperature of 180 degrees F and is thick enough to coat the back of a spoon.

5   Strain the custard through a fine mesh strainer into a metal bowl or container. Immediately place the metal bowl

MAKES 4 SERVINGS

FOR THE ALMOND ICE CREAM

2 cups whole milk

¾ cup heavy cream

1 cup slivered almonds

8 egg yolks

½ cup granulated sugar

½ teaspoon almond extract

FOR THE RUM CARAMEL SAUCE

1 cup granulated sugar

¼ cup light corn syrup

¼ cup water

3 tablespoons unsalted butter, cubed

½ cup heavy cream

2 tablespoons single-barrel rum

Kosher salt

(CONTINUED)

4 medium Red Haven
    peaches, fuzz washed
    and dried

3 tablespoons unsalted but-
    ter, at room temperature

½ cup granulated sugar

Fleur de sel

½ cup sliced almonds,
    toasted

into the ice bath. Stir occasionally until the custard cools to room temperature.

6   Add the almond extract, then refrigerate the custard until thoroughly chilled, at least 4 hours.

7   Process the custard in an ice cream maker according to manufacturer's instructions. Transfer the ice cream to a lidded container and freeze for at least 8 hours before serving.

8   To make the rum caramel sauce, in a medium saucepan over medium-high heat, combine the sugar, corn syrup, and water. Stirring frequently, cook the mixture until it becomes a golden-brown caramel. Remove the pan from the heat and very carefully whisk in the butter a little bit at a time.

9   While whisking, slowly drizzle in the cream until it is incorporated. Be careful because the caramel will sputter. Let the caramel cool until it reaches room temperature, about 30 minutes. Whisk in the rum and salt to taste.

10   Chill the caramel sauce until ready to use. It will keep in an airtight container in the refrigerator for up to 1 week. Before serving, gently rewarm the sauce in a small saucepan until it pours easily.

11   To make the lacquered peaches, preheat the oven to 350 degrees F.

12   Arrange the peaches in a baking dish. Using a pastry brush, generously coat the peaches with the butter. Sprinkle the sugar liberally over the peaches so they are well covered. Bake the peaches for 12 to 15 minutes.

13   Remove the pan from the oven and pour about 2 table-spoons of the caramel sauce over each peach. Return the pan to the oven and bake until the peaches are tender and the skins are a light golden brown, wilted, and wrinkled, 3 to 5 minutes. Set aside until you are ready to serve.

14   To serve, if necessary, warm the peaches for a few minutes in the oven. Place a peach on each of four serving plates and sprinkle with a little fleur de sel. Arrange some of the toasted almonds on the plate in a small pile and place a scoop of the almond ice cream on the almonds.

CHEF'S NOTE: Read through Ice Cream and Sorbet on page 78 for some general rules of thumb before proceeding with this recipe.

Savarins are tender, delicate, yeasted sponge cakes piped into a special ring mold (from which they take their name). The famous baba au rhum is a savarin flavored with raisins, rum, and pastry cream. My version is perfect for celebrating the bounty of summer, loaded up with berries, plums, and wine syrup.

savarin cakes

WITH BEAUMES-DE-VENISE, BLACKBERRIES, AND PLUM

1   To make the savarin cakes, first grease the savarin molds with butter.

2   In a medium bowl, combine the lukewarm milk and yeast together and let sit at room temperature for about 10 minutes. This is to make sure the yeast is still active; it should be slightly bubbly. Add 1½ cups of the flour to the bowl and stir well to combine. Set aside for about 30 minutes. The mixture should begin to form bubbles.

3   Meanwhile, in the bowl of a stand mixer fitted with the paddle attachment, cream together the butter, sugar, salt, and vanilla. Add the yeast mixture and mix again until everything is well incorporated. Beat in the eggs one at a time, scraping down the sides of the bowl with each addition. Add the

(CONTINUED)

MAKES 8 SERVINGS

FOR THE SAVARIN CAKES

9 ounces (1⅛ cups) unsalted butter, plus more for greasing molds

¾ cup lukewarm whole milk

1½ tablespoons active dry yeast

4¼ cups all-purpose flour, divided

2½ tablespoons granulated sugar

1½ teaspoons kosher salt

1 teaspoon pure vanilla extract

6 large eggs

remaining 2¾ cups flour and mix on a low speed until well combined.

4   Fill a piping bag fitted with a large round tip with the batter and pipe it into the molds so that they are filled about halfway up the sides. Cover the molds loosely with plastic wrap and place them in a warm, draft-free place to proof. Let them rise until they have doubled in height. This could take 30 minutes to 1 hour. In the meantime, preheat the oven to 325 degrees F.

5   Once the batter has doubled in height, remove the plastic wrap and bake for 8 to 10 minutes, or until cooked through and a toothpick inserted into the center comes out clean. They should rise some more and be very light golden. Let the cakes cool in the molds for at least 20 minutes. Use a paring knife to loosen the edges and gently unmold the cakes.

6   To make the macerated fruit, in a medium bowl, combine the berries. Add the Beaumes-de-Venice and sugar and fold gently until incorporated. Add the plums and stir again. Let the fruit sit at room temperature for about 30 minutes.

7   To make the whipped cream, whisk the cream, confectioners' sugar, and vanilla together. Whip until medium-stiff peaks form.

8   To serve, if necessary, warm the savarin cakes for a few minutes in a 300-degree-F oven, then dust them with confectioners' sugar. Spoon some macerated fruit into the center of each cake, overflowing on the top. Drizzle some of the wine syrup from the bowl onto the cake and let it soak in. Place a dollop of whipped cream on top.

> CHEF'S NOTE: Savarin cakes resemble medium dough-
> nuts in the sense that they are a round cake with a hole in
> the center. There are special molds for these cakes; how-
> ever, you can improvise, as we do, with a 3-inch ring mold
> and pastry tip. You can use a number of things to create
> this shape as long as it is food-safe and ovenproof.

FOR THE MACERATED FRUIT

½ cup blackberries

½ cup blueberries

½ cup raspberries

¾ cup Beaumes-de-Venise or any light, sweet wine

⅓ cup granulated sugar

½ cup sliced plums

FOR THE WHIPPED CREAM

½ cup heavy cream

2 tablespoons confectioners' sugar

½ teaspoon pure vanilla extract

Confectioners' sugar, for finishing

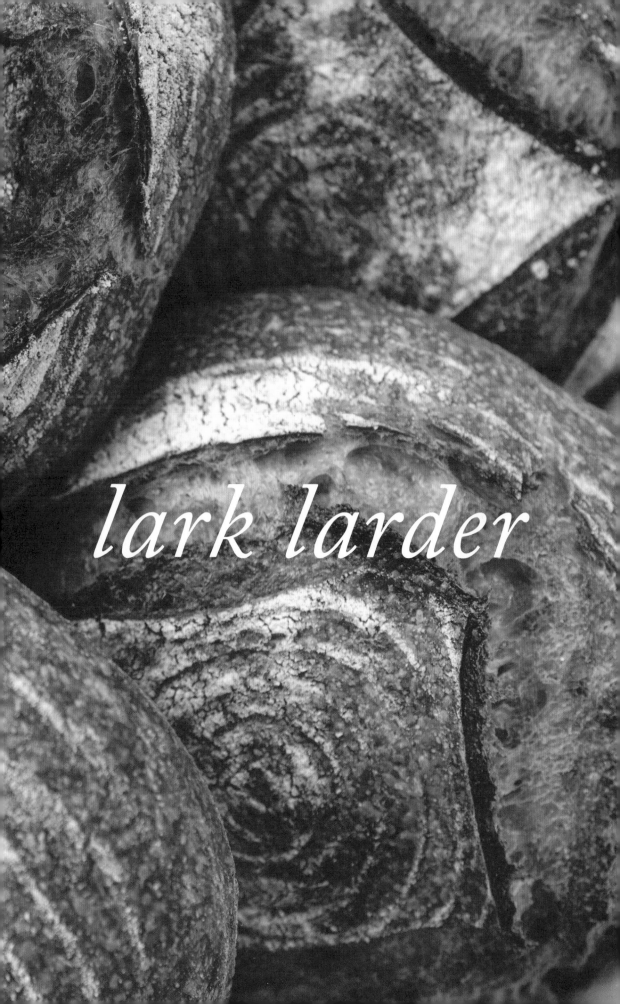

lark larder

My grandmother Estrid grew up on a farm in Idaho with seven siblings. Her dad grew potatoes and other crops to sell, but her family also grew much of what they needed to eat. I remember her telling me about meals made up of just-picked strawberries, thick cream, butter, and homemade bread. It sounded like her brothers would eat nearly everything in sight! In the cold, harsh winters I'm sure the same bread, butter, and cream would have been present. But instead of fresh peaches or berries, someone would have tramped out to the root cellar to grab a jar of preserves and maybe some pickles or relish to accompany dinner.

Our family, like most Americans at the time, were immigrants, and they brought recipes and traditions from wherever they came from to add to the evolving American lexicon of flavors. Learning to preserve the (hopefully) abundant harvest was ingrained in Estrid from a very young age. When I was kid, I wasn't too interested in the end-of-summer canning parties or the trade of jars with the neighbors in January—though I certainly enjoyed eating them. Later on, after many years of cooking, I realized that our grandmothers really had it figured out.

It's really nice to have some tasty treats stashed away for a special occasion, or just sometime when you don't want to go shopping. Now in my restaurants there is always a seasonal push to capture the best flavors of that moment for later use. There are many ways to preserve food: drying, fermenting, curing, pickling, smoking, canning, and freezing, just to name a few. Around the world chefs are being inspired by age-old preserving techniques from Japan, South America, and Scandinavia. I hope you'll find some inspiration in this chapter to try something new . . . or is that something old?

Making your own drink syrups is as easy as 1-2-3. They hold well and are a great way to spruce up a cocktail or sparkling water. Lime leaves are essential in many Southeast Asian cooking traditions, and here they're also an easy and very fragrant addition to your cocktail repertoire.

lime leaf simple syrup

1   In a stainless steel saucepan over medium-high heat, stir together the sugar and water. Bring the mixture to a simmer and cook for 5 minutes, or until all the sugar dissolves. Add the lime leaves and simmer for another 5 minutes. Remove the pan from the heat and set aside to steep and cool completely.

2   Strain through cheesecloth or a fine mesh strainer. The syrup can be stored in an airtight container in the refrigerator for up to 2 weeks.

MAKES ABOUT 1½ CUPS

1 cup (7 ounces) sugar
¾ cup water
10 to 12 makrut lime leaves

LORELEI

MAKES 1 DRINK

¾ ounce gin (I like Captive Spirits' Big Gin or Hendrick's Gin)
½ ounce Cocchi Americano
½ ounce Aperol
½ ounce freshly squeezed lemon juice
¼ ounce Lime Leaf Simple Syrup

In a cocktail shaker, combine all the ingredients with ice. Shake vigorously, then strain into a chilled martini glass.

Our good friend Rachel Marshall worked at Lark for a time before founding Rachel's Ginger Beer, and now our home and restaurant bars are never without it! Rachel would spend mornings and days off juicing lemons, crushing ginger, bottling . . . you name it! Her ginger beer was the first locally produced ginger beer that I know of and now a few years later still the tastiest: refreshing, tart with lemon, and spicy with ginger.

ginger simple syrup

MAKES ABOUT 1½ CUPS

2 small knobs ginger, scrubbed

1 cup sugar

¾ cup water

1   Using a large chef's knife, slice the ginger into thick pieces, then smash them with the side of the knife.

2   In a stainless steel saucepan over medium-high heat, stir together the sugar and water. Bring the mixture to a simmer and cook for 5 minutes, or until all the sugar dissolves. Add the ginger slices and simmer for 10 minutes. Remove the pan from the heat and set aside to steep and cool completely.

3   Strain through cheesecloth or a fine mesh strainer. The syrup can be stored in an airtight container in the refrigerator for up to 2 weeks.

MOSCOW MULE

MAKES 1 DRINK

1½ ounces vodka
¼ ounce freshly squeezed lime juice
¼ ounce Ginger Simple Syrup
3 ounces ginger beer (I like Rachel's Ginger Beer)

In a copper Moscow Mule mug, combine the vodka, lime juice, and ginger syrup. Fill the mug three-quarters full with crushed ice, and top with ginger beer.

After a trip to Milan a few years back, my respect for rhubarb grew exponentially once I tasted Zucca or more properly Rabarbaro Zucca, a spiced aperitif made with rhubarb and usually served with soda. I like to make this syrup in late May or June when the local rhubarb takes on a deep-red color. The rhubarb pulp can be repurposed into a jam or filling if desired—just fold in more sugar.

rhubarb simple syrup

MAKES ABOUT 2 CUPS

1 cup sugar

¾ cup water

½ pound rhubarb stalks, trimmed, washed, and cut into ½-inch slices

Juice from 2 lemons

1   In a stainless steel saucepan over medium-high heat, stir together the sugar and water. Bring the mixture to a simmer and cook for 5 minutes, or until all the sugar dissolves. Add the rhubarb and lemon juice and simmer for 10 minutes. Remove the pan from the heat and set aside to steep and cool completely.

2   Strain through cheesecloth or a fine mesh strainer. The syrup can be stored in an airtight container in the refrigerator for up to 1 week.

NUOVO NEGRONI

MAKES 1 DRINK

1 ounce gin (I like Captive Spirits' Big Gin or Hendrick's Gin)
1 ounce Campari
½ ounce Rhubarb Simple Syrup
½ ounce freshly squeezed grapefruit juice
Champagne or sparkling wine
Orange peel or Candied Grapefruit Peel (see recipe on page 85) (optional)

In a cocktail pitcher, combine the gin, Campari, rhubarb syrup, and grapefruit juice and stir with a cocktail spoon. Pour into a chilled coupe glass, then top with the champagne.

Garnish with a peel.

---

lark larder   **239**

Like many of the recipes in this section, making your own bitters takes a bit of advance planning and patience. But you'll save money and have a really great ingredient for your cocktail atelier. This makes a super holiday gift too—just find some dark glass bottles with eye-dropper lids, print up some labels, and you're in business!

lark bitters

MAKES 1 TO 1½ CUPS

1   In a 1-liter glass jar or bottle with a locking lid, combine all the ingredients except the filtered water. Shake well to combine. Store the jar in a cool, dark place for 3 weeks. Every second day, invert the jar to redistribute the ingredients.

2   After 3 weeks, strain the mixture through several layers of cheesecloth or a coffee filter, reserving the liquid in an airtight container for later. Wash the glass jar.

3   In a small saucepot over medium-low heat, combine the strained herb-spice mixture and the filtered water. Simmer for 10 minutes. Remove from the heat and set aside to cool completely.

4   Pour the herb-spice mixture back into the locking jar and let steep in a cool, dark place for 2 days.

5   After 2 days, strain the mixture through several layers of cheesecloth or a coffee filter. Discard the solids. Wash the glass jar. Combine the "tea" with the infused vodka mixture in the locking jar and store in a cool, dark place for 3 days.

6   Carefully decant (meaning pour out liquid without disturbing the sediment that will have collected at the bottom of the jar) the bitters into a clean, dry lidded jar or small bottles. Store at room temperature for up to 3 months.

1½ cups 100-proof vodka

4 cardamom pods, toasted and crushed

1 star anise pod, toasted and crushed

1½ tablespoons dried Seville orange peel

1½ tablespoons dried lemon peel

½ tablespoon coriander seed, toasted and crushed

½ teaspoon rhubarb root powder

½ teaspoon dried galangal powder

¼ teaspoon dried elderflower blossoms

½ cup filtered water

Ratafia is really just fortified wine with seasonal fruit. It's often made at the height of summer and consumed before the end of the year. This recipe is for plum ratafia, but really any ripe fruit that you have too much of is a good choice: peaches, apricots, raspberries, blackberries . . . you get the idea. It's a great aperitif to serve before dinner with some cheese, crackers, and salumi.

plum ratafia

MAKES ABOUT 2 QUARTS

1 pound small purple or yellow plums, halved and pitted (mine are often gleaned from neighbors' trees)

1 bottle (750 milliliters) dry white wine, such as sauvignon blanc, albariño, or grüner veltliner

1 cup brandy

1 cup granulated sugar

6 star anise pods, toasted

Peel from 1 orange, washed

1   In a 2-liter glass jar or bottle with a locking lid, combine all the ingredients. Shake well to combine and dissolve the sugar. Store the jar in a cool, dark place for 8 to 12 weeks. Once per week, turn the jar over a couple of times to redistribute the ingredients.

2   At the end of 8 to 12 weeks, strain the mixture through several layers of cheesecloth or a coffee filter. Discards the solids. Transfer the ratafia into a clean, dry lidded jar and store in the refrigerator for up to 3 months.

3   Serve chilled or over ice.

This recipe is ideal if you have your own sour cherry tree (Montmorency or Morello), though it will work with Bing, Queen Anne, or Lapins in a pinch. Plan ahead, though, since it usually takes about twelve weeks for them to get really good! These are great for your home cocktail program or as a grown-up sundae over ice cream. I've used them to liven up an apple pie or crisp filling!

brandied cherries

1   In a 2-liter glass jar or bottle with a locking lid, combine all the ingredients. Shake well to combine and dissolve the sugar. Store the jar in a cool, dark place for 12 weeks. Once per week, turn the jar over a couple of times to redistribute the ingredients.

2   At the end of 12 weeks, the color should darken and the consistency should be slightly syrupy. Store in the refrigerator for up to 3 months.

CHEF'S NOTE: For this recipe, use the best brandy you can buy—it'll make for a better cocktail!

MAKES ABOUT ¾ POUND CHERRIES

1 pound sour cherries, stemmed and pitted

1 quart (32 ounces) brandy

2 cups granulated sugar (only 1 cup if substituting a sweet cherry variety)

6 whole cloves

Peel of 1 lemon, washed and cut into wide strips

This is a Northwest play on nocino, which is a liqueur usually made with green walnuts. I like to use roasted hazelnuts and spice it with cardamom and vanilla bean. Plan ahead, though, since it usually takes about eight weeks for it to get really good! This cordial is a lovely treat for the holidays or a cold Mist evening.

hazelnut cordial

1   In a 2-liter glass jar or bottle with a locking lid, combine all the ingredients (including the vanilla bean seeds and pods). Shake well to combine and dissolve the sugar. Store the jar in a cool, dark place for 7 to 8 weeks. Once per week, turn the jar over a couple of times to redistribute the ingredients.

2   At the end of 7 to 8 weeks, the color should darken and the consistency should be slightly syrupy. Strain the mixture through several layers of cheesecloth or a coffee filter. Discard the solids. Transfer the cordial into a clean, dry lidded jar or port-type bottle with a cork. Store for up to 3 months.

MAKES ABOUT 2 QUARTS

1 pound hazelnuts, unpeeled, toasted until dark golden, and halved

1 bottle (750 milliliters) 100-proof vodka

2 cups granulated sugar

6 cardamom pods, toasted and smashed

2 vanilla beans, split and seeds scraped

This is a supereasy and incredibly flavorful dressing. Miso's deep, sweet and nutty flavor and thick, rich consistency make it a great base for sauces and dressings. It's great on summer lettuces like Little Gem or baby romaine. You will also love it slathered on green beans or grilled corn or try it on umami-rich tomatoes with shavings of Parmigiano-Reggiano.

miso dressing

MAKES ABOUT 3 CUPS

¾ cup rice wine vinegar

2 tablespoons red or brown
    miso paste

1 shallot, minced

2 cups canola oil

1 teaspoon toasted
    sesame oil

Kosher salt and freshly
    ground black pepper

1   In a medium mixing bowl, whisk together the vinegar, miso, and shallot until smooth and well combined. Slowly drizzle the canola oil into the miso mixture while whisking constantly. Whisk in the sesame oil and season to taste with salt and pepper.

2   Store the dressing in an airtight container in the refrigerator for up to 2 weeks.

Having a few homemade pickles around is absolutely necessary and easy, so get to it! Just about any green bean variety will work here, and you can use this same recipe for pickled asparagus too. I love Romano beans, Blue Lake bush beans, and haricots verts. These are delicious in a Bloody Mary or a great way to spruce up a summery salad of tomatoes, bacon, hard-cooked egg, and butter lettuce.

pickled green beans

1   Prep the green beans by washing them and removing the stems; I like to leave the tail at the other end. Arrange the beans in a large flat plastic or glass container (with lid) that will hold them all along with the brine.

2   In a large stainless steel saucepan over medium-high heat, combine the vinegar, water sugar, salt, bay leaves, garlic, and chiles. Bring the mixture to a boil, then turn down the heat to maintain a simmer for 5 minutes. Remove the pan from the heat and allow the brine to cool for about 10 minutes.

3   When the brine is still hot but not boiling (this will pre-serve the color of the green beans), carefully pour it over the beans. Be sure the beans are fully submerged; if they aren't tightly packed, you may have to weigh them down with a plate to keep them in the brine.

4   Cover with the lid, and then place the container in the refrigerator for at least 1 week to allow the beans to fully absorb the brine, and up to 3 months.

MAKES ABOUT FOUR 1-QUART JARS GREEN BEANS

2 pounds green beans

4 cups white wine vinegar or champagne vinegar

2 cups water

1 cup granulated sugar

¼ cup kosher salt

12 bay leaves

8 cloves garlic, thinly sliced

2 whole dried red chiles

At Lark we make whole milk ricotta, as opposed to ricotta made from whey. It's worth buying really good local milk for this recipe (we use Fresh Breeze organic milk from Lynden, Washington). Ricotta actually means "recooked," and is normally a by-product from making another cheese, such as mozzarella. This version will be richer and creamier than a tangy whey ricotta. The smoked ricotta version is fantastic as a spread or topped with a raw egg yolk and served with toast. It's also superb as a ravioli or lasagna filling.

whole milk ricotta

MAKES ABOUT 1 QUART

64 ounces (2 quarts) pasteurized whole milk

¼ cup heavy cream

½ teaspoon citric acid

1 teaspoon kosher salt, divided

1   Before you begin, please note that whenever making cheese or butter, you should always be sure to use very clean and sanitized utensils and equipment. Carefully dip the items in a large pot of boiling water after washing them with soapy water, then lay them out on clean towels to air-dry.

2   In a 6-quart stainless steel pot (with lid) over medium-low heat, whisk together the milk, cream, citric acid, and ½ teaspoon of the salt. Cook for 15 to 20 minutes, slowly stirring until the mixture reaches a temperature of 185 to 195 degrees F. Curds will start to form and will separate from the whey.

3   Remove the pot from the heat. Gently rotate the mass of cheese and separate it from edge of pan. Cover with the lid and let the cheese sit for 10 minutes.

4   Place a fine mesh strainer lined with cheesecloth over a large bowl or pan. Using a ladle, gently remove the curds from the pan and transfer to the cheesecloth. Don't transfer any scorched parts or scrape out curds stuck to the pan.

5   Sprinkle the strained ricotta with the remaining ½ teaspoon salt and gently fold it into the ricotta.

6   For a more moist ricotta, transfer immediately to an airtight container and refrigerate. For a dryer ricotta, continue to drain for another 20 to 30 minutes, or place the strainer and bowl in the refrigerator overnight (be sure to cover with plastic wrap), before transferring to an airtight container. The ricotta will keep for 5 to 7 days in the refrigerator.

SMOKED RICOTTA VARIATION

Place the homemade ricotta in a wide, shallow baking dish or plastic storage container.

Find a pot or a container with a tight-fitting lid that can hold both the smoker and the dish of ricotta.

Place a handful of alder or apple wood chips in a mini smoker box and place on the stove over medium-high heat to get the wood chips smoking. Once the wood chips have started to give off an abundance of smoke, place the smoker box in the pot. Place the dish of ricotta on top of the smoker. Very quickly place the lid on the pot and let it sit for 20 to 30 minutes, or until the smoke has subsided. Alternatively, you can use a smoking gun, such as the one made by PolyScience Culinary.

Making homemade butter is as easy as whipping cream until it "breaks" and separates into fat and liquid, and then kneading it. But if you're willing to culture it first, your butter can enter a new level of complexity and flavor. I like my butter for the table salted, so this is one place to use one of your "fancy" salts. You'll also end up with buttermilk to use when you're done. Using a culture adds tanginess and preserves your butter for longer. Home brew suppliers, such as MicroHomebrew.com, sell various starters and cultures. We also buy from the website SausageMaker.com.

If you want to go a step further and smoke your cultured butter, see the recipe on page 35 for instructions.

cultured butter

MAKES ABOUT 1 POUND BUTTER AND 1 QUART BUTTERMILK

32 ounces (1 quart) pasteurized heavy cream

⅛ teaspoon powdered mesophile aroma starter culture, type B

1 teaspoon fleur de sel

1 Before you begin, please note that whenever making butter or cheese, you should always be sure to use very clean and sanitized utensils and equipment. Carefully dip the items in a large pot of boiling water after washing them with soapy water, then lay them out on clean towels to air-dry.

2 In a 2-quart stainless steel pot (with lid) over medium-low heat, gently heat the cream for 7 to 10 minutes, or until it reaches a temperature of 68 degrees F.

3   Sprinkle the starter culture over cream and let it sit undisturbed for 5 minutes. Whisk the starter into cream and remove the pot from the heat.

4   Cover with the lid and let the cream sit for 12 hours at room temperature. Then transfer to the refrigerator and chill for 12 hours. (At this point you have crème fraîche, which itself has a multitude of delicious applications.)

5   When you are ready to churn the cream, set the pot at room temperature and allow the mixture to warm up to about 55 degrees F.

6   Put half of the mixture into the bowl of a stand mixer fitted with the whisk attachment, then wrap a large piece of plastic wrap around the top to prevent splashing. Beat the cream for 5 to 7 minutes, after which time the mixture should become very stiff and yellowish. Continue beating for another 8 to 10 minutes, or until the buttermilk begins to separate and flecks of butter form in the bowl. Turn off the mixer.

7   Pour the mixture into a fine mesh strainer placed over a bowl or pot. (Reserve and chill the strained buttermilk for another use.) Rinse the butter under cold water to wash away any remaining buttermilk.

8   Chill the butter for a few minutes, then gently kneed it to push out any excess water or buttermilk, and blot dry. Sprinkle the butter with half of the fleur de sel and gently knead to distribute. Repeat the beating, rinsing, and kneading process with the other half of the cream mixture, then sprinkle with the remaining fleur de sel.

9   Form the butter into logs or balls, or place it in small tubs or crocks. The butter will keep for 5 to 7 days in the refrigerator or can be frozen for up to 3 months.

When I describe how and why we do things at Lark to a new cook or waiter (or sometimes to guests), I often use the analogy of the onion. For many of our techniques and processes, we're constantly peeling back the layers of what we know and do, looking for more understanding and, ultimately, creating better tasting food. After many years of dreaming about making our own bread, we finally made it, and it has become a new "onion" for us to work on.

Our house-made loaf is earthy, crusty, and lightly tangy. It's great pretty much right from the oven (most breads do benefit from thirty to sixty minutes of resting time), but also holds up well into the next day. We use every scrap; first for the table, then as toast or crostini, and finally as breadcrumbs or as bread pudding. It's the gift that keeps on giving!

lark country bread

1   First, check the leaven for readiness with a float test. Take 1 tablespoon of the leaven and place it in 1 cup warm water. If it floats, it's ready. If it doesn't float, keep it in a warm place until it passes the float test.

2   Pour 3 cups of the warm water into a large mixing bowl. Add the leaven and break it up in the water. In a separate bowl, combine the flours and whisk. Add the flour mixture to the leaven mixture and stir with a wooden spoon until no dry flour lumps remain. The dough should be wet and shaggy. Let the dough rest for 25 to 40 minutes, or until it looks smooth and homogeneous.

3   Stir in the salt and remaining ¼ cup warm water. Incorporate into the dough, folding dough into itself, until you can no longer feel the salt in the dough. Transfer the dough to a plastic container and cover with a lid. Set the container aside in a warm, draft-free place.

4   Every 30 minutes or so, wet your hands (to prevent sticking) and turn the dough in the container. Continue these turns every half hour until the dough is fully developed. A fully developed dough will have risen about 20 percent, releases easily from the sides of the container, and holds its shape after you complete a turn. At room temperature, it usually takes about 4 hours for the dough to develop. If it is developing too slowly, you can set the container in a warm place, such as the cooktop over a warm oven.

(CONTINUED)

MAKES 2 LOAVES

⅔ cup Homemade Leaven (recipe follows)

3¼ cups warm water (90 degrees F), divided

7 cups white bread flour

¾ cup whole wheat flour

1 tablespoon kosher salt

2 tablespoons fifty-fifty blend of rice flour and whole wheat flour, for dusting the loaves

2 bannetons (proofing baskets) or mixing bowls lined with clean, flour-dusted towels

5 Transfer the dough from the container onto an unfloured counter or board. Using a bench scraper, divide the dough into two equal portions, and gently form them into rounds with the bench scraper. Cover the dough with linen or a clean kitchen towel and let it rest for 20 to 30 minutes, or until it has settled and relaxed.

6 Uncover the dough rounds and lightly flour the tops with some of the fifty-fifty flour blend. Flip the rounds over, then fold each round over into itself from the bottom, right, left, and top. Roll over again so the dough is now a ball with the seam underneath. Place, uncovered, in the refrigerator overnight.

7 The next day, preheat the oven to 500 degrees F. Place a large, deep cast-iron skillet with lid or Dutch oven in the oven until very hot—at least 15 minutes at full temperature.

8 Remove one banneton from the refrigerator and flip the dough out into the bottom of the skillet. Score the top of the dough in a square pattern with a very sharp knife or dough blade. Cover with the lid and transfer the skillet back to the oven.

9 Bake for 20 minutes, then remove the lid and lower the oven temperature to 450 degrees F. Bake for another 25 minutes, rotating the skillet halfway through. Remove from the oven when the bread is a deep caramel brown (not before) and the bread sounds hollow when thumped underneath. Cool the bread on wire rack. Return the skillet to the oven to preheat again and repeat baking with the other dough ball.

homemade leaven

Making your own leaven isn't difficult, but does take some planning and care. Allow at least three days to get started, but up to a week is not uncommon. Once it's going it needs to be maintained. But once you have the method down, it's yours forever. You might even have a starter already, which will bring history and nuance to the this recipe. The method stays the same.

1   To make the starter, combine the flour blend with the lukewarm water in a plastic container and stir to form a thick batter. Cover with a clean kitchen towel and set aside to ferment for 2 to 3 days at room temperature. The starter is ready to begin feeding when a dark crust forms on top and it smells like stinky cheese.

2   Once you've established your starters, feed the it daily by discarding three-quarters of the starting and replenishing the regain starter with 5 tablespoons water and 5 tablespoons fifty-fifty flour blend until the starter rises and falls predictably and it smells more like sweet milk or slightly overripe fruit. This should take about 2 to 4 days. The starter can be kept going indefinitely by continuing the feeding process.

3   To make the leaven, in a medium mixing bowl, combine 2 heaping tablespoons of the starter with the water and flour blend. Stir until there are no dry clumps of flour. Cover with a clean kitchen towel and set aside to rise overnight in a cool place (60 to 70 degrees F). Proceed with making Lark Country Bread.

FOR THE STARTER

⅓ cup fifty-fifty blend of white bread flour and whole wheat flour

100 grams (3½ ounces) lukewarm water (78 degrees F)

FOR THE LEAVEN

1 cup lukewarm water (78 degrees F)

⅔ cup fifty-fifty blend of white bread flour and whole wheat flour

This vinaigrette is a great way to make use of preserved lemons. In most recipes calling for preserved lemons, the only part used is the preserved peel. In this recipe, the pulp is used as well, though not the seeds or stem. This is super delicious on arugula or watercress, or drizzled over grilled chicken or asparagus.

preserved lemon vinaigrette

MAKES ABOUT 3 CUPS

3 Preserved Lemons (page 273 or store-bought), quartered and seeded (but pulp intact)

1 shallot, minced

½ cup champagne vinegar or white wine vinegar

1 cup canola oil

1 cup extra-virgin olive oil (preferably a ripe, buttery Spanish variety rather than a green peppery one)

⅛ teaspoon ground controne hot pepper or ground cayenne

Kosher salt and freshly ground black pepper

1   In a deep 2-quart container, place the preserved lemon and shallot, then puree using an immersion blender until smooth. Add the vinegar and blend well again. With the blender running, slowly drizzle in the oils and blend until emulsified. Season with the hot pepper, salt, and pepper.

2   Store the vinaigrette in an airtight container in the refrigerator for up to 2 weeks.

Garnacha *is the Spanish word for Grenache, which is a red-wine grape varietal used in the wines of southern France and Spain. Many years ago I discovered L'Estornell brand Garnacha red wine vinegar, and it's been one of my favorites ever since. The juice from Garnacha wine is acidified and aged in oak barrels for many years. It's very acidic (often I lighten it with water or another red wine vinegar) and very unique in flavor and fragrance.*

garnacha vinaigrette

1   In a medium mixing bowl, whisk together the vinegars, shallot, and Dijon. Slowly whisk in the olive oil until emulsified. Stir in the thyme leaves and season to taste with salt and pepper.

2   Store the vinaigrette in an airtight container in the refrigerator for up to 1 week.

MAKES ABOUT 1 QUART

½ cup Garnacha red
  wine vinegar

½ cup red wine vinegar

1 shallot, minced

1 teaspoon Dijon mustard

2 cups extra-virgin olive oil
  (preferably a ripe,
  buttery variety)

½ teaspoon chopped fresh
  thyme leaves

Kosher salt and freshly
  ground black pepper

Moving and expanding Lark has been amazing, and one of my favorite parts is our new sandwich shop: Slab Sandwiches + Pie. It's been great to tap into the wide variety of ingredients at our fingertips for Lark, and then turn them into amazing, delicious sandwiches! One of our new classics is this flatbread, spiced up with ground cumin and sporting house-made lamb sausage, lemony yogurt sauce, black olives, and marinated peppers. This recipe is very adaptable and can go in many directions depending on how you want to serve it.

flatbread

1 In a medium mixing bowl, thoroughly whisk together the flour and salt. Drizzle in the melted butter and stir until small crumbs form. Add the water and stir until thoroughly combined. Knead until soft, smooth dough forms, about 3 minutes.

2 Shape the dough into a disk and wrap it in plastic wrap. Set it aside to rest for 4 to 6 hours at room temperature.

3 Portion the dough into six equal balls. Cover with a damp towel and let them rest for 10 minutes.

4 One at a time, roll the dough balls with a rolling pin into very thin ovals about ⅛ inch thick. Roll the oval up into a thin, long log (like rolling a cigar), then coil the log into a circle with ends touching. Roll the dough circle flat into a large, thin oval again.

5 Store the rolled dough between greased pieces of parchment paper until you're ready to cook them. The dough can be tightly wrapped in plastic wrap and stored in the refrigerator for up to 5 days, or frozen for up to 1 month (simply thaw the dough at room temperature for 1 hour before cooking).

6 Preheat a dry griddle or cast-iron skillet over medium-high heat for 10 minutes.

7 Cook each flatbread for about 3 minutes per side, or until dark golden brown and crispy. Brush the flatbread with butter and sprinkle with fleur de sel and cumin. Serve the flatbread as is or make into a sandwich.

MAKES 6 FLATBREADS

3 cups all-purpose flour

¼ teaspoon kosher salt

6 tablespoons unsalted butter, melted

¾ cup water

Butter or olive oil, for brushing

Fleur de sel

Ground toasted cumin, crushed hot peppers, or chopped fresh rosemary or basil (or anything your heart desires!)

When most people think of pasta, there are two basic types that come to mind. For soft, rich, egg-based pasta that all sorts of ravioli shapes make use of, see the recipe on page 263. Then there is semolina-based dough, which can be served either fresh or dried. Most common extruded pasta shapes are semolina-based. It tends to be toothier and requires longer cooking. We make a few types of handmade pasta shapes using semolina dough at Lark; orecchiette (little ears) and gnocchetti are our favorites.

semolina pasta dough

MAKES 4 SERVINGS

1 pound semolina flour

¼ teaspoon kosher salt

¾ cup water

1 On a clean, dry countertop or board, thoroughly mix the semolina and salt. Make a well in the center of the flour. Using a fork, gradually mix the water into the flour until a crumbly dough forms. Knead the dough into a rough ball, then knead for 10 minutes, or until the dough is smooth and elastic. (Alternatively, using a standing mixer with the dough hook attachment, mix for 6 to 7 minutes on low speed to form a tight dough.) Shape the dough into a disk, cover with plastic wrap, and set aside to rest for 1 hour.

2 On a wooden board, cut the dough into slabs about ½ inch thick. One at a time, roll the slabs into a long, rope-shaped logs about ½ inch in diameter. Using a paring knife, cut ¼-inch-thick "coins" off of the log. Sprinkle the pasta with semolina to keep it from sticking to the board or other pieces.

3 Using the tip of a butter knife, press down on the pasta coins and roll the knife off toward you to curl the dough and create an ear shape. The dough should be quite firm before pressing. Some people find it easier to shape the "ears" by hand. Begin by pressing down with your thumb on the center of a dough coin, then press and stretch the dough outward to curl. Repeat until all of the dough has been shaped.

4 Place the orecchiette on a baking tray, and sprinkle with semolina to prevent sticking. Cooking in boiling salted water for 8 to 10 minutes. Cool the pasta on an oiled baking tray if not serving immediately. The orecchiette can also be dried. Simply leave the pasta out on the baking tray for 24 to 48 hours in a warm, dry place. Once it has dried all the way, it can bagged for storage.

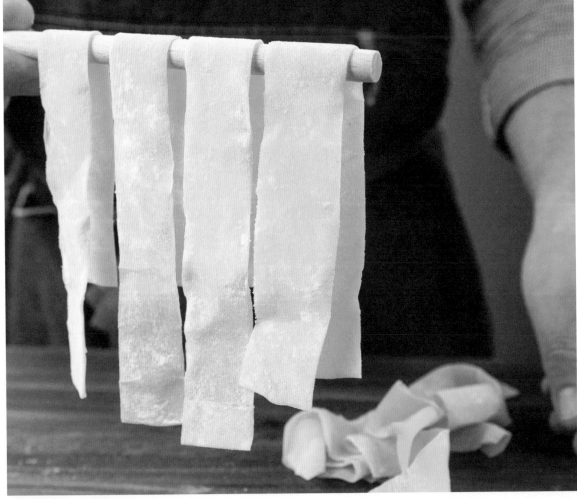

On the surface, pasta is such a simple thing, but as with most food, there are many layers of complexity that influence the taste or texture. Pasta made with eggs is richer and more tender and supple than its semolina counterpart. It's great for making ravioli or pairing with rich, creamy sauces.

egg yolk pasta dough

1   Whisk the eggs yolks in a medium bowl.

2   On a clean, dry countertop or board, thoroughly mix the flour and salt. Make a well in the center of the flour and pour in the egg yolks. Using a fork, gradually mix the yolks into the flour until a crumbly dough forms. Knead the dough into a rough ball, then knead for 10 minutes, or until the dough is smooth and elastic. Shape the dough into a disk, cover with plastic wrap, and set aside to rest for 1 hour.

3   To make pappardelle, cut the dough into slabs about ½ inch thick and roll through a pasta roller; starting with largest setting, roll the dough through each setting twice, before going up to the next one. Finish with the thinnest setting. Cut the dough sheet into 2-inch-wide strips and coil loosely on a baking tray, sprinkling the pasta with flour if it's at all sticky.

4   Cook right away in boiling salted water for 3 to 4 minutes, or freeze for up to 2 months. To store for freezing, wrap the entire tray of pasta in two layers of plastic wrap, being careful not to smash or crush the pasta. The pasta can be boiled directly from the freezer.

> CHEF'S NOTE: A couple of years ago in our never-ending search for better ingredients, we found Central Milling flours. Central Milling is located in Logan, Utah, and has been doing their thing since 1867. As a Utah boy, I had to check them out. Their organic flours are excellent!

MAKES 4 SERVINGS

10 organic egg yolks
2 cups all-purpose flour
¼ teaspoon kosher salt

The first time I had to make gnocchi on a daily basis was as a line cook at Tom Douglas's Dahlia Lounge. They were my nemesis; I could never get them right—they'd either be too tough and rubbery, or too soft and would melt away as soon as they hit boiling water. After many years of practice, and many discussions about technique, I finally have a recipe worth sharing.

potato gnocchi

MAKES 6 SERVINGS

3 pounds russet potatoes

1 large egg

2 tablespoons minced chives

1 teaspoon kosher salt

2 cups all-purpose flour,
   plus more if needed

1   Preheat the oven to 350 degrees F.

2   Place the potatoes on a baking tray and bake for 1 hour, or until tender when pierced with a fork.

3   Cut the potatoes in half and scoop out the flesh onto a clean, dry counter or board. Gently stir in the egg, chives, and salt. Add the flour and gently fold the potato and flour together to form a tender dough. Try not to overwork the dough, as this will make the gnocchi tough.

4   Flatten the dough into a rectangle 1 inch thick, then cut into 1-inch-wide "ropes." One at a time, gently roll the ropes to round the edges. Sprinkle lightly with flour if the dough is sticky. Using a bench scraper or paring knife, cut ½-inch-wide gnocchi from the rope. Each dough piece can then be rolled into a ball, or pressed with the thumb to give it a small indentation, or rolled on a gnocchi board to give it ridges. Place in a single layer on a lightly floured baking tray and refrigerate until ready to use.

5   If the gnocchi won't be cooked within a couple of hours, wrap the pan tightly with plastic wrap and freeze overnight, or until solid. Once frozen, the gnocchi can be portioned and bagged to use straight from the freezer. Cook the gnocchi in gently boiling salted water for 2 to 3 minutes if fresh, 4 to 5 minutes from frozen. Transfer directly into sauce, or toss with butter or olive oil, and serve immediately.

You might ask, why make ash? And what do I do with it? At Lark we started looking at ways to utilize scraps, or parts of vegetables that normally wouldn't have a secondary use other than as compost. What we learned is that charred or even burnt fruit and vegetables can contribute quite a lot to the flavor of a dish. This leek ash is really nice sprinkled on a soft cheese like chèvre or burrata.

leek ash salt

1   Build the fire in an outdoor barbeque, and let it burn down to gray and red embers.

2   Set a grill rack 2 to 3 inches above the coals, and arrange the leeks on the rack. Slowly char the leeks on all sides, turning periodically. Keep cooking until the leeks are mostly black and crispy, with very little green remaining. Transfer the leeks to a baking tray to cool.

3   Pulse in a completely dry food processor until a fine powder is made. Fold in the fleur de sel. Store the leek ash in an airtight container for up to 2 weeks.

MAKES 2 TEASPOONS

Wood or charcoal fire
2 leeks, split and rinsed
1 teaspoon fleur de sel

We've been making our own harissa at Lark for many years now. I love having it around for marinades, dressings, and as a side for a whole array of dishes, North African or not. This recipe has cumin and smoked paprika to give it a well-rounded flavor, rather than it just being hot.

harissa

1   In a mortar and pestle, combine the paprika, cumin, cayenne, fleur de sel, and garlic; smash together well to incorporate. Slowly drizzle in the olive oil while grinding the mixture. Store the harissa in an airtight container in the refrigerator for up to 2 weeks.

MAKES ABOUT ¼ CUP

2 teaspoons smoked paprika

2 teaspoons toasted and ground cumin seed

½ teaspoon ground cayenne pepper

½ teaspoon fleur de sel

4 cloves garlic, minced

2 tablespoons extra-virgin olive oil

There are many versions of za'atar throughout the Eastern Mediterranean; some versions call for more herbs added to the mixture, such as marjoram and parsley. I prefer this version, which is more focused on the sesame and sumac. It's often sprinkled over labne (thick, drained yogurt) as an appetizer. I love it on all types of seafood, chicken, and grilled vegetables as well.

za'atar

1   In a mortar and pestle, combine all the ingredients. Crush and stir gently to combine. Store the za'atar in an airtight container at room temperature for up to 1 week.

MAKES ABOUT ½ CUP

2 tablespoons sesame seeds, toasted golden

2 tablespoons ground sumac

2 tablespoons dried thyme leaves

2 teaspoons fleur de sel

This recipe is especially delicious using hon shimeji or oyster mushrooms but will also work well with other varieties, such as cremini, shiitake, white button, or your favorite wild types, like chanterelle, porcini, or morel. Eat them on their own or as a side, or spruce up a favorite pasta recipe or ragout.

smoked mushrooms

MAKES ABOUT 2 CUPS MUSHROOMS

1 teaspoon extra-virgin olive oil

½ pound oyster mushrooms, cleaned and torn or sliced

Kosher salt and freshly ground black pepper

2 cloves garlic, slivered

1   Preheat a large sauté pan over high heat. Once the pan is very hot, add the oil. Add the mushrooms in one handful, and let them cook for a minute or two, without stirring, then toss the mushrooms a couple of times and season with salt and pepper. Continue cooking until the mushrooms are golden brown and there is no moisture, 3 to 5 minutes. (This may take longer if the mushrooms were wet.)

2   When the mushrooms are golden brown, add the garlic, toss, and cook the mushrooms for 1 or 2 more minutes. Add more salt and pepper to taste, then remove the pan from the heat.

3   Place the mushrooms in a single layer on a baking tray, and place the tray on a rack of your smoker (stovetop or plug-in) or place in a sealable container (smoking gun). If using a stovetop or plug-in smoker, cold smoke (no more than 100 degrees) for 45 minutes. If using the smoking gun, cold smoke for 15 to 20 minutes.

4   Remove the mushrooms from the smoker and transfer them to an airtight container. The mushrooms will keep in the refrigerator for up to 1 week.

CHEF'S NOTE: I like alder, hickory, and pear chips for most things I smoke.

I used to buy my friend Mustapha's carefully sourced and produced preserved lemons from Morocco. They were so naturally sweet and salty with a deep but mellow lemon flavor. Years later when Mustapha's company's (Haddouch Gourmet) products were difficult to obtain, I decided to make my own. And what started as a stopgap project turned into a regular part of the weekly routine at Lark. We use them in the Hamachi Crudo (page 27) and Preserved Lemon Vinaigrette (page 256). They are great with seafood and chicken, and will liven up your favorite dips and spreads.

preserved lemons

1   In a medium stainless steel saucepan or stockpot, combine all ingredients and stir until the ingredients are well combined and the sugar and salt have dissolved.

2   Place the saucepan over medium-low heat and very gradually bring to a simmer. Simmer for 10 minute then remove the pan from the heat and allow the mixture to cool completely.

3   Return the pan to medium-low heat, and very gradually bring the mixture back to a simmer. Simmer for another 10 minutes then remove the pan from the heat and allow the mixture to cool completely again. Repeat the process of simmering and cooling the mixture one more time.

4   After the mixture has cooled for the third time, the liquid should be syrupy and lemony and the lemon peel should be tender and pierce easily with a fork or paring knife.

5   Spoon the lemons into two 1-quart glass or plastic containers with lids. Fill with each container with enough syrup to cover the lemons. Cover the containers lids and place in the refrigerator for up to 4 weeks.

MAKES ABOUT 2 QUARTS

- 8 lemons, halved lengthwise
- 2 cups sugar
- 2 cups kosher salt
- 4 pieces cassia bark or cinnamon sticks
- 6 whole cloves
- 6 whole star anise pods
- 1 tablespoon ground controne hot pepper or red pepper flakes
- 4 cups water

Usually when we hear the words salsa verde, *we think of Latin flavors like green chiles, cilantro, and lime. I know I did for most of my life. While a cook at Dahlia Lounge many years ago, I was introduced to salsa verde from Italy, and as it turns out, many cultures have similar sauces all based on fresh green herbs, garlic, or other aromatics and oil or fat of some kind. Now, I make this as a base sauce and then flavor it depending on the dish it's going to be part of. I love it with yuzu kosho (a Japanese yuzu peel and green chile paste) to pair with fried spot prawns and a wintery grapefruit salad. Or loaded up with extra anchovies, lemon, and pimenton to dress a Spanish-inspired warm potato salad.*

salsa verde

MAKES ABOUT 1½ CUP

1 bunch Italian parsley

½ bunch mint

½ bunch basil

8 cloves garlic, minced

2 teaspoons chopped capers

10 anchovy fillets, salted, packed in oil (1 (2-ounce) can or jar), chopped

½ cup extra-virgin olive oil (I like to use a ripe, buttery variety)

Kosher salt and freshly ground black pepper

1   Coarsely chopped by hand just the leaves of the parsley, mint, and basil. In a small mixing bowl, combine the chopped herbs, garlic, capers, and anchovies. Slowly whisk in the oil to emulsify. Season to taste with salt and pepper (go easy on the salt as the anchovies are already very salty). Store in an airtight container in the refrigerator for up to 3 days.

Again good ingredients make good food. Start with very fresh, local, organic eggs for this recipe, and wash them thoroughly. Use this mayo as is, or season as you like with chopped fresh herbs like basil or cilantro or spices like smoked paprika or ground ancho chile.

homemade mayonnaise

1 In a medium bowl, whisk the egg yolks and Dijon for 2 to 3 minutes, or until the mixture becomes pale yellow and thickened. Whisking constantly, drizzle in the canola oil until fully emulsified. The mixture will be quite thick. Whisk in the lemon juice and season to taste with salt and pepper.

2 The mayonnaise will keep in an airtight container in the refrigerator for up to 3 days.

MAKES ABOUT ⅓ CUP MAYONNAISE

2 egg yolks

1 teaspoon Dijon mustard

¼ cup canola oil

½ teaspoon freshly squeezed lemon juice

Kosher salt and freshly ground black pepper

sources

fruits and vegetables

Alvarez Organic Farms 509.830.5242 alvarezorganicfarms.com
Billy's Gardens 800.417.6387 billysgardens.com
Full Circle Farm 425.333.4677 fullcircle.com
Local Roots Farm 206.679.9512 localrootsfarm.com
One Leaf Farm 206.366.5439 oneleaffarm.org
Oxbow Farm 425.788.1134 oxbow.org
The King's Garden 509.429.3330 thekingsgarden.us
Viridian Farms 503.830.7086 viridianfarms.com

cheese and dairy

Artisanal Cheese 877.797.1200 artisanalcheese.com
Beecher's Handmade Cheese 206.956.1964 beecherscheese.com
Corsican Cellar 206.999.7381 corsicancellar.com
Cowgirl Creamery 866.433.7834 cowgirlcreamery.com
Fresh Breeze Organic Dairy 360.354.6812 freshbreezeorganic.com
Kurtwood Farms kurtwoodfarms.com
Mt. Townsend Creamery 360.379.0895 mttownsendcreamery.com
Murray's Cheese 888.MY.CHEEZ murrayscheese.com
Pleasant Valley Dairy 360.366.5398
River Valley Cheese 425.222.5277 rivervalleycheese.com
Rivers Edge Chèvre 541.444.1362 threeringfarm.com
Rogue Creamery 541.665.1155 roguecreamery.com
Samish Bay Cheese 360.766.6707 samishbaycheese.com
Tieton Farm and Creamery 509.406.3344 tietonfarmandcreamery.com
Willapa Hills Cheese 360.291.EWES willapahills.com

seafood

Fishing Vessel St. Jude 425.378.0680 tunatuna.com
Jones Family Farms 360.468.0533 jffarms.com
Lummi Island Wild lummiislandwild.com
Mikuni Wild Harvest 206.243.8201 mikuniwildharvest.com
Mutual Fish Company 206.322.4368 mutualfish.com
Penn Cove Shellfish 360.678.4803 penncoveshellfish.com
Seattle Caviar Company 206.323.3005 caviar.com

Sylver Fishing Company 206.932.2234
Taylor Shellfish Farms 360.426.6178 taylorshellfishfarms.com
Uwajimaya 206.624.6248 uwajimaya.com
Washington Trollers Association washingtontrollers.org

meats and poultry

Blue Valley Meats 509.876.4700 bluevalleymeats.com
Corfini Gourmet 206.937.3141 corfinigourmet.com
D'Artagnan 973.344.0565 dartagnan.com
Don and Joe's Meats 206.682.7670 donandjoesmeats.com
Jones Family Farms 360.468.0533 jffarms.com
Nicky USA 503.234.4263 nickyusa.com
Northwest Earth & Ocean 425.776.7800
Pleasant View Farm 253.985.0298
Rain Shadow Meats 206.467.6328 rainshadowmeats.com

charcuterie

Bavarian Meats 206.441.0942 bavarianmeats.com
Black Pig Meat Co. 707.523.4814 blackpigmeatco.com
Boccalone 415.433.6500 boccalone.com
Chop 503.221.3012 chopbutchery.com
Creminelli 801.428.1820 creminelli.com
Fra' Mani 510.526.7000 framani.com
La Española Meats 310.539.0455 laespanolameats.com
Olli Salumeria 877.OLLI.YES ollisalumeria.com
Olympia Provisions 503.954.3663 olympiaprovisions.com
Salumi 206.621.8772 salumicuredmeats.com
The Sausage Maker 888.490.8525 sausagemaker.com

spices and salts

Alaska Pure Sea Salt 907.747.7258 alaskapureseasalt.com
Le Sanctuaire 415.986.4216 le-sanctuaire.com
Sugar Pill 206.322.7455 sugarpillseattle.com
The Meadow 503.288.4633 atthemeadow.com
The Spanish Table 206.682.2827 spanishtable.com
World Spice Merchants 206.682.7274 worldspice.com

dry goods, oils, grains, and chocolate

Bluebird Grain Farms 509.996.3526 bluebirdgrainfarms.com
Caffe Vita 206.709.4440 caffevita.com
Chef Shop 206.286.9988 chefshop.com
DeLaurenti 206.622.0141 delaurenti.com
Ritrovo 206.985.1635 ritrovo.com
Theo Chocolate 206.632.5100 theochocolate.com

tools for cooks

J.B. Prince 212.683.3553 jbprince.com
Korin 212.587.7021 korin.com
Sur la Table 800.243.0852 surlatable.com
The Epicurean Edge 425.889.5980 epicedge.com

places to visit

Beach Haven 360.376.2288 beach-haven.com
Iron Springs Resort 360.276.4230 ironspringsresort.com
Rolling Huts 509.996.4442 rollinghuts.com
Sund's Lodge 800.991.SUND sundslodge.com
The Inn at Abeja 509.522.1234 abeja.net

acknowledgments

This book would never have been possible without the many wonderful and talented people I've been lucky enough to spend time with over this year and many other years.

To my wife, JM, and our son, Owen, without your love, patience and support, well, it would all be pointless. And to JM for transforming my rough, knobbly, unpeeled ideas and stories into something rich, hearty, and tasty.

To Kelly Ronan, my business partner at Lark. I'm certain we'd never have made it this far without you; thankfully you're here, and Lark is a very special place because of you.

To Jared Stoneberg, with one foot in the cooking world and one foot in the future. Thanks for sharing your vision with me and seeing all of this to fruition. I look forward to our next collaboration.

To Lauren Thompson, quite literally the huge list we created could not have been completed without your meticulous hard work and dedication.

To Zack Bent, your photos are amazing, you've made everything we do seem like our best cooking dream.

To Dan Shafer, your abilities just seem to grow every time we meet; "Oh yeah, I can do that, and that too." Always unruffled, always on time.

To Joey Veltkamp, for your joyous illustrations and map; you really brought it all together.

To the rest of our supremely talented production team, thank you!

To my mom, Joye, and sister, Sonja, and to all my family that are too far away, I wish you could eat here all the time!

To the past and current cooks and sous chefs of Lark, every day you inspire, push and sometimes torture me into being a better chef. This is all really about living up to your expectations.

To the waitstaff and front of house at Lark, without your talents and hard work, our guests would never fully grasp our intent, our process, and our care of them. Thank you, thank you!

To our Kickstarters, wow, you really came through for us! This book could never have gotten off the ground so rapidly and thoroughly without you stepping up. It's been an honor to get to know you. Your confidence and faith in us has been inspiring.

To our customers at Lark, thank you, for sustaining us! At the end of the day all a chef wants is to cook good food, have a full restaurant, and make people happy.

To Susan Roxborough and her amazing team at Sasquatch Books, thanks for all of your hard work.

index

Note: Photographs are indicated by *italics*.

conversions

VOLUME

UNITED STATES	METRIC	IMPERIAL
¼ tsp.	1.25 ml	
½ tsp.	2.5 ml	
1 tsp.	5 ml	
½ tbsp.	7.5 ml	
1 tbsp.	15 ml	
⅛ c.	30 ml	1 fl. oz.
¼ c.	60 ml	2 fl. oz.
⅓ c.	80 ml	2.5 fl. oz.
½ c.	125 ml	4 fl. oz.
1 c.	250 ml	8 fl. oz.
2 c. (1 pt.)	500 ml	16 fl. oz.
1 qt.	1 l	32 fl. oz.

LENGTH

UNITED STATES	METRIC
⅛ in.	3 mm
¼ in.	6 mm
½ in.	1.25 cm
1 in.	2.5 cm
1 ft.	30 cm

WEIGHT

AVOIRDUPOIS	METRIC
¼ oz.	7 g
½ oz.	15 g
1 oz.	30 g
2 oz.	60 g
3 oz.	90 g
4 oz.	115 g
5 oz.	150 g
6 oz.	175 g
7 oz.	200 g
8 oz. (½ lb.)	225 g
9 oz.	250 g
10 oz.	300 g
11 oz.	325 g
12 oz.	350 g
13 oz.	375 g
14 oz.	400 g
15 oz.	425 g
16 oz. (1 lb.)	450 g
1½ lb.	750 g
2 lb.	900 g
2¼ lb.	1 kg
3 lb.	1.4 kg
4 lb.	1.8 kg

TEMPERATURE

OVEN MARK	FAHRENHEIT	CELSIUS	GAS
Very cool	250–275	130–140	½–1
Cool	300	150	2
Warm	325	165	3
Moderate	350	175	4
Moderately hot	375	190	5
	400	200	6
Hot	425	220	7
	450	230	8
Very Hot	475	245	9